SŪRADĀSA

A CRITICAL STUDY OF HIS LIFE & WORK

K.C. Sharma

K.C. Yadav
&
Pushpendra Sharma

EASTERN BOOK LINKERS
DELHI : : INDIA

Publishers :
EASTERN BOOK LINKERS
5825, New Chandrawal, Jawahar Nagar,
Delhi-110007 Ph.: 2520287

First Edition : 1997

ISBN : 81-86339-47-7

Price : BOOK EASTERN EBL LINKERS RS. 500-

Laser typesetting & Printing at :
UNIQUE PRINT MEDIA
Phone : 7252362

SŪRADĀSA (1478-1583)

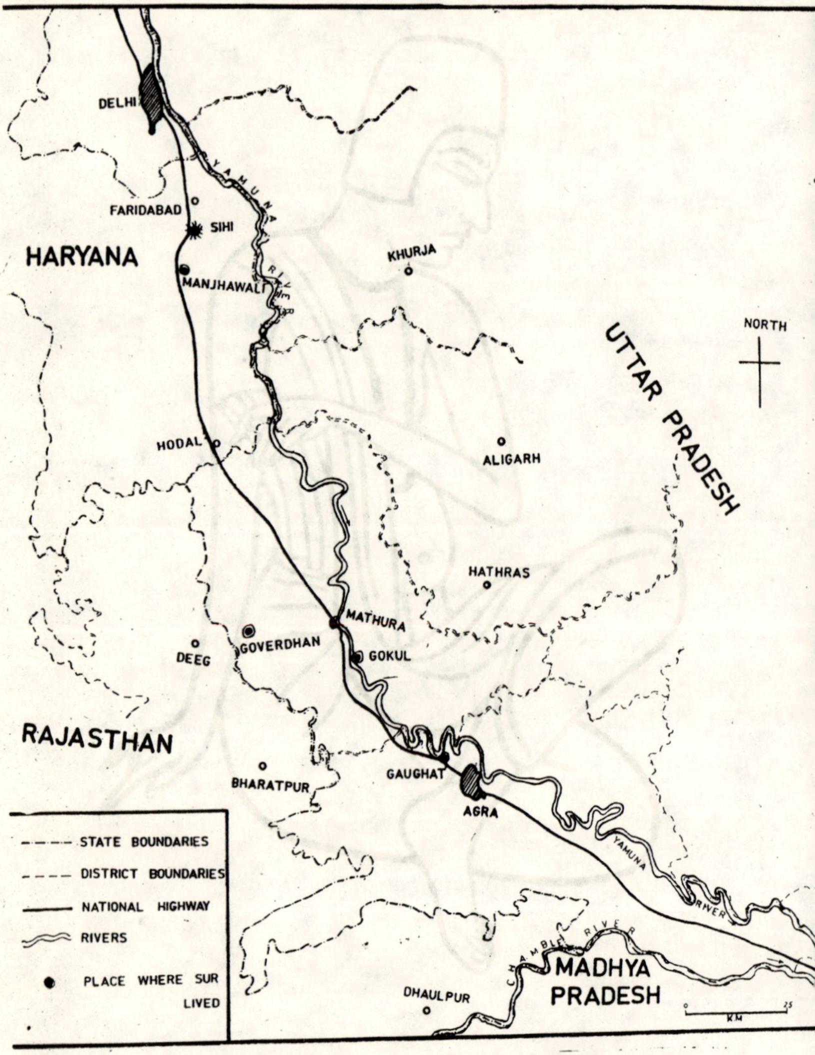

PLACES WHERE SŪRADĀSA LIVED

PREFACE

There are many books on Sūradāsa in which his biographical studies have been done in varied shades and his poetry evaluated form different angles. A careful perusal of all these works shows, however, that a real Sūradāsa—a Sūradāsa portrayed in colours true to history, does not stand before us, and many an intricate problem relating to his life and work has not been taken care of adequately in these works. Hence this monograph.

The purpose here is to paint as real a portrait of Sūra, as a man, as a poet and as a musician as is possible in the present state of our knowledge. We have put almost every generalization made so far about Sūra's life and work to serious historical scrutiny. Whatever appeared right was accepted and anything not supported by facts left out unhesitatingly. At some places, in our anxiety to reach the truth, we have controverted the conclusions drawn by many high and mighty of the scholarly world very curtly. But while doing so, we did not have the slightest idea of showing any disrespect to them or to cause any injury to their images—in fact they are beyond anybody's reach in this regard.

Several friends and colleagues have assisted us in doing this work. We are highly obliged to them. Our thanks are also due to those learned scholars whose works have been used here by us in some way or the other.

Authors

CONTENTS

Chapters I to III are done by Dr. K.C. Yadav; chapter IV by Dr. Pushpendra Sharma; and the rest by Dr. K.C. Sharma.

1

SOURCES

I

The great Indian leaders belonging to the ancient and medieval times have left, practically speaking, little evidence about themeselves. Nor were their contemporaries in any way better than them in this regard--they, too, did not write about these great personages. Regrettably, if perchance we get some passing references relevant to them in the old literature, these stand mixed up with fantasies and legends. In this circumastance, doing any biography of these great men becomes an exceedingly difficult task.

But this is in no case an impossible task to be accomplished. These forgotten 'leaders of men' can be rescued from oblivion provided scholars pay adequate attention to them. We can certainly lay our hands on the materials which can help us in constructing life-sketches of these great personages if we are really serious about the work.

II

In the present monograph, an endeavour has been made to construct a biography of Sūradāsa, who stands in a certain sense neglected so far by our scholars. The materials for the purpose come, broadly speaking, from the following three sources:

--Contemporary sources;

--Near-contemporary sources; and

--Later works.

Contemporary Sources

In the first category of sources, the place of pride goes to Sūra's own work, the *Sūrasāgara*,[1] that *magnum opus* of the blind-poet.[2] Although we do not get any direct reference to Sūra's parentage, childhood, bringing up, education or such like details pertaining to his biography in the *Sūrasāgara*, yet its utility for the present purpose is immense. For, in what one says or writes, is reflected.

---one's personality--ideas, beliefs, thoughts, and several other physical and psychic elements which constitute the 'man';

--society that one is part of---its real form, shape and colours; and above all,

--the interaction of the social, economic, cultural and religious forces of that age.

Sāgara mirrors all the three things in lively colours.

A few words of caution may, however, be given here for those who wish to study Sūra and the contemporary society in the light of verses in the *Sāgara*. In several *padas* (verses) Sūra has made references to many a thing through his own medium.[3] See, for instance, the following *pada*:[4]

Kite din Harisumirana binu khoye

Paranindā rasanā ke rasa kari, ketika janama vigoye

Tela lagāi kiyau ruchi-mardana bastara mali mali dhoye
Tilaka banāi chale swāmī hwai vishayayini ke mukha joye
Kāla bali taiṅ saba jaga kāmpyau, Brahmādikahūṅ roye
Sūra adhama ki kahau kauna gati, udara bhare pari soye

Death has shaken the whole world.
Even Brahma etc. shed tears dreading it.
What will be the fate of this degraded Sūra,
Who only ate, and slept all his life?

And one more:[5]

Kāmī kripana, kuṭila, aparādhī, aghani bharyau bahubharau,
Tīnoṅ pana meṅ bhakti na kīnhīṅ, kājarahūṅ taiṅ kārau.
Sensual, miser, crooked sinner full of wrath,
I haven't remembered God in any of
The three stages of my life.
I am darker than Kājala.

Some sholars believe that these observations were referring to Sūra's own life.[6] But we have direct evidence from contemporary and near-comtemporary sources that Sūra spent most of his life in singing devotional songs before his God. He was a highly religious man, pious and truthful. To be sure, sin, dishonesty and lust were foreign elements to him. In fact, he was just opposite to what has been depicted above. Actually in the two *padas* referred to above and in several others too, Sūra has made himself a target of rebukes on behalf of others who really indulged in such nasty activities, with a hope that the offenders would take a clue and reform themselves.

One more caution. The present editions of *Sāgara* have many interpolations, and until a new scientific edition of the great work becomes available, scholars should use it with utmost care, subjecting each *pada* to be used to a rigorous examination before accepting it as genuine.[7]

The next important work in the present category after *Sūrasāgara* is the *Chaurasi Vaishnavan Kī Vārtā* by Gokulnātha (1551-1647), a contemporary of Sūra] son of Viṭṭhalanātha and grand-son of Sūra's great guru, Vallabhāchārya. This work, as its very title indicates, provides life-sketches of 84 famous *Bhaktas* of the *Vallabha Sampradāya.*[8]

The life of Sūra has been discussed in six vignettes *(prasañaga)* in the eighty-first *Vārtā.*[9] Unfortunately, this contemporary work does not give any account of the early life of the great poet. It begins with his activities at Gaughāta (1510) and ends with his having reached the earthly extremity (1583).[10] For these years, however, the *Vārtā* is an extremely useful source of information.[11]

There is one more work of Gokulnātha, *Nijavārtā.* This work is not as useful as the above work. It contains only one biographical detail in repect of Sūra's date of birth—"He (Sūra) was younger to Āchāryaji (Vallabhāchārya) by 10 days."[12]

Besides these, another work in the present category is *Vallabhadigvijya* by Yadunātha (b. 1558), a contemporary of Sūra which throws some light on the social status of Sūra.[13] Vyāsa, a disciple of Hitaharivaṇsha and a contemporary of Sūra has commended Sūra's poetic excellence in glowing terms in his work *Vyāsavānī.*[14] Exactly the same thing has been said by Nabhādāsa, another contemporary of Sūra, in his *Bhaktamāla:*[15]

Ukti, choj, anuprāsa, varan, asthiti ati bhārī
Vachana prīti nirvaha artha, adbhuta tukadhāri
Pratibimbita divi dishti, hridaya meṅ hari līlā bhāsī
Janma, karama, guna, rūpa sabai rasanā parakāsī
Bimala buddhi guna aur kī, jo vaha guna shravanani dharai
Sūra kavitta suni kauna kavi jo nahiṅ sira chālana karai.

Near-contemporary Sources

In this category of works, the most important is the *Tīkā* (Commentary, called *Bhāvaprakasha*) of Harirāi (1591-1716), son of Gokulanātha, the author of the celebrated work *Chaurāsī Vaishṇavan Kī Vārtā* and *Nijavārtā*, and who was himself a celebrated author in the *Sampradāya*. He has supplied details of the early life of Sūra which his father had somehow missed. It is, therefore, a highly useful source for Sūra's biography.[16]

But a word of caution is needed here, too, with regard to the use of its text. At several places we find legends mixed up with facts, but fortunately the fairy tales interwoven with facts have been done in such a manner that these can be easily torn apart from one another. What we have to do is that we should have a critical eye on the text while making use of it.

There is one more work of Harirāi, *Shri Govardhananāthaji Ke Prākaṭya Kī Vārtā*, dated 1685, which helps us in computing the date of Sūra's entry into the Vallabha *Sampradāya*.[17]

The next important work in the present category is *Dhaula*, a Gujarati work by Jamanādāsa, a contemporary of Harirāi. It makes many interesting references to Sūra's life. These references, however, resemble, to great extent, the ones found in the *Bhāvaprakāsha* of Harirāi.[18] Almost of the same time is Viṭṭhalanātha Bhaṭṭ's *Sampradāya Kalpadruma*. It is not very useful, however, for it only makes a reference to Sūra being a disciple of Valllabhāchārya.[19] Unlike this, however, *Ashṭasakhāmrita*, composed about 1710 by Prānanātha is rich in details. It gives information pertaining to Sūra's birth place, caste and several other happenings.[20] Equally useful information is given by Dwārikesha (1694-1743) in his *Bhāvasaṅgraha*,[21] and by Shrīnātha Bhaṭṭa Telaṅg (1718-73) in his *Saṁskrit Vartamala*.[22]

In Santadāsa's *Chaurasī Bhaktanāmamālā*, Sūra has been depicated as a disciple of Vallabhāchārya and rated as a very great poet of his time.[23] In another work, *Nāgarasamuchchya*, Maharaja Sāwant Singh (*alias* Nāgarīdāsa) of Kishangarh (b. 1649) discusses Sūra a great deal, but his account is confusing and unreliable.[24] And so is Veni Mādhavadāsa's *Mūla Gosāiṅcharitra* where he arranged Sūra's meeting with Tulsīdāsa (in V.S. 1616).[25]

Soraha sai soraha lagai kamada giri dhigavāsa
Shuchi ekānta pradesha māṅh āye Sūra Sudāsa

....

Dina sāta rahe satsanga page
Pada paṅkaja gahe jaba jāna lage
Gahi bāṅh gosāī prabodha kiye
Puni Gokulanātha ko patra diye.

Unlike the two above works, Gopilaṅkāra (b.1840) gives many useful hints about Sūra's life in his *Vaishṇavawāhina Ke pada*. His most important statement is, however, Sūra's exact date of birth-- Vaisākha Shukla 5, V.S. 1535.[26]

Pragate bhakta siromani rāya
Mādhava shuklā pañcham ūpara, chhaṭṭa adhika sukhdāya
Saṁvata pandrahā paiṅtīsa varsheṅ krishṇa sakhā pragatāye.

Later Works

The later works are very large in number. In the light of their contents and methodology adopted by their authors in doing them, these works can be divided into two categories:

(i) Early works.

(ii) Present-day works.

In the first category come the works of Garsi de Tassy,[27] Shiv Singh Sengar,[28] Bhārtendu Harishchandra,[29] Mishra Brothers,[30] Rāmchandra Shukla[31] and Nalinī Mohan Sānyāl.[32] These pioneer works are mostly based on guesses and hearsay. In consequence, they contain many mistakes concerning Sūra's life and work.[33]

In the second category come the works of Shyām Sundar Dāsa,[34] Rāmkumāra Vermā,[35] Janārdana Mishra,[36] Rāmanātha Bhatnāgar and Vāchaspati Pāthak,[37] Hazāri Prasad Dwivedi,[38] Dhirendra Verma,[39] Ram Shankar Shukla Rasāl,[40] Premnārāyan Tandon,[41] Munshi Ram Sharma,[42] Satyendra,[43] Vrajeshwar Verma,[44] Dīn Dayāl Gupta,[45] Nand Dulāre Vājpeyī,[46] Harbans lal Sharma,[47] Dwārkādās Pārikh and Prabhu Dayāl Mittal.[48] These works[49] are in a way different from the earlier ones. The authors of these works have tried to follow modern critical approach to construct the life and to present an assessment of the works of Sūra. This is not to suggest, however, that their findings are in every case scientifically reached at and can be acceptable for our purpose. We have put almost all their conclusions to historical scrutiny in the present work and have accepted them only if these stood it.

References

1. For details about this work see chapter 3
2. Hindi scholars hold different views about Sūra's works. Some of them believe that he had authored 25 works; some others give him credit for doing only 12; and one gentleman thinks that he had actually done only three works. I do not accept any of these views and believe that Sūra has only one work to his credit—the *Sūrasāgara*. For a detailed discussion on this point, see Chapter 3.
3. See, for instance, *Sūrasāgara* (hereafter *Sāgara*) (Kashi Nagari Pracharini Sabha, 1978)—Padas 1,47,52,57,58,59,60,62,63,96,109,140,178,etc.
4. *Ibid.*, 1.52
5. *Ibid., 1.78.*
6. For instance, Brajeshwar Verma, *Sūradāsa*, (Prayag: Hindi Sahitya Parishad, n.d.), p.21:

   "Parantu nimnalikhita saṅketa atirañjanāpurṇa hote huye bhī adhika spashṭa rūpa se vyaktigata haiṅ."
7. Some modern scholars do not ragard it to have been authored by Gokulanātha. This is absurd, however. For a detailed discussion see Prabhudayal Mittal, *Ashṭachhāpa-Parichaya* (Mathurā: Agrawal Press, n.d.), pp. 74-93
8. The oldest manuscript of the book dated 1640 is found at Vidya Vibhaga, Kankroli. The published standard editions are: Dwārkādās Parikh (Ed.), *Chuarasi Vaishnavan Kī Vārtā* (Tin Janma Ki Lila Bhavanvali) (Mathura: 1961); *Prachin Varta Sahitya* (Kankroli: Vidya Vibhaga, 1940); *Chaurasi Vaishnavan Ki Varta* (Bombay: Vainkteshwar Press, V.S. 1985); Dhirendra Verma, *Ashṭachhāpa* (Prayag: Ramnarain lal,1946).

9. The oldest manuscript of the work, dated 1695, is preserved at Vidya Vibhaga Kankroli. The published standard edition is *Harirāikrita Suradasa Ki Varta*, Ed. Prabhudayal Mittal (hereafter Harirai, *Bhavanprakasha*) (Mathurā: Agrawal Press V.S 2008). English version is found in Richard Barz, *The Bhakti Sect of Vallabhācharya* (Faridabad: Thompson Press, 1976), pp. 105-39.

10. The Sūra's *Varta, op. cit.*, begins with:
So gaughāta ūpara Sūradāsa rahate... and ends with tāteṅ inkī vārtā ko pāra nāhin, so kahāṅ taiṅ kahiyai.

11. Its usefulness can be seen by a mere glance through Chapter II.

12. A manuscript of this work, dated 1794, is preserved at Vidya Vibhag, Kankroli. The reference in question is as follows: *"So shri Āchāryaji sau dina dasa chhote hote"*

13. *Vallabhadigvijyu* (Nāthadwārā: Vidya Vibhaga, V.S.1975: *Tato Ślaṅkapure samāgatāḥ tatrāvāsaḥ kritaḥ, tato braja samāgamane sāraswata sūradāso S anugrīhitāḥ.*

14. Vyāsvānī (Vrindavan: Radha Kishore Goswami, V.S. 1994), p. 14.

15. *Bhaktamāla, Mūla Chh.* 73, p. 563

16. The most authentic and well edited edition of this work is the one edited by Prabhudayal Mittal, *Sūradāsa Ki Vārtā, op. cit.* Its English version is found in Richard Barz, *op. cit.*, pp. 105-39.

17. *Shrī Govardhannāthji Ke Prakaṭve Kī Vārtā*, Ed. Mohanlal Vishnulal Pandey (Bombay: Vainkteshwar Press, n.d.), p.73.

18. The author was a follower of Harirāi and hence this similarity between the two works.

19. *Sampradāya Kalpadruma*, p.42.

20. The details are similar to those found in Harirai's *Bhavaprakasha*. See, for discussion, *Sūradāsa*, Navina Bharata, 19 May, 1948.

21. There is similarity of details between this word and Harirai's *Bhavaprakasha*. Extra detail is Sūra's date of birth: *"So Sūradāsaji mahāprabhu te dasa dina chhoṭe hate."*
22. The work consists of 125 vignettes, the 58th being devoted to Sūradāsa.
23. Santadāsa, *Chaurasibhaktanāmamālā*, (Nathdwara Collection), No. 39/3: *Sūake samāna aura bhakta nahin pāiye, sevaka Shri Vallabha Ketihūṅ loka gāiya.*
24. Sawant Singh, *Nagarasamuchchya*, Ed. Shivlal (Bombay : Jṅanasāgara Chhapakhana, V.S. 1955), is a collection of several books of the author. Sūra has been discussed in the *Padaprasangamala*.
25. Veni Madhavadas, *Mūla Gosāiṅcharitra* (Gorakhpur : Gita Press, V.S. 1993), p. 63 :
26. Gopilaṅkāra, *Vaishṇava vāhina ke pada op. cit.* So far no author had done this.
27. *Histore de la litterature Hindouvie et Hindoustan* (Paris : Academy 1839), Vol. I.
28. *Shivsinghsaroja* (Lucknow : Naval Kishore Press, 1926).
29. *Uttrardha-Bhaktamala* (Kashi : 1876-77).
30. *Mishrabandhu Vinoda* (Lucknow : Ganga Pustakamala Karyalaya, V.S. 1997)
31. *Hindi Sahitya Ka Itihasa* (Prayag: Indian Press, Ltd., V.S. 1990, V.S. 1997).
32. *Bhaktashiromani Mahakavi Sūradāsa.* (Allahabad: Ram Narain Beni Maghar, n.d.)
33. These lapses of the early authors have been pointed out at appropriate places in the following chapters.
34. HIndi Bhasha Aur Sahitya (Prayag : India Press Ltd., V.S. 1994).
35. *Hindi Sahitya Ka Alochanatmaka Itihasa* (Allahabad : Ramnarain Lal Book Seller, 1938).
36. *Sūradāsa*(Patna: United Press, Ltd. 1935).

37. *Sura Sahitya Ki Bhumika.*
38. *Sura Sahitya (Indore: Madhya Bharat Sahitya Samiti, V.S. 1993).*
39. *Ashṭachhāpa* (Allahabad: Ramnarain Lal Bookseller, n.d.)
40. *Hindi Sahitya Ka Itihasa* (Kashi : Hindi Nagri Pracharini Sabha n.d.)
41. *Sūra Ki Bhasha,* Lucknow : Hindi Sahitya Bhandar, n.d.).
42. *Sūra Saurabha* (Kanpur: Granthama, 1970)
43. *Sūra Ki Jhanki* (Agra: Shivlal Agarwal & Co., 1956).
44. Sūradāsa (Prayag: Hindi Parishad Vishvavidayalaya 1959)
45. *Ashṭachhāpa aur Vallabha Sampradāya* (Prayag: Hindi Sahitya Sammelan 1970), 2 Vols.
46. *Mahakavi Sūradāsa* (Delhi: Atmaram & Sons, 1958)
47. *Sūra aur Unka Sahitya* (Aligarh: Bharat Prakashan Mandir, 1971).
48. *Sūra Nirṅaya* (Mathura: Agrawal Press, 1962), also *Ashṭachhāpa* (Mathura: Agrawal Press).
49. This is not an exhaustive list, however. For a detailed comprehensive list see the bibliography at the end.

2

BIOGRAPHICAL SKETCH

I

The life of Sūradāsa, the great medieval saint-poet of Haryana, is shrouded in mystery and confusion. There are three main reasons for this: (i) Sūra and his contemporaries have thrown no light on any aspect of his life,[1] (ii) the near-contemporaries, literature is for the most part in Brajabhāshā and was not easily available to scholars until recently;[2] and (iii) many baseless 'facts' pertaining to various aspects of Sūra's life were 'invented' by modern Hindi scholars of early times to supply the desideratum.[3] In what follows, an attempt has been made to portray Sūra's life in colours true to history by attempting, wherever necessary, plausible resolution of problems concerning various aspects of it.

II

Birth Place

Āchārya Rām Chandra Shukla was perhaps the first man to have shed some light on the problem relating to Sūra's place of birth. In his celebrated work *Hindi Sāhitya Kā Itihāhas,* which was published in V.S. 1990 (A.D. 1933), the Āchārya held that Sūra was born at

Runaktā, a small village in U.P. on the Agrā-Mathurā Road. This view, to quote the Āchārya's own words, was based on the "*Tika* (commentary) of the *Chaurasi Vaishnavan Ki Varta*."[4] However, a perusal of the work in question—Harirai's *Ṭīkā*, popularly called *Bhāvaprakasha* gives nothing but a big surprise: the Āchārya had put forward this view on some hearsay,[5] for in the work there is no reference to Runaktā as Sūra's birth place.[6]

Āchārya Shukla came to know of this mistake right in his own life time and he corrected it in the second edition of his work (V.S. 1997), but the damage had already been done. A host of later Hindi scholars accepted the Āchārya's version to be correct by all means. Surprisingly, even such thoughtful scholars as Nizamullah Shahabi,[7] Shyāmsundar Das,[8] Munshi Ram Sharma,[9] Ramaratna Bhatnagar and Vāchaspati Pāthak,[10] Ram Shankar Shukla Rasal[11] and Hazari Prasad Dwivedi[12] did not care to put the Āchārya's statement to a scrutiny and accepted Runaktā as the birth place of Sūra. Now the view stands discarded, however.

There is yet another claim—of Mathurā. Several scholars have elected to hold this view on the basis of Mian Singh's *Bhakta Vinoda*.[13]

Although we have already exposed the worthlessness of this work elsewhere, it seems necessary, however, for the satisfaction of our readers, that the exact evidence in the present case be examined. Mian Singh says:

Mathurā prānta vipravara gehā

Bho utpanna bhakta Hari nehā.

What is Mathurā province? Neither in the time of Akbar, that is in Sūra's life time, nor later on, when the work was composed, there was any province of the name of Mathurā on the political map of India. Does it, then, mean the cultural- linguistic province? Well, then it could have been any place around Mathurā and even Sīhī, in Haryana, the actual birth place of Sūra[14]

The two great, historic cities of India, Gwalior and Lucknow are also on the list for this honour. Scholars have pressed their claims on the basis of the medieval Persian works, *Ain-i- Akbari* and *Muntkhab-ut-Twarikh,*[15] where a Sūra of Gwalior (*Ain*) and a 'Sūra of Lucknow' (*Mun*) are alleged to have been mentioned. Unfortunately, these two views are based, like the earlier views, on very light evidence. If we read the relevant accounts in the two works, we would in no time come to the conclusion that the 'Sūra of Gwalior' or the 'Sūra of Lucknow' was different from the 'Sura of Sīhī,' for the former was where a Sūra of Gwalior (*Ain)* and a 'Sūra of Lucknow' (Mun) are alleged to have been mentioned. Unfortunately, these two views are based, like the earlier views, on very light evidence. If we read the relevant accounts in the two works, we would in no time come to the conclusion that the 'Sūra of Gwalior' and the 'Sūra of Lucknow' were different from the 'Sūra of Sīhī, for the former was[16] the poet of Akbar whereas the later was the hymnist at the 'Court' of Shrinātha (Lord Krishna). In view of this, we dismiss these suppositions too.

Then, where was Sūra born? Fortunately, we have two highly knowledgeable sources to answer this question:

(i) near-contemporary authors belonging to the sect itself; and

(ii) very old tradition among the Vallabhas which remains intact even to this day.

Harirai (1591-1716), while supplying the details pertaining to the early life of Sūra which had remained amiss in his grand- father, Gokulnāth's famous contemporary work, *Chaurasi Vaishnavan ki Vārtā*, very clear terms that "Sūra was born at Sīhī,"[17] a village on the Delhi-Mathurā highway, about 2 kms. from Ballabhagarh,[18] district Faridabad, in the state of Haryana.[19] Several contemporaries of Harirai, such as Jamanādāsa,[20] Prānanāth,[21] and Dwārkesh,[22] as also a host of later authors[23] and tradition both at Shrīnāthadwārā and Sīhī confirm the view.[24] There is thus no room for doubt that Sūra was born at Sīhī.

This village, is a fairly big settlement—population about 10,000. However, a visit to the old deserted site, where the village was actually situated in the time of Sūra (15th century), gives an impression that it was a small hamlet then, comprising about 50 to 60 houses. The bulk of its population was of the Jat peasant-properietors, and the Brāhmanas, artisans, the scheduled caste people were only a few. In conformity with the general pattern of the land-holdings, the Sīhī peasants were small; there were no canals or any other means of irrigation,and, in consequence, they were poor. And so were the other castes which depended upon the peasant-proprietors for their subsistence. This is confirmed by Harirai when he says that Sūra's parents "were hopelessly poor".[25]

III

Date of Birth

Sūra's date of birth is also a controversial question. In the absence of any direct, contemporary evidence, later scholars have pur forward their own theories to answer it. A French man, Garsi de Tassy was perhaps the first person to have tried to resolve the problem, but unfortunately, he could not succeed in his venture: after much afforts he could simply say in very vague terms that Sūra was born sometime in the end of the 16th century.[26] After Tassy, Shiv Singh Sengar made some serious efforts and gave a definite date: "Sūradāsa, he says, "was born in V.S. 1440"[27]: Sūradāsa ..saṁ. 1440 mein udaya..." (A.D. 1383)." Sengar, however, does not give his source of informantion from where he got the date; and, therefore, nothing can be said about his finding. Nor can it be taken seriously in view of facts given below. Mishra brothers, on the basis of *the* following *padas* of *Sāhityalahiri and Sūrsārāwalī*, the two works ascribed to *Sāhityalahrī* :[28]

Muni puni rasana ke rasa lekha. Dasana gaurinaṅda ko likhī subala saṁvat pekha. Nandana darasa hita sāhityalahrī kini

Sūrasārāwalī:[29]—*Guru prasada hota yaha darshana sarasaṭha varasha pravīna*

The first *pada* of the *Sāhityalaharī* gives V.S. 1627 as the date of its (*Sāhityalaharī's*) composition and the second *pada of the Sūrasārāwalī* gives the age of the author at the time of the *Sūrsārawalī's* composition. Since the two works were contemprory the date of birth of their author comes to 1627-67=1540 (A.D.1843). Ācharya Ram Chandra Shukla[30] and following him a host of other later writers have accepted this, or slightly different dates[31] on the basis of these two *padas*.

The very basis of this view is not trust-worthy. In the first place, the two works, *Sāhityalaharī etc.* from which these *padas* have been taken are of doubtful authorship.[32] Secondly, there is no unanimity among scholars over their meanings—these have been interpretted in as many ways as the scholars are. Thirdly, in neither of these *padas*, do we get the date of birth of Sūra: in the first *pada* we get the date of composition of *Sāhityalahirī* and in the second is the reference to a 'meeting'—darshana when the *Sārāwalī's* author(?) was 67 years old. In view of this the two *padas* used by the protagonist of the date 1540 or for that matter even 1550 and 1560 do not prove to be authentic source of information. Consequently, the views based on them stand discarded.

Nalini Mohan Sanyal holds a totally different view: according to him Sūra was born in 1486. The basis of his contention, to quote his own words, is that "Chaitanya Mahāprabhu was born in 1485. There are some evidences, just found, which point that Sūra was born one year before him. Hence 1486."[33] Unfortunately, Sanyal does not say what these newly found evidences are: probably these were nothing but hearsay. In such circumstances, his view cannot be acceptable to us.

What could be the actual date then? The *Sampradāya* sources give some credential clues which can help us to resolve the problem. Harirāi in his *Nijavārtā* informs that Sūra "was 10 days younger to Āchāryaji (Vallabha)."[34] Dwārkesh in his *Bhāvasaṅgaraha*[35] and Jamanādāsa in his *Dhaula*[36] also confirm this view. We know for certain that Āchārya Vallabha was born on Vaisakha Krishna 11, V.S. 1535.[37] Accordingly Sūra's date of birth should be Vaisakha Shukla 5, V.S. 1535 (1478). Interestingly, Gopilankāra confirms this date in his work *Vaishṅava wāhin ke pada* in very clear cut terms.[38] And so does a very old tradition, unbroken to this date, among the Vallabha at Shrīnāthdwārā and other places connected with the *Sampradāya* according to which Sūra's birth day is celebrated on this day every year in a silent manner.[39]

IV

Name

What was the actual name of Sūradāsa? We have it on the testimony of Harirāi that besides Sūrajadāsa[40] (as Swamiji called him) Vallabha called him Sūra Viṭṭhalanātha Sūradāsa, Shrīnāthaji and Sūrashyāma.[41] All these names appear in Sūra's *padas* too. In view of this it can be safely asserted that the great blind-poet had three names: Sūradāsa, Sūrajadāsa and Sūrashyāma, Sūra and Sūraja being respectively short forms of the first two names.[42] Of these, however, Sūra or Sūradāsa became more popular.

V

Geneology

Like many other aspects of his life, Sūra's geneology is also a very controversial problem. And unfortunately most of the scholars who have tried to resolve the problem have, though unintentionally, complicated it still further.

The first to jump into the fray to give a geneology of Sūra was the Hindi scholar Bhārtendu Harishchandra.

Basing his researches on a *pada* of *Sāhityalahrī*[43] he formulated the following geneological table of Sūra:

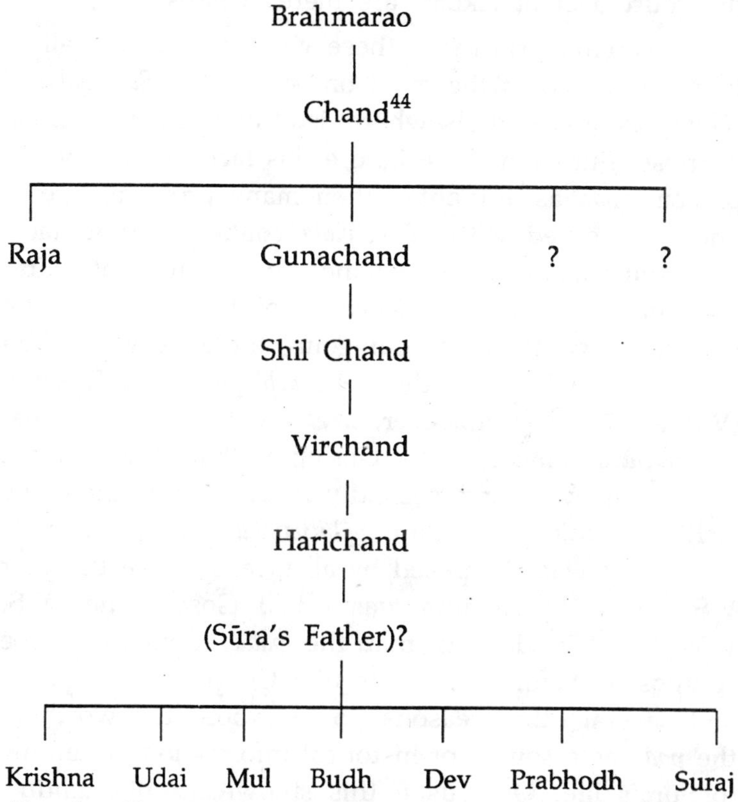

Harprasad Shastri, the famous Indologist, worked on Bhārtendu's line and supplied, with the help of a geneological table found with one Nanu Ram, a descendant of Chandra Bardai "the most useful detail" missing in Bhārtendu's table-name of Sūra's father Ramchandra.[45] Munshi Ram Sharma went a step ahead and transformed this name—Ramchandra, into its Vaishnava form— Rāmadāsa.[46] Pitambardatt Baḍathwāl went still further, and confirmed correctness of the 'great' discovery. Baḍathwāl's and Sharma's researches identifying Sīhī's Sūra with *Ain-i-Akbari's* whom Abul Fazl has described as son of the famous poet Rāmadāsa[47] the court poet of Akbar, are mere guesses.

A careful scrutiny of these views points that all of them are based in the main on *pada* 118 of *Sāhityalahirī* which, as indicated elsewhere, is of no use for historical purpose. But even if we ignore this fact and accept the present *pada* as authentic, then many problems are at once confronted with. The *pada* contains wrong facts and contradictions. For instance, it tells us that "after Sūra had the glimpse (*darshana*) of Lord Krishṇa, he desired to go to Braja. On going there he was taken into the fold of the *Aṣṭhachhāpa* by Gosāiṅji (Viṭṭhalanātha).[48] However, we know for certain that when Sūra came to Braja Gosāiṅ Viṭṭhalnātha had not been born even; and secondly it was not Viṭṭhalnātha Āchārya. One more point: *Sāhityalaharī*, as given in its *pada* 109,[49] was composed by all means before the year V.S. 1627. Viṭṭhalnātha was called Gosāiṅ after V.S. 1659 (1593).[50] How is that the *pada* supposed to be composed before 1627 calls him Gosainji then? These and several other reasons go to expose the worth of the *pada* as a source of historical information pertaining to Sūra's life. Obviously, this shipwrecks Bhārtendu's geneology[51] and other propositions of Harprasad Shastri,[52] Munshi Ram Sharma, Pitambardatt Baḍathwāl, etc., based in the main on this very *pada*.

A careful perusal of the entire literature available so far on Sūra's life and work gives us disappointment in respect of the blind-poet's geneology: we do not find any clue to either his father's, mother's or any other relative's name anywhere.

VI

Caste

What was the caste of Sūradāsa? The answers to this question are also many: different scholars hold him to be of different castes—Bhaṭṭa, Dhāḍhī, Jāt, Sāraswat Brāhmana, etc.

Bhārtendu Harishchandra has us believe that Sūra was a Bhaṭṭa (or Brahma Bhaṭṭa). Harprasad Shastri also thought likewise. This view is, however, not acceptable to us. The reasons for our so doing are simple. Bhārtendu Harish Chandra's view is based on the same notorious *pada* 119 of the *Sāhityalahirī* whose worthlessness has been already indicated. To the same category belongs the geneological table of Harprasad Shastri which he procured from Nanu Ram Bhaṭṭa, a descendant of Chandra Bardai Bhaṭṭa. This work is a very late creation of some forger.

The second view, i.e. Sūra's being a ḍhādhī (a low caste of musicians, singers or panegyrists) is also based on equally flimsy ground. In some of his *padas*, Sūra has addressed himself as a ḍhāndhī,[53] which has led many a scholar to believe that he was a ḍhādhī.[54] But a careful study of *Sūrasāgra*, as also the medieval literature of the *Bhaktas*, obliges us to negate this view at once. We find so many *padas* in his *magnum opus* where Sūra has shown that he did not believe in caste system.[55] How can we expect him to make reference to his caste in his *padas* then? Secondly,a host of medieval *Bhaktas* who belonged to different castes have referred themselves as Ḍhāḍhīs in their *padas*.[56] See, for illustration, Guru Nanak, was a Bedi Khatri: he has referred to himself as a Ḍhāḍhī at 4-5 places in his verses.[57]

The fact of the matter is that these medieval *Bhaktas,* who did not believe in caste system, posed themselves as lowly singers— Ḍhāḍhīs—before their lord in their *padas,* and as such there is no justification in our taking them to be references to their castes.

Another belief is that Sūradāsa was a Jat. Many a scholar own this belief on the basis of the following *pada:*[58]

Aise kumati Jāṭa sūraja ko
Prabhu bina koū nā dhātra.

Pārikha, Mittal[59] and Vrajeshwar Verma[60] do not accept this *pada* to be a genuine one; they rather believe it to be a later interpolation. Verma does not give any reason for rejection of the *pada,* but Pārikha and Mittal do: according to them the *pada* is not genuine because:[61]

(I) The *pada* is not found in the manuscript of the *Sūrasāgra* in the Saraswati Bhandāra, Kankroli;

(II) Sūra's *padas* do not end with such words as *pātra, dhātra,* etc.;

(III) The contents of this *pada,* especially the references to Sūra's meterial well-being, etc. found here are nowhere met with in his *padas;* and

(IV) The use of *Hari* and *duhkapātra* in the same sentence do not conform to Sūra's poetic craft.

The arguments of the learned scholars are not weighty, however. The Nāgarī Prachārinī Sabhā's edition of the *Sūrasāgara* which is supposed to be more authentic an edition than others contains this *pada.* Secondly, unless we have all the *padas* of Sūra with us, points II and III cannot be taken seriously. As regards the last point, we do not find any thing objectionable in the use of the two words in the same sentence. Nor does this usage speak any low of Sūra's poetic excellence. In view of all these points, we find no reason to doubt the genuineness of the *pada*.

Does this imply that we, too, subscribe to the above view? No. But our argument for rejecting this is different from that of Pārikha and Mittal. In the above *pada* the word 'Jat' is not used as an adjective, but it is a comparison (*upamāna*). Secondly, the argument put forward above is not acceptable because Sūra did not believe in caste system, etc. We cannot expect him to have made reference to his caste when he was opposed to this institution. Therefore Sūra cannot be taken to be a Jat on the basis of this *pada*.[62]

Then what was the caste of Sūra? Fortunately, we have a contemporary evidence to resolve this problem: Yadunātha, a contemporary of Sūra, refers him as a Sāraswata Brāhmana in his famous works the *Vallabhadigvijaya*.[63] Harirāi also says so in his *Bhāvaprakāsha*.[64] *Shrīnātha Bhaṭṭa, the author of the Sanskrit-Vārtāmanimālā*,[65] Prānanātha, in his *Ashṭasakhāmrita*[66] and Jamanādās in his Gujarati work *Dhaula*[67] also confirm this view.

Besides, there is also an additional evidence which supports this contention: the present writer's visit to Sīhī brought a strong tradition to his notice according to which Sūra's was a Brāhmana of the Sāraswata *Kula*.

In sum, Sūradāsa, as indicated above, was born on Vaisākha 5, V.S. 1535 (1478) in the house of a Sāraswata Brāhmana at Sīhī, "where Parikshit son of Janmejaya had performed snake-sacrifice (*sarpayajña*)."[68]

VII

Early Childhood

Sūra's parents already had three sons and were hopelessly poor. Unfortunately, Sūra, the fourth son was born blind.[69] Moreover, he heard many things and remembered them by heart. These remembered things were later reproduced at relevant places in his verses. In fact, as Harirāi tells us, he did not even have eye-lids—above his eye sockets had only eye brows.[70] Because of this disability Sūra was disliked in the family." None cared for him, so much so that when he grew up none even talked to him.[71] Sūra, a highly intelligent and supersensitive child, must have felt this neglect by his mother, father and brothers. The deprivation of love and care would have made him shed many a tear; and the miserable lot must have shaken him like any thing. But what was its impact? Did it shatter Sūra's personality? Did it give him a feeling of inferiority? Or did it give him guts to face the reality?

Happily, the last thing happened. The blind child effected compensation of the deprivations, equipped himself with positive materials and did not allow his personality to shatter. He created world of his own—imaginary of course, where he had a mother who loved him, a father who cared for him, brothers who were friendly to him— in sum, a happy lovable family, which existed for him and him alone, all the time bestowing their love, affection, care and all that on him as he grew up day by day.

Sūra has explained his imaginery world in his *Sāgara* in the most graphic manner through the medium of his

Ishṭadeva, Krishṇa. This has made him a master child-psychologist; and has given him a unique position in the whole range of the Indian literature: perhaps no poet before him and even after him has depicted child psychology in such a brilliant manner.

VIII

Exit form Home

Sūra, the blind neglected child, left his home at six. Here a question may be posed: Indeed Sūra's parents may be more than cruel to have closed the doors of their house upon him at so tender an age, in so pitiable a condition. An exact answer to this question is not found anywhere— not even in any traditional talk around Sīhī, Shrīnāthdwārā or elsewhere. However, the two extant stories in the old works do give us some clues which can be used for this purpose.

Harirāi[72] informs us that one day, Sūra's poor parents got two gold *mohars* from some wealthy yajamāna. They were more than pleased to have received this gift. But their pleasure vanished next day when they found that the *mohars* were 'stolen' by someone during the night. At this stage Sūra came in and said: "I can tell you where the *mohars* are, provided you permit me to leave the home thereafter." The poor people okayed the proposal. Soon after Sūra performed a sort of miracle: he told his parents where the *mohars* were; and then bagged of them to let him carry out his decision. The parents persuaded Sūra a great deal, but he would not budge. Ultimately the parents yielded.

The second story is given by Mian Singh.[73] According to him, once Sūra's parents went to Mathurā.

There Sūra came in contact with some Krishṇa- *bhaktas* and begged of his parents to permit him to remain with them. There was 'no' from the parents, but persuasion bore fruits: he was allowed to stay back to be the greatest religious hymnist of his age.

A careful perusal of the two stories indicates that the second story is complete, but the first is not. On hard insistence, Sūra's parents might have permitted him to leave home, it seems incredible that they might not have posed him a series of questions: "O blind young child, how will you go? Where will you get your food? Who will look after you?" Unless satisfactory answers to these questions were provided, how could have the parents allowed Sūra to leave them? Though the story-teller is silent on this point, yet we have to suppose the satistactory answers to these questions were found before Sūra was permitted to go. Thus in their complete form, the stories would give two important clues: (i) Sūra left his home with the consent of his parents, and (ii) he was entrusted to the care of some one. Nothing more of use than this is to be found in the stories given above. The miracle substance in the first story does not appeal to reason. And Mian Singh's sending Sūra to Mathurā is not supported by any evidence: we know for certain that the blind child was sent not to Mathurā but to a village 4 *kosa* from Sīhī.[74]

Who was the gentleman to whose care the blind child was entrusted? What was the name of village where this gentleman lived? Unfortunately, there is no material in either Sūra's *padas* or any where else which could have answered these questions.

Why Sūra is silent on both these points is quite explainable. Sūra had effected his complete surrender to Lord Krishṇa: his soul was His; his body was His.

He sang all his life in the praise of Him. How could he felicitate others, Guru,[75] or some one else, or mention the names of places connected with the activities of others than his Gopāla?

On the other hand the composers of the *Sampradāya's* literature did not think it proper to give the name of the first *Guru* of Sūra for that would have minimized the importance of their Āchārya Vallabha's contribution in the making of Sūra. Similarly, the ommission of the name of the place where the first Guru of Sūra lived can also be explained in this very light, The village, it seems, was an important centre of some Vaishṇava sect other than the Vallabha *Sampradāya,* and the saint who lived there was very famous for this learning and other such qulities. The mere mention of the place would have given a helpful clue to that Saint's name. That would have also done the same disservice. Hence this silence.

In the present state of our knowledge, it seems we shall not be in a position to know the name of the first *guru* of Sūra. But the position with regard to the identification of his village is not so hopeless. There is an indirect helpful clue supplied by Harirāi to solve the problem: Sūra went away to a village 4 *kosa* from Sīhī and stayed there for 12 years.[76] Equipped with this clue, the present writer made a survey of the area around Sīhī to trace the village in question. My first concern after reaching every village was to collect traditions regarding Sūra there, if any. Disappointment greeted me everywhere, excepting at Manjhāvali, a small village on the river Yamunā, about 12 kms from Sīhī. Here the villagers gave me the following tradition: "Sūradāsa came and did *tapa* in this village for 12 years. Lord Krishṇa got pleased with this and asked Sūra to go for any boon. "I wish to have your *darshana*", said Sūra. Lord Krishṇa okayed his *Bhakta's* proposal. The Lord first gve him sight and then *darshana*. After this, when Lord Krishṇa disappeared, Sūra again damaged his eyes and left the village. As soon as Sūra left village a deadly epidemic visited the village. The disease took a heavy toll, and the village became almost a deserted place. The villagers went to Sūra to seek his help in warding off the calmity: Sūra visited the village and health and happiness was soon restored to the villagers."

Sūra lived at Manjhāvali, as indicated above, for about 12 years under the care of his anonymous guru. Here a question may arise: What did Sūra do during these 12 years? Did he have some formal education? There are no direct answers to these questions in the extant literature. Harirāi's following clue can be of some use, however. During twelve years' stay at this place, Sūra had acquired good knowledge of omenology; he "used to recite the *Viraha (Vinaya) padas*" and had good knowledge of instrumental music.[77] Of these three things, *Vinaya padas* reveal something more: that their author was well-versed in the craft of poetics, that he had wonderful command over several languages- Brajabhāshā and even Saṁskrit; and that he was a learned *Pandita* of Indian mythology. This was by far a great acquisition which, some scholars make us believe,[78] that the blind- poet had achieved just in a casual manner through the ^company* of some wandering *sādhus*. I am afraid, one and especially one who is badly disabled owing to loss of sight, cannot learn so much, and in such an impressive manner in 12 years by just having casual company of some wandering *sādhus*. This acquisition could not have been but as a result of regular teaching by a really proficient teacher.

Sect

Another pertinent question at this stage is : to what sect did Sūra belong? This is also an exceedingly difficult question. Some attempts have been, however, made by present-day scholars to answer it. The one answer is that Sūra was a Rāmānandī at Manjhāvāli. This answer is based on Sūra's humility and entreaty found in his *Vinayapadas*. Such an element is found in the *Nirguṇa Bhāgavadīyas* of the Rāmānandī sect. The master-servant (*swāmi* and *sevaka*) relationship exhibited in these *padas* also confirms this view.[79] This theory, however, stands on no solid ground: the types are found in other Bhakti sects also. In view of this, it is difficult to accept this contention.

Another view is that Sūra was a Shaivite at this moment. This answer is based on a *pada* of *Sūrasārāvalī*: "*Shiva vidhāna tapa karyau bahuta dina taū pāra nahiṅ līna.*"[80] to which the following *shloka* of the *Bhavishya—purāṇa* adds further strength:

Sūradāsa iti jñeyaḥ Krishṇalīlākaraḥ kaviḥ Shambhurvaichandrabhaṭṭasya kule jāto Haripriyaḥ.

This view also stands on flimsy ground.[81] To begin with, both the works mentioned above are unreliable. It is a well-established fact which now every one acceptes that *Sūrasārāvalī*, if not full at least the above *pada*, is a later forgery;[82] and the later work also supplies no clear evidence: *Shambhuchandrabhaṭṭasya* does not stand for a "worshipper of Shiva" alone- it can have other meanings too.[83]

Besides, Sūra's own references in the *Vinaya padas*, which were for the most part composed during[84] this period, do not give any such clue that he held Shiva in any great esteem. At places, he even likens Shiva and other *devas* to a goat in comparison to Krishṇa, the *Kāmadhenu*.[85]

The third view is that Sūra was Harivanshi. The bases for this view are the following:

(I) Manjhāvalī, where Sūra lived for 12 years has been, according to tradition, a seat of Harivanshi order.

(II) During his stay at Manjhāvali Sūra had acquired very high excellence in music. The Harivanshis were great musicians. It is surmised that it were they who imparted this knowledge to Sūra.[86]

(III) Harirāi informs us that Sūradāsa had become a *swāmī* during his stay at the village near Sīhī (Manjhāvali).[87] Among the Vaishṇavites, the *swāmis* are found in the main among the Harivanshis alone.[88]

(IV) Sūra has held Vrindāvan and the Yamunā in very high esteem. The Vallabhas do not usually go this far. This seems to be Harivanshi influence on Sūra[89]

(V) The great importance which Rādhā has been assigned by Sūra also seems to have been inspired from some source other than the Vallabha sect. This could also have been due to Harivanshi influence.[90]

(VI) Sūra has depicted Krishṇa, mostly in the form of Vishṇu and not *Parabrahma*. This, too, seems to be due to Harivanshi influence.[91]

These points need careful scrutiny before they are accepted as final answers to the problem. Points II,IV,V and VI seem to be only small hints, which if taken individually, would not hold any weight or significance.

However, points I and III do have some convincing element about them: they present weighty proposal that Sūra could have been a Harivanshi at this moment. In this circumstance, points II, IV and VI put together with points I and III can lend further credence to this view.

IX

Renunciation

At Manjhāvalī, Harirāi informs us, that "Sūra was greatly honoured. People visited him in large numbers. Good food and costly gifts came in abundance. The hut where Sūra lived was removed and in its place a big house was constructed on the pond. He became famous...Many persons became his disciples...."[92] This way, he continues. Sūra spent ten summers here. One night, however, while he was going to sleep, he was overcome by the feeling of renunciation. In the morning he sent a *sevaka* to his village and called his parents and handed over his house and property to them. He put on one pairs of cloth on his body, took a staff club, and went away (1496).[93]

The above description makes one point : by the time Sūra had become 18, his guru had either died or left Manjhāvalī, otherwise how could he have owned a house and kept *sevakas* with him. Besides, if his guru had been there, he would not have been in a position to hand over the house and property to his parents.

After renouncing the world Sūra thought of going to Braja, the land of Lord Krishṇa. He marched with a few followers. His first halt was at Vishrāntaghāta in Mathurā. It is difficult to say how long did he stay there, but taking a clue from Harirāi it can be guessed that the stay was in any case short-lived. Harirāi, gives two reasons for Sūra's early departure from Mathurā: "Sūra did not want that he should become famous in the home land of Lord Krishṇa—all fame should be enjoyed by Him alone." And secondly, he feared interference by the Chaube Brāhamanas of Mathurā, for "once famous people would flock around him and this would mean an economic assault on the Chaubes." There seems to be contradiction in Harirāi's statement. The entire Braja where Sūra had determined to settle now has Krishṇa's land and Sūra knew that wherever he went he would become famous, thanks to his excellence in music, poetics and omenology, Secondly, how could his fame humble his Lord. In this circumstance, it seems that it was the fear of the Chaubes which might have turned him out of Mathurā.

Sūra left Mathurā no sooner than he arrived there. His next destination was Gaughāta, a small, silent, peaceful place on the bank of the Yamunā between Mathurā and Āgrā. Sūra liked the new place very much and here he lived, composing and singing hymns in praise of his Lord for 12 years.

Sūra's sweet melodies made people dance with escatsy; his divinity brought them to fall at his feet; and his wisdom captivated them beyond description. Hundreds and thousands of people became his followers and his fame reached far and wide.

Here a question may be posed: what were Sūra's achievements in these twelve years. It is difficult to provide any satisfactory answer to this question, again owing to non-availability of historical materials. Only a guess can be made, however: he remained Harivanshi; continued to compose *Vinaya padas*, matured his poetics;

gained further mastery over Saṁskrit and Indian mythology (*Purāṇas*).[94]

About 1510, Vallabhāchārya, a leader of the *Sudhādvaita* visited Gaughāta.[95] He had defeated many a learned *pandits* of *Māyāvāda* at Kāshī and in the Deccan, and was a great name in the world of religion. Sūra, who was always in the search of such learned men, seized the opportunity with both hands and called upon Vallabhāchārya.[96] On the other hand Vallabhāchārya had also known about Sūra, the greatest musician of his time; and it was quite obvious that as soon as Sūra sat before him, he demanded of him to sing a song. Sūra obeyed the Āchārya and sang the following two songs[97] full of deep penitence:

(I) *Hari, hauṅ saba patitani ko nāyaka*

ko kari sakai barābari meri, aura nahīṅ kou lāyaka

Tau vishwāsa hoi mana meraiṅ aurauṅ patita bulāūṅ

Jo prabhu ājāmila kauṅ dinhoṅ· so pāṭau likhi pāuṅ

Bachana bāhṅ lai chalauṅ gānṭhi dai pāuṅ sukha ati bhāri

Yaḥa māraga chaugunau chalāuṅ to pūrau byopārī

Yaḥa suna jahāṅ tahāṅ tai simitai, āī hoī ika ṭhāura

Ab kai tau āpuna le āyau bera bahura kī aura

Hoḍā hodī manahī bhāvate kiye pāpa bhari peṭa

Te saba patita pāya-tara ḍārauṅ, yaha hamārī bheṅṭa

Bahuta bharoso jāni tumharau, agha kīnhe bhari bhāṅdau

Lījai begi niberi turatahiṅ, Sūra patita kau ṭaṅdau.

(II) Prabhu, hauṅ saba patitanī kau tīkau

Aur patita saba divasa chāri ke, hauṅ to janamatahi kaun

Badhika ajāmila gaṇikā tārī aura pūtanāhī kau

Mohi chhāṅdi tuma aura udhāre, miṭai sūla kyoṅ jī kau

Kou na samaratha agha karive ko khaiṅchi kahata hauṅ līkau

Mariyata lāja Sūra patitani maiṅ, mohe teṅ ko ṅīkau.

The Āchārya did not like the sad, depressing note in Sūra's *padas* and said: "You are Sūra] a brave man, why are you depreciating yourself so much. Sing something expressing God's glory and grace, something that struck a positive note of realization of and fellowship with God." Sūra showed his incompetence to do so and begged the Āchārya to show him the way.[98]

But this was not possible unless Sūra joined Vallabha's sect. the Āchārya asked him to do that. Sūra accepting Vallabha's dictates immediately agreed for initiation. This must, truly speaking, be a great occasion in the life of Vallabha and in the history of his *Sampradāya* when such a great *Swāmi* was joining their order. Accordingly, Vallabhāchārya lost no time in taking Sūra to his fold.[99] He gave him eight syllabled *mantra*[100] and helped him perform *Brahmasaṁbaṅdha.*[101]

He was a Vallabha-sewaka now. Vallabha stayed with Sūra for three days and gave him gist of his Sampradāya, as was found in his writings, *Bhāgavatapurāṇa, Dashmaskandhānukramaṅikā, Subodhinī* and *Purshottmasahasranāma*. Sūra who was already well-versed in the *paurānic* lore, lost no time in getting what his *Guru* stood for. As a proof thereof Sūra composed some *padas* and sang them to Vallabha. The *padas* were so near to the Āchārya's teaching, and were sung with so great a touch of devotion that the Āchārya's joys knew no bounds. He took Sūra in his arms and showered lavish praise on him.[102]

Vallabha, to be sure, had found an asset for his church. The melody-king could spread his message to the masses in the most adequate manner. But not from Gaughāta. This remote, deserted place was not an appropriate spot for this purpose. In consequence, Vallabha decided to take Sūra to the 'bigger places' connected with the Church.

It should be sometime in the autumn of 1510[103] that Sūra, accompanined by his new guru, left Gaughāta for Gokul. Harirāi has given a vivid description of his visit to the holy land: "On entering into the bounds of Gokul, the Āchāryaji told Sūra that Gokul had come. Sūra at once threw himself on the ground in homage to Gokul, his heart became full of Krishṇa- līlā and abruptly a sweet melody began to flow in the sweetest possible tone: in it Krishṇa, Navanītaprīya was performing bāla- līlā (child-sport)."[104]

Sobhita kara navanīta liye

Ghuṭurūṅi chalata renu-tana-maṅdita mukha dadhi lepa kiye

Chāru kapola lola lochana, gaurochana tilaka diye

Laṭa-laṭakina manu matta madhupa gana, mādaka maḍhuhiṅ piye

Kaṭhulā kaṅṭha braja-kehari-nakha, rājata ruchira hiye

Dhanya sūra eko pala yehiṅ sukha, kā sata kalpa jiya.

After this, Vallabha took Sūra to Govardhan in the temple of Shrināthji. This was a great occasion in Sura's life: he was in the most sacred Church in the *Sampradāya*. It was but natural that an ocean of esctasy should have flowed from the heart of Sūra on this historic occasion. He sang the most divine *pada* which is being sung in all parts of India even to this day.[105]

Ab maiṅ nāchyau bahuta Gupāla

Kāma-krodha ko pahira cholanā, kanṭha vishaya kī māla

Mahā moha ke nūpura bājata niṅdā shabda rasāla

Bhrama bhayau mana bhayau pakhāvaja chalata asaṅgata chāla

Trshṇā nāda karati ghaṭa bhītara, nānā vidhi dai tāla

Māyā ko kaṭi-pheṅtā bāndhyau, lobha- tilaka diyo bhāla

Kotika kalā kāchhi dikharāī jala-thala sudhi nahiṅ kāla

Sūradāsa kī sabai avidyā dūri karau Naṅdalāla.

Vallabha was moved by this hymn *par excellence;* and the following words slipped out of his emotion-stirred mouth: "Sūradāsa now your mind is free of *avidyā* (ignorance), for Shrināthji has dispelled it all. Now you sing *Bhagawān's Līlā* in which there is *sneh* (love) filled with *māhātmya* (divine majesty)." The Āchārya decided the future course of his new disciple at once: "O Sūra," he said, "the tenets of the *Pushṭimārga* have borne fruits for you. You must remain here from now onwards and compose verses in praise of Shri Govardhanadhara."[106]

What else Sūra could have desired! He at once accepted the proposal of the Āchārya and he all his life that he enjoyed hereafter (1511-1583) he remained there"with his Govardhanadhara."[107]

This period is a very creative period in the life of Sūradāsa. It was during this period that thousands of verses[108] were composed by him which were, and still are, being sung throughout India. His fame reached far and wide and men and women, old and young, high and low, all sorts of people came to "drink nectar which oozed out day and night in the *Kīrtanas* from the tongue of the blind–poet."

In V.S. 1626 (1566), Sūrā went to Mathurā, for Viṭṭhalnātha had taken the *swarūpa* of Shrīnātha to this place. This was his temporary stay, however, and he returned along with the *Swarūpa* to Govardhana after a lapse of 2 months and 22 days.[109]

We have it on the testimony of the *Chaurasi Vaishṅavan Kī Vūrtū* that sometimes when Sūra was off the duty, the *Kīrtanas* being peformed by Kumbhanadāsa and Parmānandaḍāsa, he went to Gokul to have the *darshana* of *Shrī Navanītapriyā*.[110] Except for these two visits abroad, Sūra never moved out of Govardhan all his life.[111]

It was during his above-mentioned visit to Mathurā, that Sūra met Akbar, the then King of Hindustan. There goes an interesting story as to how this happened. One day Tānsen, Akbar's court singer, sang a lyric composed by Sūradāsa. It moved Akbar very much and he enquired as to whose composition that was. "It was Sura's work," said Tānsen. "Wonderful," was Akbar's response; and from thence onward, an urge to meet the great poet was born in the King's heart. This urge was quenched after sometime in 1569 when he enjoyed a great feast of music at the hands of Sūra.[112]

Gokulnātha has given a graphic account of Akbar's meeting with Sūra at Mathurā. The very first song sung by the melody- king in the praise of his *Mādhava*[113] (Krishṇa) moved Akbar beyond description. He at once measured the stature of the great singer, but this did not satisfy him. He wished to know his stature as a *Bhakta* too. "Shrī Bhagavāna," he said to Sūra, "has given me the power to rule and every man of talent has sung of my glory. You are also a talented man and, therefore, you should also sing of my fame. If you wish to get something from me (in return of this) you need only ask for it."[114] Sūra gave a sharp retort to the king in a *pada*:

"There is no room in my heart for any one else.

For here lives Krishṇa, the son of Nanda..."[115]

Akbar was mighty pleased to hear this from Sūra; and he tried to conciliate him by "giving a few villages and great wealth." But again the same experience was met with: Sūra would not accept anything. At last Akbar said: "Bābā Sahib, give a command at least." Sūra's command was in line with that of a great *Sanyāsī*: "From now on never again summon me or come to meet me."[116]

This episode shows of what moral fibre Sūra was made. Unlike many other artists of his age, he would not run after kings or queens to win favours or go to any court to seek patronage and protection. He was a singer at the grand *darbar* (court) of Lord Krishṇa, how could he go to lesser places, to smaller 'men'?

The routine Life

Sūra passed rest of his days in routine hymn-singing at the temple of Shrinātha which by now had been transformed into the main head-quarters of the *Sampradāya* by Goswami Viṭṭhalanātha, the successor of Āchārya Vallabha. Here the *bhakti* of the Lord, and preaching of the sect went on round the clock through eight ceremonials,[117] each taken care of by one of the eight great poets of the age:[118]

This routine went on uninterrupted until Sūra's death. There does not seem to have happened anything with him of historical importance[119] during this period which might deserve special mention here.

Death

Sūradāsa lived a very long life. In the year 1583, however, when he had seen 105 summers, he heard the 'divine summons'. Gokulnātha, has drawn a very lively picture of this fateful event.[120] "That day," says he, "Sri Gosāiṅji (Viṭṭhalnātha) *noticed that Sūrdasa was not sitting in his usual place singing Kīrtana. Gosāiṅji enquired of his sevakas about his whereabouts. In response, one of the sevakas said that as soon as he had darshanas at the mangala-darshana period...he had gone off towards Parsoli. Shri Gosainji at once knew that Icchā of Bhagawāna had called Sūradāsa to Pārsoli and he commanded all the Vaishṇavas: 'The ship of the Pushṭimārga is departing: who ever needs something from that ship should go now for it.'*"[121]

After this Gosainji performed *pūjā* for a while and then accompanied by Rāmadāsa, Kumbhanadāsa, Govindaswāmi, Chaturbhujadāsa and other Vaishṇavas, he too, rushed to Pārsoli where Sūra was lying in unconscious state. Gosāiṅji stirred him. This had a good effect and he at once got up and said: "Bābā! have you become very feeble. Yet he gathered all his strength that had been left behind and sang the glory of his Lord. The last *pada* of the melody-king was:

Khañjana naina rūparasa māte ।

Atisaya chāru chapala aniyāre, pala pinjarā na samāte

Chalī chalī jāta nikaṭa sravanana ke ulaṭi-pulaṭi tāṭaṅka phaṅdā te.

Sūradāsa añjana guṅa aṭake nātara abahiṅ uḍi jāte.[122]

After singing this *pada*, "meditating on the union of Rādhā and Krishṇa, Sūradāsā left his *laukika* body and entered into the external *līlā*...... the Vaishṇavas gathered over, committed his corpse to the flames"[123].

A great son of Haryana had gone; a great Bhakta of India had departed; a great poet of the world was no more.

But there was no darkness after this sun had set: his message of love, humility and equality still gives us light very much in the same way as it gave when he was alive. Sūra is dead, but he will live for ever.

References

1. This point has been discussed in detail in Chapter I.
2. No objective scholar approached this literature critically till recently. Nor was it easily available: it was hand written and was not shown to the non-Vallabhas.
3. By this I do not wish to run down or cast aspersions on these great pioneer scholars. What actually I mean to suggest here is that their methodology was defective. A perusal of their works indicates that these great scholars, to whom the original texts of several works were not available, relied on hearsay as much as on authentic records.
4. See his *Hindi Sāhitya Kā Itihāsa*, p. 155
5. Dīnadayal Gupta has pinpointed the source of this wrong evidence-he was Rādhākrishna Dāsa (See his *Ashṭachhāpa aur Vallabha Samparadāya*, Vol.I p. 192).
6. It gives Sīhī, however, as we shall see later.
7. See Satyendra, *Sura Ki Jhānkī* p. 83
8. *Hindi Bhāshā aur Sāhitya*, p.322.
9. *Sūra Saurabha*, p.22
10. *Sūra Sāhitya Kī Bhūmika, p. 17*
11. *Hindi Sahitya Ka Alochanatmaka Itihasa*, p. 605
12. *Hindi Sahitya, p.22*
13. See Chapter I for the nature of this work.
14. Harbans lal also thinks likewise. See *Sūra aur Unkā Sāhitya*, pp.22-23.
15. Abul Fazl, *Ain-i- Akbari*, Eng. Tr. H Blochman, Vol. I,pp.680-82 mentions one Sūradāsa, son of Ramadāsa, a great singer as a court poet of Akbar (Position No. 19).

Badaoni has, however, nowhere made any reference to this Sūradāsa in his *Muntkhab-ut-Twarikh,* though he mentions his father-Rāmadāsa (Eng Tr. W.H. Lowe, Vol.II.p.37). I do not know how Hindi scholars (Munshi Ram Shrama, *op. cit.* p.58; Vrajashwar Verma, *Sūradāsa,* p.40) have created Sūra's footnote in the *Ain* Without seeing *Muntkhab*. This note reads as follows:"...Badaoni (II,42) says Rāmadāsa came from Lucknow....His son Sūradāsa is mentioned below (in the *Ain* not *Muntkhab*)", (Vol.I.p.682).

16. Rāmadāsa of Lucknow and of Gwalior were not two persons as some scholars have us believe. He was one person who first lived at Lucknow and later shifted to Gwalior.

17. Harirāi, *Bhāvaprakasha* (hereafter abbreviated as *Bhāva* if it is tīkā of Harirāi; and *Vārtā* if it is the original work of Gokulnath), *pp.1-2. "So Sūradāsaji dilli pāsa chāra kosa ure meṅ Sīhī gāma hai...so tā gāma meṅ ...pragate."*

18. Harirāi places Sīhī at a distance of 4 *kosa* (Approx, 13kms) form Delhi (*Bhāva* p.1). The distance is, however, about 32 kms. This discrepancy has led many a scholar to doubt the present identification of Sīhī. The doubt is, however, misplaced. In the first place, there is no other village Sīhī, except the present one identified here, around Delhi. Secondly, this village holds a strong tradition of being the birthplace of Sūra. Thirdly, Harirāi tells us (p.1) that Sūra's Sīhī was the place where Janmejaya had performed Snake-sacrifice. This tradition is also alive at this Sīhī: There is a pond outside the village which is called 'Nageshwarī Talāba and villagers hold it to be the spot where the snake-sacrifice was performed. Why has Harirāi written 4 *kosa* then? In olden days the distances were written just by guesses. These were not measured correctly unless a government was involved in the process. Harirāi's statement is also based on a guess, which is slightly wrong. Or may be referred

to by Harirāi was a bigger measure than what we take it to be at present.

19. Some scholars have, however, misidentified Sīhī, probably knowingly, as "some village in district Mathurā." There is no village of this name in district Mathurā (see Satyendra *op.cit.*, p.86). Moreover, Harirāi has given Sīhī's proximity to Delhi (4 *kosa*). How could this place be in Mathurā district?

20. See Jamnādāsa, *Dhaula*, *pada* 1:
Sri Sūradāsa param bhakta shiromani,Ārhatā te to Dillī Sīhī grāma jo
Bālapane Sri hari bhakti karatā sadā, Atraṇakāla nā janami rākhe haiṅ jo

21. Prānanātha, *Ashṭasakhāmrita: Sri Vallabha prabhu lādale Sīhī sara-jala jāta.*

22. Dwārkesh,*Bhāvasangrha: So Sūradāsa ji Sīhī...grāma ke Vāsī.*

23. Almost every scholar holds this view these days. The conficting views put forward by the scholars of the previous generation stand discarded as seen above.

24. The present writer came across very strong tradition to this effect at both these places.

25. *Bhāva*, p.3.

26. Garsi da Tassy, *vide* Dīndayal Gupta, *op. cit.*, vol. I. p. 193.

27. Shiv Singh Saroja, *op.cit.* p.502

28. *Sāhityalaharī* (Mathurā: Sahitya Sansthana), 109.

29. *Sūrasārāwali* (Mathurā: Agrawal Press). 1002.

30. Ram Chandra Shukla, *op. cit.*, p.140

31. The different views based on this *pada* are: Bhartendu Harish Chandra: Muni=7, Rasana-=1 Rasana Ke rasa=6, dasana Gauri Nandan Ko=1 (=1617 VS. in reverse order); Munshi Ram Sharma=Muni=7, Rasana=2, Rasa=6, Nandan=1 (=1627 Vs.).

32. These works are no longer believed to have been done by Sūra. See chapter3.
33. Nalini Mohan Sanyal, *Bhakta Shiromani Sūradāsa*, p.6.
34. "So Sūradāsaji Sri Ācharyaji so ye din dasa chhote hute"
35. "So Sūradāsa Sri Ācharyaji Mahāprabhu teṅ dasa din chhote hute"
36. Rūpa baṭuka sadā chhe chunāṅ ātāra thī ye divasa dasa mahān jo
37. Yadunātha, Vallabhadigvijaya p.7
38. Pragate bhakta shiromani rāya
    Mādhava shuklā paṅchmī upara chhaṭṭha adhika sukhadāya
    Samvat pandraḥ paiṅtīsa varsheṅ Krishṇa sakhā pragatāye
    Kari hai līlā pheri, adhika sukha mana manoratha pāya
39. For tradition see Dīndayal Gupta, *op. cit.*,Vol. I, p.212
40. Ibid
41. Śri Āchāryaji āpa tauṅ "Sūra" kahata aur Śri Gosāiṅji āpa
    Sūradāsa kahate...aur teesaro inko nāma Surajā Dāsa hai Sūrashyāma... so yā prakāra Sūradāsa ke chāra nāma prakaṭa bhaye. so Sūradāsaji ke Kīrtana meṅ yeṅ chāroṅ bhoga kahe hain"
42. Some scholars have also given the following more names of Sūra: Suraj chand, Sūrasuman, Sūrasaras, Sūrjashyām and Suraj Shyām Sujān, but since their contentions are based on unreliable and flimsy evidence, these names cannot be accepted.
43. Prathama hī pratha jagate, bhe pragata adbhuta rūpa,
    Brahmarāva vichāri brahmā nāma rākhi anūpa.
    Tāsu baṅsa prasaṁsa shubha meṅ bhau chanda chāru navrīna
    Tāsu baṅsa anūpa bhau Harachanda ati vikhyāta
    Āgare rahi, gopāchala meṅ rahyo tā sutabīra

Putra janame sāta tāke mahābhaṭa gambhīra
Bhayo sāto nāma sūraja chanda manda nikāma
Vipra pratha te jāga ko hai bhāva sura nikāma
Sūra hai nandananda jū kou, liyo mola gulāma

44. Chandra Bardai, author of the celebrated work *Prithvīrāja-rāso.*

45. Harprasad Shastri has given this information. This is of little value, however.

46. See Munshi Ram Sharma *op. cit.*, p.25

47. *Sūradāsa Jīwan Sāmagri*, Ed. Bhagirath Mishra (Lucknow: Avadh Publishing House).

48. Mohi manasā ihai, vraja kī basai sukha chitta thāpa
Thāpī Gosāyi kari meri āṭha madhya chhāpa

49. For other reasons see Dwārkādāsa Pārikha, Prabhu Dayal Mittal, op. cit., pp. 5-7.

50. This title was in all probability given by King Akbar, for we do not come across this title in any other document, secular or religious prior to Akbar's firman of grant to Viṭṭhalnātha dated 1593. See M.C. Parikh, *Sri Vallabhā-chārya* (Rajkot: Sri Bhāgavata Dhruva Mission, 1943), pp. 227-28.

51. See above for discussion

52. See above for discussion.

53. See, for instance: (i) Haun to tihāro ghara kau ḍhāḍhī Sūradāsa merau nāun. *Sāgara* 1, 653

54. Even so careful and critical an author as Vrajeshwar Verma has faltered here. He, in the light of these *padas*, is inclined to believe that Sūra was probably a ḍhādhī. See his *Sūra, p.26*

55. For instance see the following: Jāti, gota, kula, nāma ganata nahin ranka hoyi kai rāno 1, 11
Jāti pānti kula kāni na mānata Veda, purānana sākhe 1,15
Jāti pānti kou pūchhata nāhī Śripata ke darabāra 1, 119
Ūncha nīcha Hari ginata na doī. 1, 124

56. See Dwarkādas Parikh,and Prabhudayal Mittal, *op.cit.*: "Krishnadāsa-Vallabh kula ko ḍhāḍhī..." Chaturbhijadāsa—Hauṅ ḍhāḍhī kabhī na aghāuṅ...." Nandadāsa—"Nanda dāsa Nandarāu ko ḍhāḍhī...."

57. D.S. Narula, *Guru Nanak Sangītāchārya* (Jullundur: 1978) p.110.

58. *Sāgara*, 1,216.

59. See Dwarkadas Parikh and Prabhudayal Mittal, *op. cit.* p.13

60. Vrajeshwar Verma, *op. cit.*, pp.5.20.

61. Dwarkadas Parikh and Prabhudayal Mittal, *op. cit.*, p.13

62. For details see Satyendra, *op. cit.*, p.91

63. *Vallabhadigviljya* p.50.

64. *Bhāva*, p.3. "So Sūrdāsaji....eka Sārasvata Brāhmaṇa ke ghara pragate,"

65. Shrinātha Bhaṭṭ *op. cit.*, in *Sūrapada* I, calls him *'prāchya Brāhamaṇa'*.

66. Prānanātha, *op. cit.*, calls him *Sarsutiduja* i.e. *Saraswatadwija* (Brāhmaṇa).

67. Jamanādāsa, *op. cit.*, *pada*, 2: "Pragatyāye to Brahmā Sārasvata kula māṅ."

68. "So Sūradāsaji Dillī pāsa chāra kosa ure meṅ Sīhī gāma hai, jahāṅ rājā Parākshita ke betā janmejaya ne sarpa yajṅa kiyau hai, so tā gāma meṅ eka sāraswata brāhmaṇa ke yahāṅ pragate... so tina betā vā sāraswata brahāmṇa ke āgai ke hate aur ghara meṅ bahauta nishkaṅchana hato" *Bhāva*, pp. 1-2.

69. In view of his lively, graphic poetry many people do not think that Sūra was born blind. It is surprising that even such a critical scholar as Hazari Prasad Dwivedi (p.175); Deendayal Gupta (Vol. I. p. 202) and Vrajashwar Verma (pp. 12-13) have also fallen prey to such a doubt in utter disregard of a great deal of contemporary and near-contemporary evidence to the contrary. See Sūra's

own evidence:
Sūradāsa sauṅ kahāṅ nihārauṅ nainanahīṅ kī hāni. *Sāgara,135.; Sūradāsa kura āṅdharau main dwāra paryo gāūṅ Ibid.*166.
Kāto na phaṅda mo andha ke, aba bilamba kāraṇa kavana *Ibid.*,180.; Sūrajadasa andha aparādhī so kāhe bisarāyau *Ibid.*,1,190.; Aiso andha, adhama avivekī khotani karata khare. *Ibid.*, 1,198.
The Learned scholars ought to know that an intelligent, blind person makes fullest possible enquiry about things to understand them. For instance, 'to understand' one colour, he must know about all the colours. To know about one sweet-meat, he should know about all others and then how these are prepared, and so many other details about their different contents. An unblind person would normally not make so many enquiries on seeing a thing and hence his knowledge is limited. Sūra, a highly intelligent and inquisitive man who possessed powerful memory had gathered encyclopaedic knowledge just by asking about different things from men around him.

70. *Bhāva*, p.2

71. "So mātā pitā ghara ke sab koi insoṅ prīti kareṅ nāhīṅ. Jāṇeṅ, jo netra binā kau putra kahā, tāsoṅ in soṅ koī bolatau nāhīṅ.

72. *Ibid.*,pp.3-4.

73. Mian Singh, *op. cit.*,

74. *Bhāva*, p.5.

75. Gokulanātha, Sūra's contemporary, informs us that while Sūra was about to die Chaturbhujadāsa. his colleague, said: "Sūradasāji..has composed at least a hundred thousand *padas* for Shri Thākurji. But Sūradāsaji has never described the glory of Shri Ācharyaji Mahaprabhu" (*Vārtā*, p.60). In the light of this, we cannot expect Sūra to have sung in praise of his former Guru.

76. *Bhāva,* p.5
77. *Ibid.,*pp.6-7
78. See, for instance, Dwarkādāsa Parikh and Prabhudayal Mittal, *op. cit.,* p. 82
79. For this see Satyendra, *op. cit.,* p.105.
80. *Sūrsārāwali, pada* 1002.
81. *Bhavishyapurāṇa, Pratisargaparva, III, 30.*
82. See Satyendra, *op. cit.,* p.102.
83. *Ibid.*
84. See, for instance, Sāgara, 1.3;1.11;1.34;1.44;1.54;1.94; 1.201;etc.
85. *Ibid.,* 1.43
86. The present writer's finding.
87. Satyendra, *op. cit.,* p.101.
88. Ibid.
89. *Ibid.*
90. *Ibid.*
91. *Ibid.*
92. *Bhāva, pp.6-7.*
93. *Ibid.,* p.8. Not only this, Here there is anti-climax too. First God's consideration and then of the lowly Chaubes:
94. His *padas* bear a testimony to this.
95. *Bhāva,*pp.9-10
96. *Ibid.*
97. *Bhāva,* pp.10-11.
98. *Vārtā,* p. 11.
99. *Ibid.,*p.12.
100. Śrīkrishṇaḥ sharaṇam mam.
101. This is a highly important ceremony in the sect for without having performed this none is entitled to the worship of Lord Krishṇa. The ceremony is performed by

offering *Tulisīdala* to the *Swarūpa* of Lord Krishna by the *sevaka*

102. *Vārtā* pp. 11-17

103. *Ibid.*

104. *Ibid.,p.19*

105. Bhāva, p.10

106. *Ibid.*

107. *Bhāva,* p.56, Sūra's permanent abode was at Pārsoli, a small village in close proximity of Govardhan. His hut was on a pond called Chandrasarovara.

108. *Vārtā,* p.23.

109. Dwārkadāsa Parikh and Prabhudayal Mittal, *op. cit.,* pp. 80

110. *Vārtā,* p.16.

111. Dwārkādāsa Parikh and Prabhudayal Mittal *op. cit.,* 88-90 also think that he had visited Brindāban too. But there is no evidence to support this point.

112. *Vārtā,* pp.28-29.

113. *Ibid.*

114. *Ibid.,* pp.30-31

115. *Iibd.*

116. *Ibid.,*p.31.

117. These eight ceremonials were as follows: (1) *Mangla* (The morning levee): The image being washed and dressed is taken from the couch, where it is supposed to have slept during the night, and placed upon a seat about half an hour after sun-rise: light refreshments are then presented to it, with betel: lamps are generally kept burning during this ceremony. (2) *Śringāra:* The image having been anointed and perfumed with oil, camphor and sandal, and splendidly attired, now holds his public court: this takes place about an hour and a half after the preceding.

or when four *gharis* of the day have elapsed. (3) *Gwāla*: The image is now visited, preparatory to his going out to attend the cattle along with cow- herd; this ceremony is held about forty eight minutes after the last or when six *gharis have passed. (4) Rājabhoga*: Held at mid-day, when Krishṇa is supposed to come in from the pastures, and dine: all sorts of delicates are placed before the image and both those and other articles of food dressed by the ministers of the temple are distributed to the numerous votaries present and not infrequently sent to the dwellings of worshippers of some rank and consequence. (5) *Uthāpan* (The calling up): The summoning of the god from Siesta: this takes place at six *gharis or* between two and three hours before sun-set. *(6) Bhoga*: The afternoon meal, about half an hour after the preceding. (7) *Sandhyā*: (About sun-set): The evening toilet of the image when the ornaments of the day are taken off, and perfume etc. applied. (8) *Sāyam* (retiring to repose): The image, about eight or nine in the evening, is placed upon a bed, refreshments and water in proper vastes, together with the betel box and its appurtenances, are left near it, when the votaries retire, and the temple is shut till the ensuing morning. See H.H.Wilson, *Religious Sects of the Hindus*, Ed. B.R. Rost (Calcutta: Sushil Gipta Pvt. Ltd.,1958),pp.72-73.

118. These eight great poets of whom Sūra was the most prominent, are known as *Ashṭachhāpakas* or *Ashṭakāvyakāras* (Eight poets). Sūradāsa, Chhītaswāmī, Paramānandadāsa, Govindaswāmī, Chaturbhujadāsa, Kumbhanadāsa, Krishṇadāsa and Nandadāsa.

119. Some scholars believe, however, that the great poet went to Chitrakūṭa to meet another great poet Tulsīdāsa in V.S.1616 (1559). Some others reverse the order: According to them Tulsīdāsa came to Govardhan. Both these views are based on no evidence which can be acceptable to any students of history.

120. *Vārtā,* pp.56-65
121. *Ibid.*
122. *Ibid.*
123. *Ibid, page 65.*

3

THE WORK

I

Sūradāsa had powerful intellect, prodigious memory and cyclopaedic knowledge. He was a great *paṁdita* of Saṁskrit, and his mastery over Brajabhāshā and his acquisition of ancient and medieval Indian lore were simply enviable. In sum, he was a literary giant of his age.

II

How many works did Sūra compose? There is a great deal of controversy among scholars over this question. But to me it seems the problem is not as complicated as it has been made: we have direct historical evidence which throws useful light on this apparently difficult problem.

Gokulanātha, the fourth son of Viṭṭalanātha was, as indicated else-where, a contemporary of Sūra. He was a great scholar who wrote able commentaries on the works of his grand-father, Vallabha, and produced a lot of *Vārtā* literature. He has been considered the third great leader of the *Sampradāya* by its followers. A careful perusal of his celebrated work, the *Vārtā* makes it crystal clear that this man had no knowledge of any work of *Sūra except for the Sūrasāgara.*[1] What does this mean? Simply this, that Sūra composed no work other than *Sāgara,* otherwise these would not have remained concealed from this most knowledgeable contemporary of his.

Secondly, there is important evidence of Harirāi (1591-1711), one of the greatest names in the literary history of the *Sampradāya.* He wrote hundreds of books on various subjects concerning his church; and was "so deep in his treatment of them that one might well find all the knowledge and edification he wants in regard to the Vaishṇavism and Vallabha in his writings."[2] This great author also makes reference to just one work of Sūra-*Sūrasāgara.* No other work of Sūra is known to him.[3] This implies that at least until one hundred years after Sūra's death no other work of his, excepting *Sāgara* was available, otherwise Harirāi would have mentioned them in his literature.

III

Nevertheless, we find several works ascribed to Sūra. The *Survey Reports* of the Nāgarī Prachāriṇi Sabhā, Kāshī, refers to the following 12 titles ascribed to him: *Bhāgavata Bhāshā,*[4] *Dashama Skandha Tīkā,*[5] *Sūradāsa Ke Pada,*[6] *Nāgalīlā,*[7] *Govardhana Līlā,*[8] *Sūra-Pachisi*[9] *Prānapiyari,*[10] *Vyahalo,*[11] *Sūrasāgarasāra,*[12] *Sūra- Shataka,*[13] *Rāmajanma*[14] and *Ekadashi Māhātmya,*[15] In the *Sampradāya's* library at Nāthadwārā we find other works ascribed to Sūra. These works are: *Sevāphala*[16] and *Sūradāsa Ke Drishtakūta pada.*[17] The Odor Aufrecht refers to one more work of his *Harivaṅsha* tīkā in the *Catalogus Catalogrrorum.*[18]

Besides, the following 13 books ascribed to Sūra are available in the published form:[19] *Sūrsārāwali, Sāhityalahari, Bhramaragīta, Sūra Rāmāyaṇa, Dānalīlā, Sūra-Sakhi, Mānalīlā, Vinaya, Dānalīlā, Driṣtantalilā, Mayurabhaja Raja Ki Katha, Gopalagari* and *Sūrasāgararatna*.

A careful scrutiny of all these works yields the following coclusions about them.

(I) All the above works excepting *Sūrasārāwalī, Sāhityalahari, Harivaṅshaṭikā, Sevāphala, Rāmajanama, Nala-Damayanti* and *Ekadashi Māhātmya* are not independent treatises. These are parts of *Sūrasāgara* which have been formed into separate works by later editors/compilers.

(II) The *Harivaṅshaṭīkā* is a Saṁskrit work. Not only Sūra but none of the *Bhakta* poets of the *Ashṭachhāpa* wrote any work in Saṁskrit. This work is, therefore, not of Sūra

(III) The *Rāmajanma* and *Ekādashīmāhātmya,* written in *dohas* and *chaupais,* are in Avadhi dialect. The works conform neither to Sūra's style nor approach. Besides, Sūra wrote in *Brajabhāshā* and not in Avadhi. These works are, therefore, of some Avadhi-speaking Sūrajadāsa.

(IV) The *Sevāphala* is also not of Sūra for its language, style and contents are of very low standard.

(V) The two other works, the *Surasārāwalī* and the *Sāhityalahiri* whom most of the present day authors believe to be Sūra's works are in fact not his. Their language, poetic craft, and subject matter are pretty different from what we come across in *Sūrasāgara.*[20] Besides, we find in them several *padas* which are at variance with historical details pertaining to Sūra's life and personality,as reflected in reliable contemporary and near-comtemporary literature.

To conclude, Sūra as pointed out by the *Vārātākāras* composed only one work, the *Sūrasāgara*. All other works ascribed to him are either parts of the *Sāgara* or are later forgeries or are works of some other Sūradāsa or Sūrajadāsa wrongly ascribed to Sūra.

IV

How did Sūra compose the *Sāgara*? Why did he do it? How many *padas* did he really compose for the *Sāgara*? There is no unanimity among scholars over these questions. Why is it so? Answer to this question is not beyond comprehension, however; for we find very clear-cut clues to answer these questions in an adequate manner in the contemporary and near-contemporary literature.

Sūra was a religious hymnist. He was not an author whose aim it was to compose books. He composed *padas* for and sang them to his *Ishṭadeva*. This process went on uniterrupted all through his life. Gokulnātha, his contemporary, tells us that he had taken a vow to compose and sing one and a quarter lakh *padas* before his Lord. However, at the fag end of his life, when he knew that his end had come, he became very unhappy, for he had composed only one lakh *padas*. But his *Ishṭdeva* could not make his *Bhakta* feel likewise and he composed 25 thousand *padas* for him. Thus Sūra's vow was fulfilled and he died a happy contented man.[21]

In modern parlance the above account may be taken in a slightly different way. When Sūra had composed one lakh *padas*, he grew very weak and his end seemed very near. He knew that now he would not be able to fulfiḷ his vow, and became painfully restless. Sūra's disciples or some single talented disciple helped him out of this agony by composing for him the rest of the 25 thousand *padas*. On Sūra's enquiry as to who did it for him, the desciples/ desciple seem/seems to have told him that it was done by the grace of God. These *padas* bearing the *signatures (bhoga)* of 'Sūra-Shyāma' are in no way different from Sūra's own *padas*, for these were done by his followers/follower who had taken instructions from him in composition of *padas*. In sum, we can believe that Sūra had composed one lakh *padas*, and that 25 thousand were added to them by some of his very able desciples/desciple right in Sūra's own life-time.

Sura's *padas* had begun to be recorded in Sūra's own life- time at least at two places: (I) Shrīnātha temple in the *chauparas*;[22] and (II) at Akbar's court.[23] Unfortunately we have not been able to lay our hands on these two versions of Sūra's *padas* so far.

V

Where did Sūra get inspiration for his *padas* in the *Sāgara*? Obviously, from the *BāgvataPurāṇa*, as Sūra himself admits: "God gave four *shlokas*[24] to Brahmā. Brahmā gave the *shlokas* to Nārada and Nārada to Vyāsa who composed the twelve-*Skandha Shrimad Bhāgavata* on the basis of these *shlokas* and recited it to his son Shukadeva. I am singing the very same *kathā* of the *Bhāgavata* in Brajabhāsā."[25] We come across such like expressions in almost all the twelve *Skandhas of Sāgara*., for instance, *Sāgara*[26]*— I.225,27,60,85; II. 379; III. 387,90; IV. 398, 401,2,3; V. 406,9,10,11; VI. 416,18,19;VII. 426; VIII. 438; I Pūr. 446,47,52,53,59, 617,18; X(Utt.) 138;XI. 5; XII. 2.4.5. Besides this, the Vārtākāra*, a contemporary of Sūra also confirms this fact: "Sūradāsa's heart was filled with all the līlā of the *Bhāgavatapurāṇa* and he composed *Kīrtanas* describing the *dānalīlā* and the *mānalīlā* and all the other *līlās* contained in the *Bhāgavatapurāṇa* from the first *skandha* to the twelfth and the last *skandha*."[27]

In view of such a strong evidence, and that too, of the contemporary and first hand nature, it can be said without any reservation that Sūradāsa received ample inspiration from the *Bhāgavatapurāṇa* and his *Sāgara* was to a great extent based on it. Some scholars, however, object to it, chiefly on two grounds: First, although there is equal number of *Skandhas* in the two works, the number of *shlokas* and *padas* in them vary to a frightening degree. They usually give the following table in support of their contention:

TABLE I28- COMPARISON OF BHāGAVATA AND SūRASāGARA

SKANDHA	BHĀGAVATA SHLOKAS	SŪRASĀGARA PADAS
1.	1692	343*
2.	392	38
3.	1502	13
4.	1407	13
5.	666	4
6.	851	8
7.	750	8
8.	931	17
9.	963	174
10. *Pūrwārdha*	1935	4160
10. *Uttarārdha*	1516	149
11.	1374	4
12.	566	5
Total	14,615	4936

In the second place, differences in the contents of the *Skandhas* of the two works are pointed out: many incarnations, Bharata and other *rājās,* and such like things mentioned in the *Bhāgavata* are conspicuous by their absence in the *Sāgara*. Besides, several episodes given in the *Sāgara* do not find place in the *Bhāgavata* at all.[29] The works are, therefore, independent of each other as far as their contents are concerned.

We do not accept these contentions, for these are without any historical basis. We do not get complete *padas* of Sūra, then how can we compare the number of its *padas* with the *shlokas* of the *Bhāgavata*. The same can be said about the differences in their contents too. But of things; there is difference between the two works in their Kathās which are available. Take, for instance, the *Kathā* of the *Kālīya-damana.* Although the episode has been taken from the *Bhāgavata,* its plot is totally different. This can be owing to two reasons. In Sūra's days the *Bhāgavata* was not easily available. It's *kathās* were for the most part recited orally. And in such circumstances, there had got to be a vast difference in the versions of different reciters.[30] May be the kathā which Sūra had heard was this distorted version which we come across in the *Sāgara*. Secondly, Sūra was a great original poet. Naturally such a man would change any account if it did not fit in with his scheme of things. Sūra has done this at many places in his *Sāgara*.

In sum, we cannot, in the present circumstances when all the *padas* of Sūra are not available, help but accept the above-quoted statement of Sūra that in his *Sāgara* he "was reciting the story of the *Bhāgavata* in Brajabhāshā." He did not say, however, that "he was translating the latter in the former." He has nonetheless kept his originality alive even while the well-known stories of the *Bhāgavata* are retold; he has made them more down-to- earth type, more colourful, and more lively by his original touch. Hence at variance with the great *Purāṇa*.

VI

We have indicated above that Sūra had composed one lakh *padas* during his life-time. Despite the best efforts on the part of modern scholars, however, even one-tenth of these *padas* are not available today. So far 119 manuscripts, both incomplete as well as complete, of *Sūrasāgara* are available in libraries and collections of institutions and individuals in India and abroad.[31] These are 16 standard publised editions[32] based on these manuscripts of these editions. The one published by the Nāgarī Prachārini Sabhā Kāshī is by far the most authentic.[33] It consists of twelve *skandhas* (chapters), the contents of which are as follows:

Skandha I: The *Skandha* begins in the usual traditional manner with the following invocative verse (*maṅgalācharaṇa*):

Charaṇa kamala baṅdauṅ harirāī

Jāki kripā paṅgu giri laṅghai, andhe ko saba kachhu darasāī

Bahirau sunai guṅga puni bole, raṅka chalai sira chhatra dharāī

Sūradāsa swāmī kruṇāmaya, bāra-bāra baṅdauṅ tihiṅ pāī.

This is followed by 212 *padas* of *Vinaya* (humility) which according to the popular belief were composed by the great poet before he came into contact with Vallabhāchārya. These *padas*, as their very title suggests, are full of deep notes of penitence. Then comes a set of 12 *padas* where the objectives of the *Bhāgavatapurāṇa* are described very briefly; some stories found in the first *skandha* of the great *Purāṇa* as related to the birth of Shukadeva, incarnation of Vyāsa, Bhīshma's death, Krishṇa's visit to Dwārikā, Yudhishtra's renunciation, Pāṅdavas going to the Himālayas, Parikshit's birth and *Kaliyuga's* chastisement, are told in equally brief terms.

Skandha II: This *Skandha* consits of 38 *padas*. In the beginning the importance of *bhakti* (devotion). *satsaṅga* (association with pious men), *sādhanā* (spiritual endeavour) etc. has been highlighted; and subsequently the origins of the world, *Virāṭa-Purusha* (God), twenty-four *avatāras* (incarnations) of God, etc. have been described.

Skandha III: This is a small *Skandha*, having only 13 *padas*, wherein the repentance of Uddhava, dialogue of Maitreya and Vidura, incarnation of Shaṅka, Kapiladeva, Varāha etc; origin of Rudra, Saptarishīs, Dakshaprajāpati and Swayambhu Manu, Jai-vijaya's story, Kardama's demise, dialogue of Devahuti and Kapila, etc. have been described on the basis of the *Bhāgavata*. The *Skandha* ends with a very impressive *pada*, wherein the importance of *bhakti* (devotion to God) has been highlighted.

Skandha IV: This *Skandha* is also very small, like the earlier one, consisting of 13 *padas*. The *Skandha* opens with a description of Daṭṭātreya's incarntion, followed by Yajṅapurusha's incarnation, Pāravati's marriage, Dhruva's story, Prithu's exploits. In the last the importance of knowledge and *guru's* greatness have been emphasized.

Skandha V: This *Skandha* has only 4 *padas* in which the *Bhāgavata's* story of Rishabhadeva and Jaḍabharata is given very briefly.

Skandha VI: This *Skandha* is almost of the double the size of the *skandha V*. In its 8 *padas* the stories of Ajāmila, Brihaspati, Vishvarūpa and Vritāsura are given in brief. There is also a *pada* wherein the importance of *guru* is highlighted. In the end the exploits of Nahusha and the dialogue between Indra and Ahilyā are discribed.

Skandha VII: This *Skandha* also consists of 8 *padas* carrying in brief the stories of Narisiṁha *avatāra*, murder of Tripura and exploits of Nārada.

Skandha VIII: This *Skandha* is a little more than double the size of the preceding *Skandha* (17 *padas*). The stories of Gajamochana, incarnation of kūrma, sea-churning and securing nectar by the devas, incarnation of Vāmana and Matsya etc., are told in brief. In the end, there is a *pada* of Veda Uddhava whose Shaṅkhāsura has replaced Hayagrīva of the *Bhāgavata*.

Skandha IX: This is a big *Skandha* containing 174 *padas*. Here we find, unlike in the preceding *Skandha*, detailed description of the exploits of King Puraravā, Seer Chyavana, Haladhara, King Ambarish, seer Saṁbhari, the Gaṅgā's descent and activity of Parashurāma. This is followed by an account of the exploits of Rāma, in a much more detailed and impressive manner than what we get in the *Bhāgavata*

Skandha X: The *Skandha* is divided, like the *Bhāgavata, into two parts: (I) Pūrvārdha*; and (II) *Uttarārdha* In the former we have 4130 *padas* which for the most part depict Krishṇa's birth, childhood, murder of Kaṅsa and Akrūra's meeting with the Pāṅdavas. The *uttarārdha* part has relatively smaller number of *padas* (149). Here, too, we find Krishṇa's exploits described in detail. Of these the important ones are those related to Rukamaṇi's acquisition, battle with Jarāsaṅdha and his liquidation, birth of Pradumna, Pradumna's and Anirudha's marriage, Rājā Nriga's bliss, murder of *rākshasas*, and *Sudāmācharitra*.

In the *Skandha* Sūra has not followed *Bhāgavata* very strictly, His originality, creativity, the great poet in him have in a way forced him to be independent in his descriptions. Here there is life, colour and depth in his *padas* which give Sūra an enviable position among the world-poets.

Skandha XI: This is again a very small *Skandha* (4*padas*). In the first two *padas* Uḍdhawa has been shown in great *bhakti* of Lord Krishṇa and in the remaining two the incarnations in Nārāyaṇa and Haṅsa are described.

Skandha XII: This is the last *Skandha* which consists of 5 *padas* in all. In these *padas* the incarnation of Buddha, advent of Kāli, Parīkshita's attainment of *moksha* and Janmejaya's snake-sacrifice have been described briefly.[34]

In sum, we can safely declare that of the several works ascribed to Sūra only one is his and that is *Sūrasāgara*. This work comprised one lakh *padas*. None of its present editions is complete. A serious 'hunt' on scientific lines be made by scholars to procure lost *padas* of Sūra. Complete success is out of question, but at least some more *padas* can certainly be had.[35]

References

1. We have it on the testimony of the *Vārtā* that Sūra composed and sang Kirtanas in thousands. These had begun to be recorded in a book called *Chauprar* in Sūra's own life time under the direction and supervision of Sūra himself. These hymns formed Sūra's *Sāgara*. See Harirāi, *Bhāvaprakasha (Vārtā)*, p.55
2. M.C. Parikh, *Sri Vallabhāchārya*, pp. 307-10
3. See *Vārtā*, pp. 53-54, where he says that Sūra had composed one lakh *padas*.
4. *Survey Report*, 1912-14,p.233.
5. *Ibid.*, 1906-8 p.325.
6. *Ibid.*, p.324.
7. *Ibid.*, 1906-8, p.234.
8. *Ibid.*, 1917-19; p.372
9. *Ibid.*, 1912-14, p.233.
10. *Ibid.*, 1917-19, p.373.
11. *Ibid.*, 1906-8, p.323.
12. *Ibid.,1909-11, p.421*
13. *Ibid.*, 1900, p.6
14. *Ibid.*, 1917-19, p.437.
15. *Ibid.*
16. *MS*. No. 46/5.
17. *MS*. No. 16/10.
18. See pp.731,761
19. *Ibid*
20. For a detailed discussion, see Vrajeshwar Verma, *op. cit.*, p.80

21. *Vārtā*, pp. 53-55
22. *Vārtā*. p.54
23. *Ibid.*, p.33.
24. *Shrīmadbhāgavata*, II, 9.32-35
25. *Sāgara*, 1,225.
26. See Harbans lal Sharma, *op.cit.*, p.143.
27. Vārtā,p.17
28. See Harbans lal Sharma, op. cit., p. 143.
29. She Bhanwarlal Joshi, *Sūradās aur Narsiṅgha Mehta* (Ahmedabad: Grujarabharati, 1968), pp.29-31
30. Not to speak of differences in verbal accounts, even manuscripts of different works usally do not tally with one another.
31. The oldest of these Mss. is of VS. 1639 (1572). It's title is *Sūrapadāwalī* and it is prescrived at the Pothikhānā of Jaipur. For details of various MSS. see Jawahar Lal Chaturvedi, *Sūradāsa Adhyayana Sāmagrī* (Mathura:, A.B. Braja Sahitya Mandala, VS.2016), pp. 5-17.27-31.
32. For details see *Ibid.*, pp.21-23;27-31; also see Krishṇāchārya, 'Unnisaviṅ shati me prakāshita *Sūrasāgara'*, *Sūra Sahitya Sandarbha* Eds. Ram Sarup Arya and G. Agrawala (Bijnore: Sūra Pañchāshati Samāroha Samiti, 1976). pp. 42-48
33. The edition, published in 1958 in two volumes, has been edited by the great linguist and litterateur Jagan Nath 'Ratnākara'.
34. This pada is based on the following *Shloka* of the *Bhāgavatapurāna*:

    Mūkam karoti vāchālam paṅgum langhayate girim
    Yatkripā tamahaṁ vaṅde paramānandamādhawam
35. Interestingly, Tulsidāsa has also taken inspiration from this verse for the *maṅgalācharaṇa* of his *Mānasa*:

    Mūka hoyi vāchāla, paṅgu chaḍhai girivara gahana
    Jāsu kripā so dayālu, dravahu sakala kalimaladahana.

4

THE POET

I

Before we discuss Sūrā as a poet it seems pertinent to have a brief resume of his views—philosophical, religious and social for the correct understanding and assessment of the poet.

Sūra lived and wrote his poetry during such a time which witnessed the fall of the Afghans and the rise to power by the moghals, resulting in the establishment of a stable empire by Akbar, who brought about an all round unity and harmony in all the sections of Indian society. That the period which marked the clash of centrifugal and centripetal forces and also that of the conservative and liberal outlook sensing the mood of the general masses of his days Sūra too fought against those discordant tendencies or factors and opened the portals of bhakti (devotion) to one and all irrespective of caste or creed.

It is believed that to begin with Sūra was a Rāmānandī. This assumption is based on Sūra's 'humility' and 'entreaty'noticed in his Vinaya-padas[1]. Another view is that Sūra was Shaivite. This belief is borne out by a pada of 'Sūrasārāvalī' to which all the shlokas of Bhavishya Purāṇa adds further credence.[2] On close scrutiny these views are untenable.[3-4] In the opinion of some other scholars Sūra seems to have followed Harīvanshī sect[5] for some time during his stay at Majhāvalī.[6] But about 1510 A.D. he met a great saint—Vallabhāchārya and joined his sect. Vallabhāchārya's[7] thoughts and dogmas exercised a tremendous influence on Sūra. He became a great Vaishṇava of the *Puṣṭimārga—the cult of grace,*[8] as propounded by Vallabhāchārya. In the second *Skandha* of *Bhāgavata Purāṇa Puṣti* is defined as Poshaṇa and Poshaṇa is nothing but the other name for 'God's grace'. God's grace is two fold-*Sādhanarūupā* (as a cause or means) and Sādhyarūpa (as an effect or end). In the former the devotee has to make efforts for the attainment of *God—Parabrahma* but in the latter the devotee completely surrenders himself to Him. With his deep involvement in *Puṣti-Bhakti,* the almighty God himself takes care of his devotee with the result that the devotee, having reposed full and exclusive faith in his Lord, feels quite contented and does no longer bother at all for anything. In *Puṣti-Bhakti* God's grace for the devotee plays a very significant role. It is His grace alone through which the devotee after crossing over the illusory world attains His abode of enternal bliss and is finally freed from the shackles of birth and rebirth (Jīvana-mukta) for ever:

(i) Jāpara Dīnānātha dharai,

Soi kulīna baḍau sundara soi, jāpara Kṛpā Karai[9]

— — — —

— — — —

Sūradāsa Bhagavanta-bhajana bina phiri phiri Jahara Jarai

जा पर दीनानाथ ढ़रै ।

सोइ कुलीन, बड़ौ सुन्दर सोइ, जापर कृपा करै।

सूरदास भगवंत-भजन बिन फिरि फिरि जहर जैरे।

____ ____ __ __ ____

____ ____ ____ ____

(ii) Jākau Dīānātha nivājai

Bhavasāgara maiṅ Kabahuṅ na jhūkai,

abhaya nisānai bājai

जाकौ दीनानाथ निवाजै।

भवसागर मैं कबहुं न झूकै, अभय निसानै बाजै[10]

(iii) Hari kī kṛpā jāpara hoi,

Tāhi kachhu yaha bahuta nāhīṅ hṛdaya dekhau joi,

Harana karana samartha eī kahauṅ bāraṁbāra,

Sūra Hari-Kṛpā taiṅ khala tari gaeṅ saṅsāra.

हरि की कृपा जापर होइ

ताहि कछु यह बहुत नाहीं हृदय देखौ जोइ।

हरन, करन समर्थ एई, कहौं बारंबार।

सूर हरि-कृपा तैं खल तरि गएं संसार।।[11]

According to Vallabhāchāya the *Puṣti-Bhakti* is of four kinds—*Pravāha Puṣti, Maryādā-Puṣti, Puṣti-Puṣti* and *Ṣuddha Puṣti. In Pravāha Puṣti* the devotee while leading worldly life here devotes whole-heartedly himself to the worship of God. In *Maryādā Puṣti* the devotee after withdrawing his mind from the material pleasures hands himself over to the service of God by listening to discourses about Him and chanting His name which is a mighty force. The third entitled as *Puṣti-Puṣti* concerns those devotees who though having secured His grace still remain engaged in his adoration. According to *Ṣuddha Puṣti* the devotee mentally becomes one with the līlās (divine sports) of God. His mind is thus completely transformed into His *Līlāsthalī* (sport-ground). Cows, Cowherds, Gopīs, the Yamunā, the Kadamba tree, Rādhā and Krishṇa all merge their identities in Him. Sūra followed the path of *Ṣuddha Puṣti* as the sole means of his emancipation The main basis of Sūra's *Bhakti* thus lies in 'God's grace'. All these, in Sūra's opinion, are illusory (bhramātmaka).[12] There is no place of *jñāna*, yoga, karma and even for upāsanā there.

It is the Vallabhāchārya's philosophy of *Ṣuddhādvaita* (pure monism or non-dualism) as different form Shaṅkar's *Advaitavāda* that appeals to Sūra. Accordingly Sūra holds that Krishṇa is nothing but 'Para-brahma' in the subtle form who is all-pervasive. He is the creator, protector and also the destroyer of the whole universe. He is the root cause of the world. He assumes whatever form he desires by the process of evolution (āvirbhāva) and disappearance (tirobhāva) of His attributes. Vishṇu, Rāma and Hari are all but His other names. There is no essential difference between Krishṇa with attributes (*saguṇa*) and Krishṇa without attributes (*nirguṇa).* Krishṇa is acceptable to sūra in both the *saguṇa* and *ṇirguṇa* mode of worship. He looks upon Brahma as the whole (aṅshin) and the individual soul (*jīva*) as part (*aṅsha*). As Brahma he manifests Himself of His own free will in the form of *Jīvas*. There is, in essence, no essential distinction between the two. Sūra does not treat *Māyā* also as something distinct from *Brahma*. It is totally subservient to Him (*So Hari māyā jā vasa māhiṅ*—Skandha 3, pada 13/394) and finally submerges into Him after *Pralaya* (total annihilation of the universe). Sūra does not consider

Māyā in its visible form as unreal but on the other hand regards it as the creative energy of Brahma. This *Māyā* is quite different from *Avidyā* (ignorance) which stands as a great hinderance in the attainment of final goal. Lord's grace is required to overcome the deep impact of this kind of *Māyā*. *Mukti* (salvation) can only be achieved through bhakti which means ardent and intense love of Krishṇa. Sūra has deviated from the philosophy of Vallabha in giving a great importance to Rādhā in the worldly or mundane life of Krishṇa as a part of Krishṇa's self neither independent from or fully identical with him and also as a symbol of his *Shakti* which is the prime source of divine bliss.[13] Sūra regards Rādhā as embodiment of supreme love and beauty.

Truly speaking, Sūra did not propound any philosophy in general or any particular system. He was basically out and out a poet who kept himself always engaged in chanting the name and glory of God (Krishṇa). He was an enlightened man having liberal and cosmopolitan views. He was tolerant, truthful and thoughtful. The blind dogmas and convictions had no place in the life of this great blind poet of Haryana. He had no ill-will, jealousy or hatred towards any one. He could well feel the pulse of the masses and dive deep into the human psyche. He was in fact a true son of God. All his children were his brothers. The portals of *bhakti* he propagated were open to all irrespective of any caste or sex. He was bold enough to raise his voice against tyranny and injustice done to the common people. He symapathized with them in their sufferings. He was a true humanist in the real sense.

Sūra had infinite faith in social eqaulity. For him the *rājā* (King) and raṅka (beggar) were equal. Not only that even *Bhagavāna* (God) and his *bhakta* (devotee) stood on equal footing. Krishṇa, the Supreme Lord, is depicted as roaming about in the company of *gopas* (cowherds) in the streets of Braja, indulging in all sorts of sportive activities with them. He (Krishṇa) mixes with the lowly freely, caring the least for their caste or creed. Neither the *gopas* have a feeling that Krishṇa was the son of a *rājā*, a superior one for that matter, They stand on equal footing, exchange pleasantries and quarrels amongst themselves. The *gopas* at times go even to the extent of challenging Krishṇa thus:

(i) Āju hauṅ eka-eka kari ṭarihauṅ,

Kai tumahī kai hamahīṅ, mādhāu apuna bharose larihauṅ.

(ii) hauṅ tau patita sāta pīḍhina kauṅ, patita hwai nistarihauṅ.

आजु हौं एक एक करि टरि हौं ।

कै तुम ही कै हमहीं, माधौ अपुन भरोसे लरि हौं ।।

हौं तो पतित सात पीढ़िन कौं, पतित ह्वै निस्तरहौं ।[14]

(iii) Aba hauṅ ughari nachyau chahata hauṅ, tumhaiṅ virada binu karihauṅ

Patita pāvana Hari, virada tumhārau konaiṅ nāma dharyau.

अब हौं उधरि नच्यौ चहत हौं, तुम्हैं विरद बिनु करिहौं ।

पतित-पावन हरि, विरद तुम्हारौ कोनैं नाम धर्‌यौ ?[15]

(iii) Tuma kaba moso patita udhāryau,

Kāhe kauṅ prabhu virada bulāvata bina masakata ko tāryau.

तुम कब मो सो पतित उधार्यौ ।

काहे कौं प्रभु विरद बुलावत, बिन मसकत को तार्यौ । ।[16]

Again when he takes up Rādhā-Krishṇa love episode, Sūra places the two—a son of a rājā and an ordinary woman from an ordinary family on an equal footing. Unlike Krishṇa of other poets, Sūra's Krishṇa even marries Rādhā. Even Rukmiṇī, the queen, embraces her 'as if she was the sister born of the same father'.[17]

Indeed Sūra was a man who took the concept of social equality to such an extent that he brought his 'God' even to the same level. This approach puts an end to master-serf relationship between man and God.

The superiority of the upper castes, Brāhmaṇas etc. was also challanged by Sūra, though not in so strong terms as was done by Kabīra for obvious reasons:

Jāpara Dīnānātha ḍharai,

Soī kulīna baḍau sundara soī jāpara kṛpā karai.

Sūra patita tari jāya tanika meṅ jo prabhu naika ḍharai

जापर दीनानाथ ढरै ।

सोई कुलीन बड़ौ सुन्दर सोई जापर कृपा करै ।

सूर पतित तरि जाय तनिक में जो प्रभु नैक ढरै ।[18]

Anyone on whom the lord of the poor bestows His grace is well-born (superior) and beautiful. Says Sūra, all those fallen men and women who receive even a little of the lord's grace, are able to cross the sea of sin instantly.

Sūra shows hollowness of religious rituals etc. which create differences between different people. An individual's love for God who performs līlā on earth, in human form is sufficient to mitigate one's sin, if any, and one does not need to follow religious rituals, accepted methods of worship, intellectual discourses, etc. (that is, the religious courses prescribed by the Brāhmaṇa priests are irrelevant):

Karmayoga puni jñāna upāsana saba hī bhrama bharamāyau.

Shrīvallabha gurutatva sunāyau līlā bheda batāyau.

कर्म योग पुनि ज्ञान उपासन सब ही भ्रम भरमायौ ।

श्रीवल्लभ गुरुतत्व सुनायौ लीला भेद बतायौ[19]

Unlike his Guru, Vallabhāchārya, who imparted all the reasonings behind his philosophy of love, duly substantiated by scriptures, Sūra used it in his own way. For this poet, love needed no reasoning; it was its own justification. For him it was an inner urge, as it always happened in relations between a mother and her son, a young woman and her lover. It was this element that made Sūradāsa a most sensitive and sensuous poet.[20]

Almost in every verse Sūradāsa reminded his reader that though the story of Krishṇa's *līlā* looked very much human, it was a divine act, and yet, what his readers derived from his verses represented the best of the pleasures of man and woman relationship. More significant was the fact that Sūra's concept of relationship between man and woman, on the one hand, rejected libertinism that was quite prevalent under feudalism and, on the other, almost recognised equality of both the sexes as the true basis. Rādhā was no slave to the highest of the feudal lords, Krishṇa, but a friend, a childhood friend. And, for this woman, her love felt the same pains as she felt for him when they got separated.[21]

A question may arise here: From where did, Sūradāsa imbibe those concepts which were missing in Bhāgvata Purāṇa which were in a way contrary to the teaçhings of that sacred book? Sūra had it from the folk tradition which already contained songs that treated Rādhā-Krishṇa theme as a commoner's love-story. Of course, Sūradāsa refined it both on the level of language and also on the philosophical level in the light of Vallabhāchārya's teachings.[22]

It is in fact difficult to give any definition to the religion of Sūradāsa. For the ruling classes, religion had been a conspiracy against the toiling people to subjugate them, but the common man converted it in their own way to meet the needs of their matrerial life, and endeavoured to fill the gap that lay between their dreams and the immediate reality. Saints like Vallabhāchārya and Rāmānanda felt the need for a popular religion. Though they attempted to take it up to the classical level and even substantiated it by readings from the scriptures, it basically remained epicurean in spirit, and more so after receiving poetic touch from poets like Sūra, Kabīra and even Tulsī. In Sūradāsa *lokadharma* (popular religion) once again marked its victory over the hypocrisy of the religions of the ruling and oppressive classes. Further, it marked an era of another advance in the refinement of sensibilities and thus another leap forward in enrichment of humanist values of life.[23]

Sūra's Vaishṇavism remained wedded to *Lokadharma*, while others of the same school reached nearer to gratification of libertinism of the upper classes. This is why Sūradāsa remains relevant to the toiling people of our times too.[24]

Before we discuss at length the poetic content of Sūra's works, it is proper to have some idea of the language that he has composed his *padas* in. It is *Braja Bhāṣā,* the language of the masses *(loka-bhāṣā)* which the poet has himself termed as *bhāṣā*:

Ṣrīmukha chāri sloka diye Brahmā ko samujhāi,

Brahmā Nārada sauṅ kahe, Nārada Vyāsa sunāi,

Vyāsa kahe Sukadeva sauṅ dwādasa skandha banāi,

Sūradāsa soī kahe padabhāṣā kari gai,

श्रीमुख चारि स्लोक दिए ब्रह्मा को समुझाइ ।

ब्रह्मा नारद सौं कहे, नारद व्यास सुनाइ । ।

व्यास कहे सुकदेव सौं द्वादस स्कंध बनाइ ।

सूरदास सोई कहे पदभाषा करि गाइ । ।[25]

The credit of shaping the 'Loka Bhāṣā' into a literary form, in fact, goes to Sūra alone. He has chosen soft, easy and emotive words in his works and he is much sensitive in his choice of appropriate words. Sūra's works are abundantly rich in different kinds of figures of speech which lend an additional charm to his diction simplicity, delicacy, fluency, ingenuity, musical rhythm and life-like portrayls are other characteristics noticeable in his poetry.

Language Complexion

Sūra has used the same vowels and consonants as found in Brajabhāṣā in his poetry. The use of au, aī, ae, āi, āī, āū, ia,uā, oi, oī—ending words e.g. tārau, kārau, dārau—Sk. 1/178, aisau Sk. 10/1364 dekhou—Sk. 10/1300; sikhau 10/1352; baī naī—Sk. 1/185; tau, 1/117; nae, bhae- 1/286; āī—10/1133; dhāi-1.295 parāī—1/147; baṭāū—9/489; suniata—10/4632;

dtārau—Sk 1/753; joi, roi- 1/286; soī—1/117 etc. and that of the nasalized forms viz khāeṅ- Sk. 2/32; ihāuṅ- Sk. 3/383 etc., noticeable in abundance, has made the poet's language extremely melodious. In place of 'ऋ' 'रि (ri)' is commonly employed. Successive repetition of even three vowels is also seen at some places e.g. so āe (सोआए)—Sk. 10/626. as for the consonant ṇ (ण),Sūra has retained it as such at places but generally he has changed it to n (न).Similarly both ṣ (ष) and Ś (श) also have sometimes been retained as such but more often he has changed into s(श)also. There are some words where '(ड़)' is changed to 'ra (र)' (Ghorā for Ghoḍā in)- Sk. 9/9); 'y' and 'v' are generally changed into 'j' and 'b' respectively. Sūra's language is very rich in noun and verbal forms. His choice of adjectives and adverbs too is very apt.

Vocabulary

Tadbhava words (derived from Sanskrit) are used in high frequency by the poet but saṁskrit words in their original form (tatsama) are also found in abundance in his poetry. Sūra has employed tatsama words in Vinayapadas and also at places where he has portrayed static descriptions of Krishṇa's physical beauty or playing on flute (muralī-vādana) or the Dance Divine (Rāsa līlā). He has used the tatsama words not only in case of noun-forms alone but also in respect of verbal forms. But at some places tatsama verbs are also found either in their masculine or feminine forms in accordance with the grammar of Braja Bhāsā viz. Gati sudhaṅga nrityati braja nāri (1675), nrityata syāma nānā raṅga (10/1674), Syāma tanu rājati pīta picchaurī (10/1672). On the contrary tadbhava words are used to depict childhood pranks and frolicks (Bālalīlā) of Krishṇa or dynamic thoughts and feelings of gopīs (milk-maids). Such colloquial forms of words are found in plenty in 'Bhramaragīta.' A few examples given below will testify this.

***Vinaypada* (विनयपद)**

Charana *kamala* bandauṅ hari rāī.

jākī *kripā paṅgu giri* laṅghai aṅdhe ko saba kuccha darsāī.

Bahirau sunai, gūṅga puni bolai, *raṅka* chalai sira *chhatra* dharāī.

Sūradāsa *swāmī karunāmaya* bāra-bāra bandauṅ tihi pāī.

चरन कमल बन्दौं हरि राई।

जाकी कृपा पंगु गिरि लंघैं, अंधे को सब कुछ दरसाई।

बहिरौ सुनै, गूंग पुनि बोलै, रंक चलै सिर छत्र धराई।

सूरदास स्वामी करुनामय बार-बार बन्दौं तिहि पाई।[26]

***Physical beauty* (रूपवर्णन)**

Sobhatī *kara navaneeta liye.*

Ghuṭurani chalana renu-*tana-maṅdita, mukha dadhi Lepa kie*

Chāru kapola, lola *lochana, gorochana-tilaka* die.

Laṭa-laṭakani manu *matta madhupa-gaṇa, mādaka* madhuhiṅ pie.

Kaṭhula-Kaṅṭha, bajra—kehari-*nakha,* rājata *ruchira* hie.

Dhanya Sūra ekau pala ihiṅ sukha, kā sata *kalpa* jie.

सोभति कर नवनीत लिए।

घुटुरुनि चलन रेनु-तन-मण्डित, मुख दधि लेप किए।
चारु कपोल लोल लोचन गोरोचन-तिलक दिए।
लट-लटकनि मनु मत्त मधुपगन मादक मधुहिं पिए।
कठुला-कंठ, बज्र केहरि-नख, रजत रुचिर हिए।
धन्य सूर एकौ पल इहिं सुख, का सत कल्प जिए। [27A]

and

Giridhara, vajradhara,muralīdhara, dharnidhara, mādhauṅ *pītāṁbaradhara.*

Saṅkhachakradhara, gadāpadmadhara, sīsa*mukuṭadhara, adharasudhādhara kaṅbukaṅṭhadhara, Kaustubhamanidhara vanamālādhara muktamālādhara.*

Sūradāsa *prabhu gopaveṣadhara,* kālīphana para *charanakamaladhara.*

गिरिधर, दज्रधर, मुरलीधर, धरनीधर, माधौं पीताम्बरधर।
संखचक्रधर, गदापद्मधर, सीसमुकुटधर, अधरसुधाधर।
कंबुकण्ठधर कौस्तुभमनिधर, बनमालाधर, मुक्तमालाधर।
सूरदास प्रभु गोपवेषधर, कलीफन चरनकमलधर। [27B]

Childhood pranks (बाल लीला)

Khelana dūri jāta kata kānhā?

Āju sunyo maiṅ hāū āyo tuma nahiṅ jānata nānhā.

Ika larikā abahiṅ bhaja āyo rovata dekhyo tāhi.
kāna tori vaha leta sabani ke, larikā jānata jāhi.

खेलन दूरि जात कत कान्हा?
आजु सुन्यो मैं हाऊ आयो, तुम नहिं जानत नान्हा।
इक लरिका अबहिं भजि आयो, रोवत देख्यो ताहि।
कान तोरि वह लेत सबनि के, लरिका जानत जाहि। [28]

As a result of the influence of Vīragāthā Kāla the poet has also used *Prākrit* words, though very rarely, like sāyara (सायर),sāara (साअर)from sāgara (सागर)—skandha 1,125; puhupa (पुहुप) from puṣpa (पुष्प) etc.— skandha 10,2110. Words from *Bundelakhaṅdī-gahibī* (गहिबी), jānibī (जानिबी), dekhībī (देखिबी), *Avadhī— khoisa-खोइस, soisa-सोइस, hoisa-होइस, ihivāṅ-इहिवां, jini-जिनि; Gujarātī—pelā-पेला, ḍhorī-ढ़ोरी, biyo-बियो and Rājasthānī*-pūrabalī (पूरबली) also find a place in his padas. Loan (Arabīc and Persian) words are found in great number but in their modified from viz. masakata (मसकत), khasama (खसम), khavāsa (खवास), saratāja (सरताज),nāhaka (नाहक),bakasīsa (बकसीस),dāmanagīra (दामनगीर), taratāzā (तरताजा), gumāna (गुमान),rukkā (रुक्का), garībanavāja (गरीबनवाज), kharāda (खराद), amala (अमल), gunahagāra (गुनहगार), amānata (अमानत), sandooka (सन्दूक), akala (अकल), dagābāja (दगाबाज) etc. in order to keep the melody and flexibility of Braja Bhāṣā in tact. Sūra has freely used rural (desī) words too like auchaṭa (औचट),indurī (इन्डुरी), abāra (अबार),ghīṅcha (घींच),chiriyā (चिरिया),chhohrā (छोहरा),kacchautī (कछौटी),jhagā (झगा),chutiyā (चुटिया),achagiri (अचगिरी),laḍabaurī (लडबौरी), khutilā (खुटिला), jhāma (झाम) etc. in tune with the spirit of the language. In short Sūra has generally used the words in their current forms. But he has not hesitated even to modify them as per provision of the metre or to maintain the rythm such as–paṅga (paṅgu) lavanī (navanīta), keta (ketu), gaiyā (go), barīsa (varṣa), gauna (gagana), kilakī, hilakī, silakī, milakī, etc. पंग (पंगु), लवनी (नवनीत), केत (केतु), गइया (गो), बरीस (बर्ष), गौन (गगन), किलकी, हिलकी, सिलकी, मिलकी etc. This has made the language more effective and musical.

In addition to this he has tried to coin new words as well by combining Arabic-Persian and Sanskrit words. For example, lonaharāmī, faujapatī etc. The enigmatic verses reflect the poet's keen learning and admirable skill in playing on words. He has freely used the various derived forms of the same word such as झकझोर-झकझोर, झकझोरि,झकझोरत or ति,झकझोरै; झलक—झलक,झलकत,झलमलात,झलकाइ etc.

The use of onomatopoeic (ध्वन्यात्मक) words lends peculiar charm and elegance to the language. This is quite evident from the description of the *dāvānala* (forest conflagration) and also that of the *Govardhana Līlā* given in the following *padas*:

(i) Bhaharāta Jhaharāta dāvā (nala) āyau.

Gheri chahūṅ ora, kari sora andora bana, dharani ākāsa chahūṅ pāsa chhāyau.

Barata bana-bāṅsa, tharaharāta kusa-kāṅsa, jari uḍata hai māṅsa, ati prabala dhāyau.

Jhapaṭi Jhapaṭati lapaṭa, phūla-phala chaṭa-chaṭaki, phaṭata laṭa laṭaki druma druma navāyau.

भहरात झहरात दावा (नल) आयौ।

घेरि चहुं ओर,करि सोर अन्दोर बन, धरनि आकास चहुं पास छायौ।

बरत बनबांस थरहरात,कुस कांस जारि उड़त है मांस,अति प्रबल धायौ।

झपटि झपटति लपट,फूल- फल चट- चटकि,फटत,लटलटकि द्रुम-द्रुम नवायौ।[29]

(ii) Dasahuṅ disā dusaha dāvāgni upajī hai ihi kāla.

Paṭakata bāṅsa, kāṅsa kusa chaṭakata, laṭakata tāla tamāl.

Uchaṭati ati aṅgāra, phuṭata kara, jhapaṭata lapaṭa karāla.

दसहुं दिसा दुसह दावाग्नि, उपजी है इहि काल।

पटकत बांस, कांस कुस चटकत, लटकत ताल तमाल।

उचटति अति अंगार, फुटत कर, झपटत लपट कराल।।[30]

(iii) Suni meghavartta saji saina āye

. . . .

Ghaharāta, gararāta, daradarāta, hararāta, tararāta jhaharāta mātha nāye

सुनि मेघवर्त्त सजि सैन आए।

. . . .

. . . .

घहरात, गररात, दररात, हररात, तररात झहरात माथ नाए।[31]

and

(iv) (Gagan) megha ghaharāta thaharāta gātā.

Chapalā chamachamāti chamaki nabha bhaharāta rākhi kyoṅ na brajanaṅda tātā.

Sunata karunā baina, uṭhe hari bala-aina, naina kī sain giritana nihāryau.

Sabana dhīraja diyau, uchaki mandira liyau, kahyau girirāja tumaka ubāryau.

(गगन) मेघ घहरात थहरात गाता।

चपला चमचमाति चमकि नभ भहरात, राखि क्यौं न ब्रजनंद ताता।

सुनत करुना बैन, उठे हरि बल-ऐन, नैन की सैन गिरि-तन निहार्‌यौ।

सबन धीरज दियौ, उचकि मंदिर लियौ, कह्यौ गिरि-राज तुमक उबार्‌यौ।।[32]

The words in the above *padas* fully suggest the outbreak of wild-fire all around, the thundering of dense clouds and the tumultous storm. They provide a musical flow and echo the sense to be conveyed. Herein such harsh sounds are used. Contrary to this soft sounds are employed in depicting the innocent beauty of Krishṇa. In erotic unions and all other soft moments as well the poet makes use of words with softer sounds.

Sūra's language is replete with idioms and proverbs for they provide brevity, expressiveness and grace to the language. Their frequent use has also contributed towards infusing force and vitality into the poet's expressions. At times the poet floods them in one and the same verse. They are available in large numbers in his poetry, especially in 'Bhramaragīta' as the following will show.

Idioms (मुहावरे)

Tau lagi saba *pāni kī chuparī.*

Gūṅge kau gura kiyo sabani.

Nanda braja *lījai thoki bajāi.*

Kāṭe ūpara *launa chaḍhāvata.*

Jāgata *ginata gagana ke tāre.*

Phūṅka phūnka hiyarau sulagāta.

Sūradāsa prabhu hamahiṅ nidari, *dāḍhe para lona lagāvata.*

Sūra para sauti hamāre kubjā *chāma ke dāma chalāvai.*

Khelana aba merī *jāta balaiyā.*

Aṅkhiyāṅ hari ke *hātha bikānī.*

Gura kī chīṅtīṅ jyoṅ pāgī.

Dhura hī taiṅ khotī khāyau hai.

Naṭinī lauṅ kara lie lakuṭiyā, kapi jyoṅ *nācha nachāvai.*

Sūrasyāma taji aura na sūjhai jyoṅ *Khere kī dūba.*

Sūradāsa prabhu tumhāre milana bina bhai *bhusa para kī bhīti.*

Sūra su kata *haṭhi nāva chalāvata ye* saritā hai sūkhī.

तौ लगि सब पानी की चुपरी ।[33]

गूंगे कौ गुर कियो सबनि ।[34]

नंद ब्रज लीजै ठोकि बजाइ ।[35]

काटे ऊपर लौन चढ़ावत ।[36]

जागत गिनत गगन के तारे ।[37]

फूंक फूंक हियरौ सुलगात ।[38]

सूरदास प्रभु हमहिं निदरि, दाढ़े पर लोन लगावे ।[39]

सिर पर सौति हमारे कुब्जा चामके दाम चलावै ।[40]

खेलन अब मेरी जात बलैया ।[41]

अंखियां हरि के हाथ बिकानी[42]

गुर की चींटीं ज्यों पागी[43]

धुर ही तै खोटी खायौ है[44]

नटिनी लौं कर लिए लकुटिया, कपि ज्यौं नाच नचावे[45]

सूरस्याम तजि और न सूझै, ज्यौं खेरे की दूब[46]

सूरदास प्रभु तुम्हारे मिलन बिन भई भुस पर की भीति[47]

सुर सु कत हठि नाव चलावत ये सरिता है सूखी[48]

Proverbs *(लोकोक्तियां)*

Mana kī mana hī māṅjha rahī.

Āpana kiyo āpahiṅ bhugatahiṅ.

Kahau kauna pai kaḍhata kanukā, jina haṭi bhusī pacchaurī.

Sūradāsa prabhu tumhare darasa ko *karavata laiṅhe kāsī.*

Kahā kathana māsī ke āgeṅ, jānata nānī nānana.

Kākī bhūkha gaī bayāri bhakhi, binā dūdha ghrita māṅde.

Dāī āgeṅ peta durāvati.

Jo buniyai soī puni luniyai.

Yaha jobana barṣā kī nadī jyoṅ

Jaiseṅ ghaṭa pūrana na dolai adhabharī dagadaura.

Jākau mana mānata hai jāsauṅ so tahaṅī sukha mān.

मन की मन ही मांझ रही ।[49]

आपन कियौं आपहिं मुगतहि[50]

कहौ कौन पै कढ़त कनूका जिन, हठि भुसी पछौरी[51]

सूरदास प्रभु तुम्हारे दरस कौ, करवत लैहे कासी ।[52]

कहा कथन मासी के आगें, जानत नानी नानन ।[53]

काकी भूख गई बयारि भष[54]

दाई आगें पेट दुरावति ।[55]

जो बुनियै सोई पुनि लूनियै ।[56]

यह जोबन बरषा की नदि ज्यों[57]

जैसें घट पूरन न डोलै अधभरी डगडौर[58]

जाकौ मन मानत है जासौं, सो तहंई सुख मान ।[59]

There is regular flow in Sūra's language. The words strike to him spontaneously and consequently the language moves on uninterrupted. See, for instance:

Aise bādara sajala, karana ati mahābala, chalata ghahairāta kari andhakālā.

Chakita bhaye Nanda, saba mahara chakrita bhaye chakita nara-nāri hari karata khyālā.

Ghaṭā ghanaghora laharāta, ararātā dararāta thararāta braja loga darape

Taḍita-āghāta tararāta, utapāta, suni, nāri-nara sakuchi tana prāna arape.

ऐसे बादर सजल, करन अति महाबल, चलत घहैरात करि अंधकाला ।

चकित भए नंद, सब महर चक्रित भए, चकित नर नारि हरि करत ख्याला ।

घटा घनधोर लहरात, अररात, दररात, थररात, व्रज लोग डरपे ।

तड़ित आघात. तररात, उतपात, सुनि, नारि-नर सकुचि तन प्रान अरपे ।[60]

Bādara bahu umaḍi ghumaḍi, baraṣata braja āyeṅ chaḍhi, kāre dhaure dhumareṅ, dhāre ati hīṅ jala.

Chapalā ati chamachamāti brajā-jana saba ati darāta, ṭerata sisu-pitā mātu, braja meiṅ bhayau galabala.

Garajata dhuni pralaya kāla, gokula bhayau aṅdhajāla, chakita bhaye gwāla-bāla, ghaharata nabha halachala.

बादर बहु उमड़ि, बरषत ब्रज आए चढ़ि कारे घौरे धूमरें धारे अति ही जल।

चपला अति चमचमाति, ब्रज-जन सब अति डरात, टेरत सिसु-पिता मातु ब्रज मैं भयौ गलबल।।

गरजत धुनि प्रलय काल, गोकुल भयौ अंधजाल, चकित भए ग्वाल-बाल, घहरत नभ हलचल।।[61]

These passages are suggestive of the thundering of the stormy thick clouds and flash of lightning, terrifying all the inhabitants of Braja:

Yashodā's words *'Thoki Bajāi'* etc. (take charge of your Braja. You are very fond of it. Bid me farewell) addressed to her husband (Nanda) in the famous pada given below:

Nanda Braja lījai ṭhoki bajāi

Dehuṅ bidā mili jāhiṅ madhupurī jahaṅ gokula ke rāi.

नन्द ब्रज लीजै ठोकि बजाइ।

देहुं बिदा मिलि जाहिं मधुपुरी जहं गोकुल के राइ।। (सूरसागर, स्कन्ध 10,3786)

are quite apt and forceful and at the same time are expressive of her mixed feeling of anger, resignation and humiliation.

Sūra has a peculiar knack of using appropriate language at appropriate time. The format of language also changes with the change in the situation. In describing the emotion of heroism he uses harsh and effective language as is quite evident in the pledge made by *Bhīshma* to fight to the last.

Āju jau harihiṅ na sastra gahāūṅ.

Tau lājauṅ gaṅgā jananī kauṅ sāṅtanu-suta na kahāūṅ.

Syaṅdana khaṅdi mahārathi khaṅḍauṅ, kapidhwaja sahita girāūṅ.

Pāṅḍava-dala-sanmukha hvai dhāūṅ, saritā rudhira bahāūṅ.

Iti na karauṅ sapatha tau hari kī, kṣhatriya-gatihiṅ na pāūṅ.

Sūradāsa ranabhūmi vijaya binu jiyata na pīṭhi dikhāūṅ.

आजु जौ हरिहिं न सस्त्र गहाऊं ।
तौ लाजौं गंगा जननी कौं, सांतनु-सुत न कहाऊं ।
स्यन्दन खंडि महारथि खंडौं, कपिध्वज सहित गिराऊं ।
पाण्डवदल सन्मुख है धाऊं, सरिता रुधिर बहाऊं ।
इति न करौं सपथ तौं हरि की, छत्रिय गतिहिं न पाऊं ।
सूरदास रनभूमि विजय बिनु, जियत न पीठि दिखाऊं ।[62]

He is very alive to the most suitable correct usage of words. His choice of words in expressing the emotion of anger is worth-mentioning in the utterance of Rādhikā's mother when she finds that Rādhā is engaged all the time loitering about shamelessly in the company of Krishṇa.

Krodha kari sutā sauṅ kahati mātā.

Tohiṅ barjati marī, achagarī sira parī,

Garba gaṅjana nāma hai vidhātā.

Tohiṅ kacchu doṣa nahiṅ, bhramati tū jahāṅ tahiṅ,

Nadī doṅgara, banahiṅ patā pātā.

Mātu pitu loka kī kāni mānai nahīṅ.

Nilaja bhaī rahati nahiṅ lāja gātā.

क्रोध करि सुता सौं कहति माता।

तोहिं बरजात मरी, अचगरी सिर परी,

गर्ब गंजन नाम है विधाता।

तोहिं कछु दोष नहिं, भ्रमति तू जहां तहिं

नदी डोंगर, बनहिं पात पाता।

मातु पितु लोक की कानि मानै नहीं,

निलज भई रहति नहिं लाज गाता।[63]

Wherever Sūra depicts erotic or comic sentiment, he makes use of soft words as produce the desired effect. The milkmaids do not even feel any hesitation whatsoever in taunting or villifying Uddhava when he poignantly calls him a big merchant who had come to Braja for unloading his commodity of Yoga, demanding gold in return of his chaff.

Āyau ghosa baḍau vyaupārī

lāda khepa guru jṅāna joga kī, braja meiṅ āni utārī.

and

Udhau jāhu, tumahiṅ hama jānai

Syāma tumahiṅ hyāṅ kau nahiṅ paṭhyau, tuma hī bīcha bhulāne

____ ____ ____ ____ ____

Sūra syāma jaba tumahiṅ paṭhāyau, taba nekahu musakāne.

आयौ घोस बड़ौ व्यौपारी।

लादि खेप गुरु ज्ञान जोग की, ब्रज में आनि उतारी।।[64]

ऊधौ जाहु, तुमहिं हम ज्ञानै।

स्याम तुमहिं ह्यां कौ नहिं पठ्यौ, तुमही बीच भुलाने।

__ __ __ __ __

सूर स्याम जब तुमहिं पठायौ, तब नेकहु मुसकाने । ।[65]

Sūra has an effective control and command over language.Even though the same theme is repeated in his padas, every time it is presented in different lights and shades with renewed freshness.This does not in any way make the readers feel bored.

In a nutshell Sūra's language is an example in itself. Actually it is a kind of a current language of the age which heightens our awareness, intensifies our experience and sharpens our sensibilities. The later poets are greatly indebted to Sūra's language pattern, content and form.

III
Figures of speech (Alaṁkāra)

In Sūra's poetry figures of speech are noticed frequently. They have played a major role in making the language more impressive, attractive and graceful. They come to the poet in a natural effortless manner and form an integral part of the language. His figures of speech are plain, straight and self-speaking. He is fond of *Anuprāsa* (Alliteration) and *Yamaka* (Repetition of words similar in sound with different meanings) among *shabdālaṁkāras* and *Upamā* (simile), *Rūpaka* (Metaphor), *Utprekshā* (Poetical fancy), *Rūpakātishayokti* (Metaphorical hyperbole), *Drishtānta* (Illustration, *Vyatireka* (Contrast), Vyājokti (Artful concealment), *Viṣeshokti*, (Specific or peculiar statement) among *Arthālaṁkāras*. Some examples are quoted below:

Anuprāsa *(अनुप्रास)*

Arabarāi kara pāni gahāvata, dagamgāi dharani dhare paiyā

Tarapata nabha surapata brajā loga.

अरबराइ कर पानि गहावत, डगमगाइ धरनी धरे पैया [66]

तरफ्त नभ सुरपत, ब्रज लोग[67]

Here the underligned words are repeated.

Yamaka *(यमक)*

Sāraṅga sāraṅgadharahiṅ milāvahu,

Sāraṅga vinaya karati, *sāraṅga* sauṅ *sāraṅga* dukha bisarāhu.

सारंग सारंगधरहिं मिलावहु ।

सारंग विनय करति, सारंग सौं, सारंग दुख बिसरावहु ।।[68]

Here the same word सारंग has been repeated but with different meanings every time i.e. Friend, Krishṇa, Sky, Vishṇu and Kāmadeva respectively.

Upamā *(उपमा)*

Parama biyoginī saba ṭhāḍhī.

Jyoṅ jalahīna dīna kumudini bana, ravi prakāsa kī ḍaḍhī.

Jihiṅ vidhi mīna salila taiṅ bicchurai, tihiṅ ati gati akulāni.

परम बियोगिनी सब ठाढ़ी ।

ज्यौं जलहीन दीन कुमुदिनि बन, रवि प्रकास की डाढ़ी ।

जिहिं विधि मीन सलिलतैं बिछुरै, तिहिं अति गति अकुलानी ।।[69]

Gopīs feeling the pangs of separation *look like* the forest of lilies in the tank without water which is dried up with the sunbeams. Here love-lorn gopīs are compared with dried up lilies.

Utprekṣā *(उत्प्रेक्षा)*

Chalita kuṅdala gaṅda maṅdala jhalaka lalita kapola.

Sudhā-sara *janu* makara krīḍata, indu ḍaha ḍaha dola

चलित कुंडल गंड मंडल झलक ललित कपोल।
सुधा-सर जनु मकर क्रीड़त, इन्दु डह डह डोल।।[70]

The tremulous reflex of the ear-rings hanging on the bright cheeks of the gopis appears as if the crocodile is playing about in the ocean of nectar and also as if the moon is moving there slowly and slowly. Here the reflex of the ear-rings on the cheeks has been imagined as crocodile moving in the ocean of nectar and so on.

Rupaka *(रूपक)*

Charana-kamala baṅdauṅ harirāi.

Maiyā meiṅ to *chaṅda-khilaunā* laihauṅ.

Kamala-naina bali jāūṅ suchita hvai.

चरन-कमल बन्दौ हरि राइ[71]
मैय्या मैं तो चन्द-खिलौना लैहौं।[72]
कमल-नैन बलि जाऊं सुचित ह्वै।[73]

In the underlined words here there is complete resemblance between the object compared to (upamāna) and the object compared (upameya).

Rūpakātishayokti *(रूपकातिशयोक्ति)*

Adbhuta eka anupama bāga.

Jugala kamala para gaja bara krīḍata tāpara siṅha karata anurāga.

Hari para sarabara, sara para girivara, giri para phūle kañja parāga.

अद्भुत एक अनुपम बाग।

जुगल कमल पर गज बर क्रीडत तापर सिंह करत अनुराग।

हरि पर सरबर, सर पर गिरिवर, गिरि पर फूले कंज पराग [74]

Rādha's body is compared with a wonderful garden. The constituents of upameya (object compared) such as feet, thighs, waist etc. are implied here and they are expressed through the medium of upamānas (standard of comparison) such as lotus, elephants, lion etc. respectively.

Drishṭānta *(दृष्टान्त)*

Mero mana piya jīva basata hai, piya jiya moṅ maiṅ nāhiṅ.

Jyoṅ chakora chandā kauṅ nirakhata, ita uta drishṭi na jāi.

मेरो मन पिय जीव बसत है, पिय जिय मों मैं नाहिं।

ज्यों चकोर चन्दा कौं निरखत, इत उत दृष्टि न जाइ।।[75]

The idea expressed in the first line corresponds to the one in the second line. The two are not the same but there is some similalrity between them as there is between the original and the reflected image *(bimba pratibimba)*.

Vyājokti *(व्याजोक्ति)*

Maiṅ jānyoṅ yaha ghara apano hai, yā dhoke meṅ āyau

Dekhata ho gorasa meṅ chīntī, kāḍhana koṅ kara nāyau.

मैं जान्यों यह घर अपनो है, या धोखे में आयौ ।
देखत हो गोरस में चींटी, काढ़न कों कर नायौ । ।[76]

Krishṇa's statement here that he entered the gopī's house to take out the black ant from the earthen pot is just made by way of pretext to defend himself.

Vyatireka *(व्यतिरेक)*

Dekhi rī Hari ke chañchala naina,

....

Rājiva dala, indīvara, satadala, kamala kusesaya jāti

Nisi mudrita, prātahi vai vikasata, ye vigasata dina-rāti.

राजिवदल, इन्दीवर, सतदल, कमल, कुसेसय जाति ।
निसि मुद्रित, प्रातहि वै विकसत, ये विगसत दिन-राति । ।[77]

Krishṇa's tremulous eyes bloom day and night whereas the petals of all kind of lotuses remain closed at night and bloom only in the morning. The distinctive contrast is quite clear here. Krishṇa's eyes are represented as superior to the lotuses.

Viśeshokti *(विशेषोक्ति)*

Syāma rūpa nirakhata naina nibhari mohana phaṅdaparī.

Aba gayī chhabi samāi hiya maiṅ ṭārata hūṅ na ṭarī.

स्याम रूप निखरत नैन निभरि, मोहन फंदपरी ।
अब गई छबि समाइ हिए मैं टारत हूं न टरी । ।[78]

Krishṇa's charm has penetrated deep into the hearts that it can by no means be dislodged from there. Here the act of dislodging remains unaccomplished even though the cause i.e. determined effort is there.

Thus illustrations of Transferred Epithet (विशेषण विपर्यय) and Personifiction (मानवीकरण) are also seen in frequency in Sūra's poetic works. A few examples are given below:

Transferred Epithet

Aṅkhiyāṅ hari darsana kī bhūkhī

अंखियां हरि दर्सन की भूखी (10,4175, 3557)

The adjective 'bhūkhī (hungry) is always used for living beings who are able to eat but Sūra uses it for the eyes and suggests that as a living being is unable to survive without food similarly the eyes are unable to survive without their food viz. a view of Krishṇa.

Aṅkhīyāṅ hari darasana kī pyāsī

अंखियां हरि दरसन की प्यासी (10,4176, 3558)

Here the poet uses the word pyāsī (thirsty) for the eyes in the same context.

Personification

Nisidina barasata naina hamāre

निसिदिन बरसत नैन हमारे (10, 3856)

The root 'barasanā' in 'barasata' is used for clouds but Sûra has used it for the eyes of the love-stricken maidens just to show that tears go on dropping ceaselessly from their eyes.

At another place Sūra uses the root 'Arujhnā' (to be entwined) for the mind whereas it is always used for ropes etc.

प्यारी सौं चित रहो अरूझाइ (10,717, 1335)

IV

As noted ealier, Sūra had composed one lakh *padas*. Unfortunately, however, most of the great treasure of art done by this illustrious blind son of Haryaṇā is not available to us. As such we base our opinions about him as a poet on the basis of whatever little has reached us so far. But even ṭhis tip of the ice-berg is enough to take us to the conclusion that Sūra was by and large a very effective poet who was gifted with immense creativity and originality. His compositions are characterized by overflow of powerful emotions and feelings, spontaniety, obliquity, subjectivity and musical content. He has done all this with masterly tact and artistic beauty and fareness.

Vātsalya Rasa

Sūra's poetic art has varied aspects. he is at his height when he takes to *Vātsalya rasa* (sentiment of filial affection) while describing the childhood of Lord Krishṇa in his immortal padas. He starts by portraying different playful activities full of fun and frolics and traits of demeanour of Krishṇa as a child with the help of his imagination. He has made them appear natural, lively and colourful by his original touch. His descriptions are so real and devoid of any trace of exaggeration and artificiality that one cannot but help praising him (Sūra) in the highest terms. This has made him a master Child-Psychologist and has also given him a unique position not only among the Indian poets but also among the world-poets. Perhaps no poet before and even after him has depicted child-psychology in such subtle and splendid manner. Like an expert psycho-analyist Sūra fully understands the nature and behaviour of a child. Throwing about his feet and turning over in the cradle, sometimes crying aloud continuously without any reason, holding his toe or thumb and sucking it, pressurizing his mother to get the moon, crawling on the floor of the courtyard, covering his body with dust and also eating a handful of it, insisting on his going out in open for playing with his fellow friends in spite of his mother's forbidding him not to go breaking curdpots and toppling milk jars, exposing of rivalry and jealousy with his playmates, especially with his brothers & sisters, expressing of mother's filial love and affection for her progeny etc. are some of the innate tendencies of a child. Sūra has very successfully depicted them in case of Krishṇa.

Vātsalya Rasa is twofold—Saṁyoga (Union) and Viyoga or Vipralambha (Separation). Portrayals in respect of Krishṇa's union with his parents while at Gokula and those of separation from them on leaving from Gokula to Mathurā exhibit the poet's keen insight even into the minutest details of human life. Sūra is very well acquainted with the feelings and emotions of children and those of their parents. He has given a vivid account of the eye-catching physical charm of Krishṇa as a child. The following three padas clearly show the exuberance of ecstasy which Yashodā is deriving from the sight of the natural beauty of Krishṇa. Covering the body with mud, crawling on knees, tossing of the curly locks of somewhat brownish hair on the forehead, tinkling sound of the anklets and that of the small bells in the girdle around the waist, hanging necklace of lion's nails and a lotus-garland round the neck, dangling jewelled rings in the ears, lovely nose-rings, singing and dancing in coutyard with graceful movements of the eyes, holding some butter in the hand with his lips and mouth besmeared with curd–all these go to add an additional attraction to his person. Having a view of her dear son's physical charm Yashodā thinks herself as very lucky to have such an attractive child. Other young ladies of Braja also are extremely overwhelmed with joy on seeing the extraordinary charm of Krishṇa. None of them is in a mood to part company with him even for a moment.

(i) Āṅgana syāma nachāvahīṅ jasumati naṅdarānī.

Tārī dai-dai gāvahiṅ madhurī mridu bāṇī

Pāinu nupura bājai, kaṭi kiṅkini kūjai.

Nāṅhīṅ eḍiyani arunatā phala-bimba na pūjai.

Kehari-nakha ura para lasai, suṭhi sobhākārī.

Mano syāma ghana madhya maiṅ nava sasi ujiyārī.

Gabhuāra sira kesa haiṅ bara ghuṅgharawāre.

Laṭakana laṭakata bhāla para vidhu madhi gana tāre.

Jasumati sutahiṅ nachāvahiṅ chhavi dekhata jiya taiṅ.

आंगन स्याम नचावहीं जसुमति नंदरानी।
तारी दैन्दै गावहिं, मधुरी मृदु बानी।।
पाइनु नुपुर बाजई, कटि किंकिनि कूजै।
नान्ही एडियनि अरुनता फल बिम्ब न पूजै।।
केहरि-नख उर पर लसै, सुठि सोभाकारी।
मनो स्याम घन मध्य मैं, नव ससि उजियारी।।

गभुआरे सिर केस हैं बर घूंधरवारे ।
लटकन, लटकत भाल पर, बिधु मधि गनतारे ।।
जसुमति सुतहिं नचावहिं, छवि देखत जियतैं ।[79]

(ii) Hauṅ bali jāūṅ chhabīle lāla kī.

Dhūasari dhūri ghuturuvani reṅgani bolani bachana rasāla kī

Chhiṭaki rahīn chahuṅ disi ju laṭuriā laṭakana laṭakani māla kī.

Motini sahita nāsikā nathunī, kaṅtha kamaladala māla kī.

हौं बलि जाऊं छबीले लाल की ।
धूसरि धूरि घुटुरुवनि रेंगनि, बोलनि बचन रसाल की ।।
छिटकि रहीं चहुं दिसि जु लटुरियां, लटकन लटकनि माल की ।
मोतिनि सहित नासिका नथुनी, कण्ठ कमलदल माल की ।।[80]

(iii) Sobhita kara navanīta lie.

Ghuṭuruni chalana renutanamaṅdita mukha dadhi lepa kie.

Chāru kapola, lola lochana. gorochana tilaka die.

Dhanya Sūra ekau pala ihiṅ sukha kā sata kalpa jie.

सोभित कर न नवनीत लिए ।
घुटुरुनि चलन रेनुतनमंडित मुख दधि लेप किए ।।
चारु कपोल, लोल लोचन गोरोचन तिलक दिए ।
धन्य सूर एकौ पल इहिं सुख, का सत कल्प जिए ।।[81]

Good-looking tiny fingers with sparkling nails, striking bangles on the arms, curly tufts of hair, broad and radiant eyes filled with collyrium, pleasing face, jingling sound of the anklets, toddling on the smooth and resplendent courtyard, dancing on small legs with graceful eye-gestures accompanied by snapping with the thumb and the fingers, laughing with shrill shrieks–all these are amply suggestive of Sūra's insight into the physical form and patterns of behaviour of child-Krishṇa.

(iv) Chhoṭi-chhoṭi guḍiyāṅ aṅguriyāṅ chhoṭi chhabīlī.
Nakha joytī motī mānauṅ kamaladalni para.
Lalita āṅgana khelaiṅ ṭhumuka ṭhumuka dolai.
Jhunuka jhunuka bājai paiṅjanī mridu mukhara.
Kiṅkanī kalita kaṭi, hāṭaka ratana jaṭita
. . . .
Aṅjana raṅjita naina chitavana chitachorai
Chuṭuki bajāvati nahāvati Yasodā dharanī.
. . . .
Kilaki kilaki haṅsai, dvai dvai danturiyāṅ haṅsai.
Sūradāsa mana basaiṅ totare bachana bara.

छोटी- छोटी गुड़ियां अंगुरियां छोटी छबीली,
नख ज्योती मोती मानौं कमलदलनि पर ।
ललित आंगन खेले ठुमुक-ठुमुक डोलै,
झुनुक- झुनुक बाजै पैंजनी मृदु मुखर ।
किंकनी कलित कटि, हाटक रतन जटित,
....…
अंजन रंजित नैन, चितवन चितचोरैं
चुटुकि बजावति, नचावति यशोदा धरनी,
....
किलकि किलकि हंसै, द्वै द्वै दंतुरियां हंसै,
सूरदास मन बसैं तोतरे बचन बर ।[82]

The poet depicts Krishṇa as fretting, crying. chattering and insisting on getting the moon like a normal child.

Sūra has surpassed in drawing a clear pen-picture of the different situations of Krishṇa as a child, such as murmuring to himself a song, crawling on the ground briskly, lisping, calling out cows black and white by raising his little arms, feeding with butter his own shadow in the translucent pillars, caressing and cajoling his mother for having his way.

Hari apanaiṅ āṅgana kachhu gāvata

Tanaka tanak charanan sauṅ nāchata manahīṅ manahiṅ rijhāvata.

Bāṅha uṭhāi kājarī dhaurī gaiyani ṭera bulāvata.

. . . .

Kabahūṅ chitai pratibimba khambha maiṅ launī liye khavāvata

Duri dekhati Jasumati yaha līlā, haraṣa anaṅda baḍhāvata.

हरि अपनैं आंगन कछु गावत।

तनक तनक चरनन सौं नाचत मनहिं मनहिं रिझावत।

बांह ऊठाइ काजरी धौरी गैयनि टेरि बुलावत।

. . . .

कबहुं चितै प्रतिबिम्ब खम्भ मैं लौनी लिए खवावत।

दुरि देखति जसुमति यह लीला, हरष अनंद बढ़ावत।।[83]

It is universally acknowledged that mother is the greatest repository of filial affection. Yashodā is so highly overpowered with the emotion of maternal love that milk starts oozing out of her breasts. She at once takes the baby Krishṇa in her lap and after covering him under the outer fringe of her sārī starts feeding him without losing any more time.

Kilakata kānha ghuturuvani āvata

. . . .

Bāla dasā sukha nirakhi jasodā puni puni naṅda bulāvati.

Aṅcharā tara lauṅ ḍhāṅki Sūra Ke prabhu kau jananī dūdha piyāvati.

किलकत कान्ह घुटुरुबनि आवत।

....

बालदसा-सुख निरखि जसोदा पुनि- पुनि नंद बुलावति।
अंचरा तर लौं ढ़ांकि सूर के प्रभु कौ जननीं दूध पियावति।।[84]

Persuading children to sleep by singing lullabies and by patting them gently in the cradle is a common device employed by mothers all over. Yashodā is no exception to this.

Jasodā Hari pālanaiṅ jhulāvai,
Halarāvai dularāi malhāvai, joi-soi kachhu gāvai
Mere lāla kauṅ āu nidariyā, kāhiṅ na āni suvāvai.

जसोदा हरि पालनैं झुलावै।
हलरावै, दुलराइ मल्हावै, जोइ-सोइ कछु गावै।
मेरे लाल कौं आउ निदरिया, काहिं न आनि सुवावै।।[85]

Day by day child Krishṇa grows more sportive and prankish. Like all other playful children he wants to go out and play with his fellow-cowboys but the mother does not allow him to go. She has always in mind the well-being of her son. She is extremely pained to see him even in the slightest distress. Whenever he is late in reaching home after playing with his freinds, she is very much upset and asks *Nanda Bābā* as to why he had been so late.

Hari kauṅ ṭerati haiṅ Nandarāṇī,
Bahuta abāra bhai kahaṅ khelata rahai mere sāraṅgapāṇī.

हरि कौं टेरति हैं नंदरानी।
बहुत अबार भइ कंह खेलत, रहै मेरे सारंगपानी।।[86]

Even on the occasion of *'Karṇachhedana'* (Piercing of the ear) ceremony, Yashodā's heart begins to palpitate, thinking about the excess of pain her son Krishṇa would have to suffer.

Kānha kuṅvara ko kanacchedanau hai, hātha suhāri bhelī gurta kī

Vidhi Vihaṅse harasata heri heri, Jasumati kī dhuka-dhukī su ura kī.

कान्ह कुंवर को कनच्छेदेनौ है, हाथ सुहारी भेली गुर की।
विधि विंहसे हरसत हेरि हेरि, जसुमति कप धुक धुकी सु उर की।।[87]

Sūra has not only described the paternal affection for the son but also for the daughter. Yashodā is thrilled on seeking the extraordinary beauty of Rādhā when the latter happens to visit the former's house along with Krishṇa. It then occurs to her that both would be a befitting match for each other and prays to 'Sun God' for the fulfilment of her wish.

Naina bisāla badana ati sundara, dekhata nīkī chotī.

Sūra mahari savitā sāuṅ vinavati bhalī syāma kī joṭī.

नैन बिसाल, बदन अति सुन्दर, देखत नीकी चोटी।
सूर महरि सविता सौं विनवति भली स्याम की जोटी।।[88]

Sūra has very vividly described Krishṇa playing with the milk–maids and teasing them in his own style or even breaking their milk-pots and also his adulthood amorous sports with them during *Rāsa līlā* on the sandy banks of the Yamunā under the famous *Kadamba* tree to the music of his flute. All these are, actually, a part of his līlās in which the milk-maids seem to be the willing partners. In consequence he takes the full liberty of playing with them. One evening when it is pitch dark the naughty lad enters the lonely house of a gopī stealthily. As soon he tries to put his hand in the earthen pot containing curd, the gopī catches him red-handed. She then puts him a straight question if he has to say something in his defence. Krishṇa then readily replies in an innocent manner that he had entered the house taking that to be his own and as such dropped his hand in the earthern pot to take out the small black ant from inside.

Syāma kahā chāhata se dolata?

Puchhe taiṅ tuma badan durāvata sūdhe bola na bolata.

Pāe akele ghara maiṅ dadhi-bhājana maiṅ hātha.

Aba tuma kakau nāūṅ leuge, nāhiṅ na koū sātha

Maiṅ jānyo yaha ghara mero hai, tā dhokhaiṅ maiṅ Āyau.

Dekhata hauṅ gorasa maiṅ chīnṭī kaḍhana ko kara nāyau.

स्याम कहा चाहत से डोलत ?
पूछे तैं तुम बदन दुरावत, सूधे बोल न बोलत ।
पाए अकेले घर मैं, दधि-भाजन मैं हाथ ।
अब तुम काकौं नाऊं लेउगे, नाहिंन कोऊ साथ ।
मैं जान्यौ यह घर मेरों है, ता धोखैं मैं आयौ ।
देखत हौं गोरस मैं चींटी, काढ़न को कर नायौ ।

Highly impressed by his presence of mind the gopī smiles and closes the matter at that.

Padas beginning with the burdens such as: Maiyā maiṅ nahiṅ mākhana khāyau, maiyā mohiṅ dāū bahuta khijāyau, moṅ sauṅ kahata mola kau līnhau tū Jasumati kaba jāyau, maiyā kabahūṅ baḍhaigī choṭī, kitī bāra mohiṅ dūdha piyata bhaī yaha ajahūṅ hai chhoṭī, maiyā maiṅ to chanda-khilaunā laihauṅ. मैया मैं नहिं माखन खायौ,[90] मैया मोहिं दाऊ बहुत खिजायौ, मो सौं कहत मोल कौ लीन्हौं तू जसुमति कब जायौ,[91] कबहुं बढ़ैगी चोटी ? किती बार मोहिं दूध पियत भई यह अजहूं है छोटी,[92] मैया मैं तो चन्द खिलौना लैहौं,[93] are amply expressive of Krishṇa's feelings of infantile simplicity, jealousy, rivalry, competition, sharpwittedness and obstinancy, a reality which cannot be challenged. Krishṇa like a normal child complains to his mother that his elder brother teases him in the presence of other cow-boys. This he does just to win her affection and sympathy.

Krishṇa is happily living with his mother Devakī at Mathurā but Yashodā is still feeling concerned and restless to know about his welfare and does not even hesitate to send a message to Devakī requesting her to look after the poor chap with utmost care. Yashodā naturally believes that she is the only one person in the world capable of taking care and looking after the comfort of her dear child.

Sandesau Devakī sāuṅ kahiyāu,

Hauṅ to dhāi tihāre suta kī mayā karata hī rahiyau.

....

Joi-joi māṅgata soi-soi detī, krama krama kari kai nhāte,

Sūra pathika suni mohiṅ raini dina baḍhyau rahata ura socha.

Merau alaka laḍaito mohana, hvai haiṅ karata saṅkocha.

संदेसौ देवकी सौं कहियौ ।

हौ तो धाइ तिहारे सुत की मया करत ही रहियौ ।

....

जोइ-जोइ मांगत सोइ-सोइ देती, क्रम क्रम कर कै न्हाते।

'सूर' पथिक सुनि मोहिं रैनि दिन बढ़यौ रहत उर सोच।

मेरौ अलक लड़ैतो मोहन, ह्वै हैं करत सकोच।।[94]

She further conveys her concern through any of the wayfarer who happens to go to Mathurā.

Kahiyo jāya pathika ghara āvahu, rāma-syāma doū bhaiyā,

Sūra syāma kata hota dukhārī, jinake mosī maiyā.

कहियो जाय पथिक घर आवहु, राम-स्याम दोऊ भैय्या।

सूर स्याम कत होत दुखारी, जिनके मोसी मैय्या।।[95]

On Krishṇa's leaving for Mathurā along with Akrūra, Yashodā's heart bursts out with grief and asks people of Braja to persuade Krishṇa not go to Mathurā. She is feeling worried as to why the king has sent for him.

Jasodā bāra-bāra yauṅ bhākhai

Hai kou braja maiṅ hitū hamārau chalata gopālahiṅ rākhai.

Kahā kāja mere chhagana magana kauṅ nripa madhupurī bulāyau.

Suphalaka suta mere prāna harana kauṅ kāla rūpa hvai āyau

. . . .

Kamala nayana guna ṭerata ṭerata adhara badana kumḥlānī.

Sūra kahāṅ lagi pragaṭi janāūṅ, dukhita naṅda jū kī rānī.

जसोदा बार-बार यौं भाखै।

है कोऊ ब्रज मैं हितू हमारौ चलत गोपालहिं राखै।।

कहा काज मेरे छगन मगन कौ नृप मधुपुरी बुलायौ।

सुफलक सुत मेरे प्रान हरन कौं काल-रूप ह्वै आयौ ।।

कमल नयन गुन टेरत टेरत, अधर बदन कुम्हिलानी ।।

सूर कहां लगि प्रगटि जनाऊं। दुखित नंद जू की रानी ।।

Nanda returns from Mathurā all alone leaving behind Krishṇa in Mathurā. The mother Yashodā is all the more highly upset and in a fit of anger and frustration is much irritated and behaves harshly even towards her husband Nanda.

Jasodā kānha kānha kai būjhai

Phūṭi na gaī tumhārī chārauṅ kaisaiṅ māraga sūjhai

Ika tau jarī jāta bina dekhaiṅ aba tuma dīnhauṅ phaṅki.

. . . .

Dhika tuma dhika ye charana ahau pati, adha bolata uṭhi dhāye.

Sūra syāma bichhurana kī hama pai. daina badhāyi āye.

जसुदा कान्ह कान्ह कै बूझै ।

फूटि न गई तुम्हारी चारौं कैसें मारग सूझै ।।

इक तौ जरी जात बिनु देखैं अब तुम दीन्हौं फंकि ।

धिक तुम धिक ये चरन अहौ पति, अध बोलत उठि धाए ।

सूर स्याम बिछुरन की हम पै, दैन बधाइ आए ।।[97]

It can now safely be said that Sūra has excelled in all respects while describing the psychological subtleties and sensibilities essential for the description of *Vātsalya rasa*.

जसोदा बार-बार यौं भाखै।
है कोऊ ब्रज मैं हितू हमारौ चलत गोपालहिं राखै।।
कहा काज मेरे छगन मगन कौ नृप मधुपुरी बुलायौ।
सुफलक सुत मेरे प्रान हरन कौं काल-रूप ह्वै आयौ।।
कमल नयन गुन टेरत टेरत, अधर बदन कुम्हिलानी।।
सूर कहां लगि प्रगटि जनाऊं। दुखित नंद जू की रानी।।

Nanda returns from Mathurā all alone leaving behind Krishṇa in Mathurā. The mother Yashodā is all the more highly upset and in a fit of anger and frustration is much irritated and behaves harshly even towards her husband Nanda.

Jasodā kānha kānha kai būjhai

Phūṭi na gaī tumhārī chārauṅ kaisaiṅ māraga sūjhai

Ika tau jarī jāta bina dekhaiṅ aba tuma dīnhauṅ phaṅki.

. . . .

Dhika tuma dhika ye charana ahau pati, adha bolata uṭhi dhāye.

Sūra syāma bichhurana kī hama pai. daina badhāyi āye.

जसुदा कान्ह कान्ह कै बूझै।
फूटि न गई तुम्हारी चारौं कैसैं मारग सूझै।।
इक तौ जरी जात बिनु देखैं अब तुम दीन्हौं फंकि।
धिक तुम धिक ये चरन अहौ पति, अध बोलत उठि धाए।
सूर स्याम बिछुरन की हम पै, दैन बधाइ आए।।[97]

It can now safely be said that Sūra has excelled in all respects while describing the psychological subtleties and sensibilities essential for the description of *Vātsalya rasa*.

Shrīṁgāra Rasa (Erotic sentiment)

Like *Vātsalya rasa Shriṁgāra rasa* is also of two kinds, *saṁyoga* and *vipralambha* or *viyoga*. Let us deal with *saṁyoga rasa* first. It is a common experience that love or friendship of childhood lasts long and is not to be normally forsaken. The case of Krishṇa and Rādhā is just the same. Their love of childhood grew into that of adoloscence. The childhood youthful pranks gradually changed into youthful amorous sports. To start with Krishṇa and Rādhā both meet each other in a dramatic way. Krishṇa holding *chaka-dorī* (top and string, a play-toy) in his hand comes out in the narrow alleys of Braja and accidently comes across a young pretty girl with broad and graceful eyes:

Khelata hari nikase braja-khorī
Kaṭi-kācchanī pītāmbara bāṅdhe, hātha liye bhauṅrā chakadorī

. . . .

Sūra syāma dekhata hīṅ rījhai naina-naina mili parī ṭhagorī

खेलत हरि निकसे ब्रज खोरी।
कटि-काछनी पीताम्बर बांधे, हाथ लिए भौंरा चकडोरी।
. . . .
सूर-स्याम देखत हीं रीझै, नैन-नैन मिलि परी ठगोरी।।[98]

Krishṇa (Shyāma) then asks her, " O fair one! who are You? Where do you hail from? Whose daughter are you? You were never seen before in the lanes of Braja." To this the fair girl replies, "Normally why should I come to Braja. I have my own street to play at. We of course hear that Nanda Bābā's son Krishṇa is in the habit of stealing curd and butter."

Krishṇa then retorts, "What is that you have which I shall steal? Come let us play together."

The innocent Rādhā is attracted towards him and this meeting at first-sight, gives rise to their mutual love and they start exchanging visits. Sometime later Rādhā accepts an invitation from Krishṇa and agrees to reach there in the streets of Braja (Skandha 10, pada 674). Both of them are keen on finding more opportunities of meeting each other and exchanging visits under this or that pretext. They have by now begun to realize that the path of love is very slippery and hazardous. Rādhā somehow takes the liberty of speaking out her mind one day to her mother, "Give me the milkpot. *Ahīrs* (cowherds) first milk their cows in the cow-sheds and then milk our cows. If you give me the milkpot I will get my cows milked first. If I am a bit late in coming from there do not be in a hurry to go there." Imagine how much impatient, restless and dejected lovers are in case they were to meet late even for a moment. Rādha, as per mutual agreement, reaches the spot but to her utter disappointment she finds Krishṇa nowhere. In the meanwhile on noticing Krishṇa coming with Nanda Bābā, she returns to her normal self. Nanda feels happy to find Rādhā there. He at once asks her to play with Krishṇa and also to mind that the cows do not hurt him (Krishṇa) in any way. This naturally serves as a fillip and enocourages Rādhā to have a heart-to-heart talk with Krishṇa. She accordingly makes full use of the opportunity and remarks that she would not allow him to leave and go away from her.

Mohiṅ chhāṅdi jau kahūṅ jahuge, lyāūṇgī tuma kauṅ dhari.

Bhalī bhaī tumahaiṅ sauṅpi gae mohiṅ gāna na daihauṅ tuma kauṅ.

Bāhuṅ tumhārī naiṅku na cchāṅḍauṅ, mahara khījihaiṅ hama kauṅ.

मोहिं छांडि जौ कहूं जाहुगे, ल्याऊंगी तुम कौं धरि।

भली भई तुम्हैं सौंपि गए मोहिं, गान न देहौं तुम कौं।।

बाहुं तुम्हारी नैंकु न छांड़ौं, महर खीझिहैं हमकौं।।[99]

Love knows no bounds. Consequently one day when Krishṇa is engaged in embracing Rādhā in a very jovial mood, Yashodā happens to be there per chance. Rādhā is upset but it is Krishṇa who has saved the whole situation with his sagacity and has thus given a sound proof of his being a perfect gentleman. He says, "O Mother, look Rādhā has stolen my ball but she refuses to give it back to me."

Dekhau ḍhīṭhi deti nahīṅ mātā, rākhyau geṅda churāi.

देखौ ढ़ीठि देति नाहीं माता, राख्यौ गेंद चुराइ।।[100]

On this Rādhā's reply is worth noticing. She ends the matter by agreeing to tell him the location of the ball.

Taba briṣabhānu sutā haṅsi bolī hama pai nāhīṅ kanhāi.

Kāhe ko jhakajhorata nokhe, chalahu na deūṅ batāi.

तब बृषभानु सुता हंसि बोली हम पै नहिं कन्हाइ।

काहे को झकझोरत नोखे, चलहु न देऊं बताइ।।[101]

One more meeting between Krishṇa and Rādhā is worthy of mention. Krishṇa gets a last chance of his life when he meets Rādhā on reaching *Kurukshetra* from *Dwārikā* along with Yashodā, Nand and others from

Braja. Rādhā is also with them. Rukmiṇī herself recognised Rādhā standing in the midst of gopīs and embraced her like sisters who had met after a long interval. Krishṇa was wonderstuck to see her graceful figure. When they saw each other they met with so much warmth that they both merged into one soul. Rādhā became Krishṇa and Krishṇa became Rādhā. Krishṇa then smiled and told Rādhā to go back to Braja. Rādhā finally repented and she was so much stunned at that moment that she could not utter a single word to Krishṇa again. Only tears rolled down her cheeks.

Rādhā mādhava bheṅṭa bhaī

Rādhā Mādhava, Mādhava Rādhā kīṭa bhriṅga gati hvai ju gaī.

Mādhava Rādhā ke raṅga rāṅchai, Rādhā Madhava raṅga bhaī.

. . . .

Vihaṅsi kahyau hama tuma nahiṅ antara, yaha kahi kai braja paṭhaī.

and

Karata kacchu nāhiṅ āju banī

Hari āe hauṅ rahī ṭhagī sī jaiseṅ chitra ghanī.

राधा माधव भेंट भई ।

राधा माधव, माधव राधा, कीट भृंग गति ह्वै जु गइ ।।

माधव राधा के रंग रांचै, राधा माधव रंग भई ।

— — — — —

विहंसि कह्यौ हम तुम नहिं अंतर, यह कहि कै ब्रज पठई ।।[102]

करत कछु नाहिं आजु बनी ।

हरि आए हौं रही ठगी सी, जैसें चित्र घनी ।।[103]

In short Sūra has thus vividly portrayed various occasions and moments of Krishṇa's union with Rādhā.

Viyoga Shrimgāra

As far as the description of *Viyoga Shrimgāra* is concerned, there is no denying the fact that Sūra has no equal in the realm of Indian literature. His 'Sūrasāgara' is replete with innumerable references where various types of mental situations caused by unbearable pains of separation have been portrayed so vividly. Gopīs are the main target in respect of Sūra's description of *Viyoga Shrimgāra* since it is the gopīs who long and pine for the love of their beloved Krishṇa more than Krishṇa longs for them. Separation from Krishṇa even for a moment is extremely afflicting and unendurable for them. This becomes all the more intolerable when on Krishṇa's leaving for Mathurā for good, Yashodā falls down on the ground senseless again and again and other gopīs stand like statues, motionless and speechless with their faces turned pale and eyes flooded with tears flowing down incessantly.

Rahīṅ jahāṅ so tahāṅ saba ṭhāḍī.

Hari ke chalata dekhiyata aisī manahuṅ chitra likhī kāḍhī.

Sūkhe badan, sravata naina teṅ jaladhārā ura bāḍhī.

Kaṅdhani bāṅha dhare chitawati druma manahuṅ beli dava-ḍāḍhī.

रहीं जहां सो तहां सब ठाड़ी।

हरि के चलत देखियत ऐसी मनहुं चित्र लिखी काढ़ी।

सूखे बदन, स्रवत नैन तें जलधारा उर बाढ़ी।

कँधनि बांह धरे चितवति द्रुम मनहुं बेलि दव-डाढ़ी।।[104]

The gopīs are so much distressed that they intend to drop the idea of going to Braja, since Krishṇa is no more with them.

Pācchaiṅ hī chitavata mere lochana, āge parata na pāi.

Mana lai chalī mādhurī mūrati kahāṅ karauṅ braja jāi.

पाछैं ही चितवत मेरे लोचन, आगे परत न पाइ।

मन लै चली माधुरी मूरति कहां करौं ब्रज जाइ।।[105]

The house which used to look very much pleasing and comfortable in his company earlier looks now quite dreadful. All its happiness and prosperity have vanished into thin air like a dream. Besides, gopīs have not been able to have a wink of sleep at night and have passed the whole night in counting the stars.

Rī mohiṅ bhavana bhayānaka lāgai, māī syāma binā

___ ___ ___ ___ ___ ___ ___ ___

Sūradāsa mohana darasana binu sukha-sampati sapanā

and

Āju raina nahīṅ nīṅda parī.

Jāgata ginata gagana ke tāre rasanā raṭata gobinda harī.

री मोहिं भवन भयानक लागै माई स्याम बिना।

सूरदास मोहन दरसन बिनु सुख-सम्पति सपना।।[106]

आजु रैन नहिं नींद परी।

जागत गिनत गगन के तारे रसना रटत गोबिन्द हरी।।[107]

In Krishṇa's absence the whole Braja presents a deserted look, devoid of all happiness and good fortune. Every body particularly Yasodā and Nanda feel as if mortified with intense grief. The cows have ceased eating grass and roots and have also stopped yielding milk.

Taba taiṅ miṭe saba ānaṅda

Yā Braja ke saba bhāga, sampadā lai ju gae naṅdanaṅdana.

Vihvala bhaī Jasodā ḍolati dukhita Nanda upanaṅda.

Dhenu nahiṅ paya sravati ruchira mukha charati nāhiṅ triṇakaṅda.

तब तैं मिटे सब आनन्द ।
या ब्रज के सब भाग, सम्पदा, लै जु गए नंदनन्दन ।।
विह्वल भई जसोदा डोलति, दुखित नंद उपनंद ।
धेनु नहिं पय स्त्रवति रुचिर मुख चरति नाहिं तृणकंद ।।[108]

Gopīs, cowherds and cows all feel sad and distressed as if they have lost their guardian. Old memories viz. Krishṇa's home-coming at this hour after grazing the cows in the fields, his playing of some musical tune on the flute, his singing of songs in a pitched and raised voice , his stealing of curd and butter, his bidding of cows both black and white to come with raised arms and other child-like playful activities and his amorous sports with Rādhā and other gopīs amidst the cluster of trees, creepers, groves and the lush green meadows of Vrindāban on the banks of Yamunā during autumnal glittering moonlight and his *Rāsa* performances are revived which make them restive.

Ihiṅ biriyāṅ bana taiṅ Braja āvata.

Dūrahiṅ taiṅ ye benu adhari dhari, bāraṁbāra bajāvata.

Kabahuṅka kāhūṅ bhāṅti chatura chita, ati ūnche sura gāvata.

Kabahūṅka lai-lai nāma manohara dhaurī dhenu bulāvata.

Ihiṅ vidhi bachana sunāya syāma ghana, muracche madana jagāvata.

इहिं बिरियां बन तैं ब्रज आवत।

दूरहिं तैं ये बेनु अधरि धरि, बारं-बार बजावत।।

कबहुकं काहूं भांति चतुर चित, अति ऊंचे सुर गावत।

कबहुंक लै-लै नाम मनोहर, धौरी धेनु बुलावत।।

इहिं विधि बचन सुनाय स्याम धन, मुरछे मदन जगावत।।[109]

Krishṇa is omnipresent for the gopīs. They find him always hovering around them. They cannot even imagine that Madhubana can remain as green and verdant as ever in Syāma's separation . On the contrary it should have been burning with pain. They reprimand and curse the green trees of Madhubana and claim that they had better withered away by now.

Madhubana tuma kata rahata hare

Viraha viyoga syāma suṅdara ke ṭhaḍhe kyauṅ na jare.

Mohana benu bajāvata drumatara sākhā ṭeki dhare.

Mohe thāvara aru Jaḍa jaṅgama, muni jana dhyāna ṭare

—— —— —— —— —— —— ——

Sūradāsa prabhu viraha davānala nakhasikha lauṅ na jare.

मधुबन तुम कत रहत हरे।

विरह-वियोग स्याम सुन्दर के ठाढ़े क्यौं न जरे।।

मोहन बेनु बजावत द्रुमतर साखा टेकि धरे ।

मोहे थावर अरु जड़-जंगम, मुनि जन ध्यान टरे । ।

— — — — —

सूरदास प्रभु विरह दवानल, नखसिख लौं न जरे । ।[110]

On receving the letter through Uddhava written in the hand of Ṡyāmasundara (Krishaṇa) Rādhā embraced it again and again out of intensity of love. Tears rolling down her eyes then drenched the letter which was turned black due to the spreading of the ink on it (10,4105). The eyes of gopīs too have an unending flow of tears. Their situation becomes all the more of a mockery when they receive a letter from their darling Krishṇa after a long time. They are very anxious to read it but because of the intense mental agony they are neither able to touch it for fear of its being burnt by the hot finger of the hand nor to have a look at it for fear of its being moistened with tears in their eyes.

Naina sajala kāgada ati komala kara aṅgurī ati tātī

Parasaiṅ jarai, vilokaiṅ bhījai, duhūṅ bhāṅti dukha chhātī.

नैन सजल कागद अति कोमल कर अंगुरी अति ताती ।

परसैं जरै, विलोकैं भीजै दुहुं भांति दुख छाती । ।[111]

The gopīs (milk-maids) are so much plunged in inexpressible grief that they send messages after messages to Mathurā but whosever carries their messages never returns. Nor is any reply received. The messengers have, perhaps, either been dissuaded by Shyāma or have breathed their last somewhere on the way.

Saṅdesani madhubana kūpa bhare

Apane tau paṭhavati nahiṅ mohana, hamare phiri na phire.

Jite pathika paṭhaye madhubana kauṅ bahuri na sodha kare

Kai vai syāma sikhāi pramodhe kai kahūṅ bīcha mare

संदेशनि मधुबन कूप भरे।

अपने तौ पठवति नहिं मोहन, हमरे फिर न फिरे

जिते पथिक पठए मधुबन कौं, बहुरि न सोध करे।

कै वै स्याम सिखाइ प्रमोधे, कै कहुं बीच मरे।।[112]

In the meantime rainy season also sets in. The thundering clouds make the gopīs feel tormented on account of the agony of separation (10,3921). Sometimes the gathering cloud while raining give solace and happiness to them due to thier resemblance with Syāma

Baru ye badarāū baraṣana āye

Apanī avadhi jāna naṅdanaṅdana garaji gagana ghana cchāye

—— —— —— —— —— —— ——

Sūradāsa prabhu rasika siromani madhubana basi bisarāye.

बरु ये बदराऊ बरषन आये।

अपनी अवधि जान नंदनंदन, गरजि गगन घन छाये।

— — — — — — — — — —

सूरदास प्रभु रसिक सिरोमनि मधुबन बसि बिसराये।।[113]

The sky is overcast with dense dark clouds on a rainy night but sometimes they are seen scattered, giving a full view of the moon—light. In the moonlight the gopīs are writhing in pain due to their separation from Krishṇa so much that no other remedy could give any relief to them.

Piya binu nāgini kālī rāta

Kabahūṅ jāmini uvati junhaiyā ḍasi ulti hvai jāti.

Jaṅtra na phurata maṅtra nahiṅ lāgata prīti sirānī jāta

Sūra syāma binu bikala birahinī muri–muri laharaiṅ khāta.

पिय बिनु नागिनि काली रात ।
कबहुं जामिनि उवति जुन्हैया, डसि उल्टी ह्वै जात ।।
जंत्र न फुरत मंत्र नहिं लागत प्रीति सिरानी जात ।
सूर स्याम बिनु बिकल बिरहिनी, मुरि-मुरि लहरैं खात ।।[114]

Sweet notes of chātaka, papeehā, pik (Cuckoo) and peacocks too which seemed to be delightful and soothing in *saṁyoga* have now turned into foes in *Viyoga*. Not only this the creepers which used to provide a cooling touch earlier now appear to be emitting out flames of fire which cannot be extinguished even by the cold flowing water of the river Yamunā. Neither lotus flower nor camphor nor even moonlight is able to end this burning sensation.

Binu gopāla bairani bhaī kuṅjaiṅ.

Taba ye latā lagati tana sītala aba bhai viṣama jwāla kī puṅjaiṅ.

Brithā bahati yamunā khaga bolata, brithā kamala phulaiṅ ati guṅjaiṅ.

Pavan, pāni, ghanasāra sumana dai daḍhisuta kirana bhānu bhaī bhuṅjaiṅ.

बिनु गोपाल बैरनि भई कुंजैं ।
तब ये लता लगति तन सीतल अब भई विषम ज्वाल की पुंजैं ।।
बृथा बहति यमुना, खग बोलत, बृथा कमल फूलैं अति गुंजै ।

पवन, पानि, घनसार, सुमन दै दधिसुत किरन भानु भई भुंजैं । ।[115]

Gopīs have thus been anxiously awaiting Krishṇa's return since long but in vain. They have now left all hopes of Krishṇa's return. They feel completely broken-hearted and helpless. The wayfarers too have all stopped taking that course. All birds and animals have also fled Braja, leaving it to be a lonely and dreary place.

Saṁskrit scholars have mentioned eleven states of mind of human beings in respect of *Viyoga* viz. *Abhilāshā,* (longing or Desire), *Chintā* (Anxiety), *Smaraṇa* (Remembrance), *Guṇakathana* (Narration of qualities), *Udvega* (Perplexity), *Unmāda* (Insanity), *Vyāḍhi* (Disease), *Jaḍatā* (Stupidity), *Mūrchhā* (Unconsciousness), and *Maraṇa* (Death). We come across such illustrations in abundance in Sūra's poetry. A few examples:

Abhilāṣā (अभिलाषा)

lai āvahu gokula gopālahiṅ.

Pāṅina pari kyoṅhūṅ binatī kara, chhala bala bāhu bisālahiṅ.

Aba kī bāra naiṅku dikharāvahu naṅda āpane lālahiṅ.

Chintā (चिन्ता)

Pācchaiṅ hī chitavata mere lochana āge, parata na pāṅya.

Mana lai chalī mādhurī muarti, kahā karauṅ braja jāya

Pawana na bhaī patākā ambara, bhaī na ratha ke aṅga.

Dhūri na bhaī charana lapaṭātīṅ, jātīṅ uhaṅ lau saṅga.

Udvega (उद्वेग)

Kahāṅ lauṅ mānauṅ apanī chūka

Binu gopala sakhi rī ye chhatiyāṅ, hvai na gaī dvai tūka

. . . .

Hridaya jarata hai dāvānala jyoṅ kaṭhina biraha kī hūka

Jaḍatā (जड़ता)

Nisidina kalamalāti suni sajanī gājata manamatha ara

Sūradāsa saba rahīṅ mauna hvai, atihiṅ maina ke bhara.

अभिलाषा: लै आवहु गोकुल गोपालहिं।

पांइन परि क्योंहू बिनती कर, छल बल बाहु बिसालहिं।

अब की बार नैंकु दिखरावहु नंद आपने लालहिं।।[116]

चिन्ता: पाछैं ही चितवत मेरे लोचन, आगे परत न पाय।

मन लै चली माधुरी मूरति, कहा करौं ब्रज जाय।।

पवन न भई पताका अंबर, भई न रथ के अंग।

धूरि न भई चरन लपटातीं जातीं उहं लौ संग।।[117]

उद्वेग: कहाँ लौं मानौं अपनी चूक।

बिनु गोपाल सखी री ये छतियां, ह्वै न गई द्वै टक।।

हृदय जरत है दावानल ज्यों कठिन बिरह की हूक।।[118]

जड़ता: निसिदिन कलमलाति सुनि सजनी गाजत मनमथ अर।

सूरदास सब रहीं मौन ह्वैं, अतिहिं मैन के भर।।[119]

Bhramaragīta (The song of the Black-bee)*

Krishṇa perhaps wanted to change Uddhava's ideology of *jñāna* and *yoga* to that of *prema* and *bhakti*. Consequently he sends his companion Uddhava to the gopīs. As soon as he arrives in Braja, they (gopīs) mistaking him to be Krishṇa's emissary surround him. Uddhava then commences his long discourse, eulogising the importnce of the philosophy of *jñāna* in the attainment of *Nirguṇa Brahma* (Krishṇa). He asserts that mukti (salvation) can be attained only through the *nirguṇa mode of worship* in which *Brahma* (Krishṇa) is treated as invisible and not through the *saguṇa* mode of worship where *Brahma* (Krishṇa) is regarded as having a human form.

Gopī sunahu hari saṅdesa.

Kahyau purana brahma dhyāvahu, triguna mithyā bheṣa.

Jṅāna bina nara mukti nāhīṅ, yaha vishaya saṅsāra.

Rūpa rekha, na nāma jala thala, barana abarana sāra.

---

* Once it so happened that a black-bee (bhramara) came flying and began to hum around the gopīs when they were mutually locked in arguments and counter-arguments. The gopīs then, ignoring Uddhava started addressing the black-bee expressing to it all about love for Krishṇa and hurling harsh and unpleasant words. They were thus, in fact, conveying their feelings to Uddhava through the medium of black-bee. That is why these plaintive remarks are styled as 'bhramaragīta'.
Uddhava does not relent and continue harping on the same tune. The Gopīs are thus highly enraged and ask him to divert to any topic other than that of philosophy of jṅāna.

and

Sunau gopī hari kau saṅdesa

Kari samādhi aṅtaragati dhyāvahu, yaha unakau upadesa.

Tatvajṅāna binu mukti nahīṅ hai, veda purānani gāi

Saguna rūpa taji niraguna dhyāvahu ika chita ika mana lāi.

गोपी सुनहु हरि संदेस।

कह्यौ पूरन ब्रह्म ध्यावहु, त्रिगुन मिथ्या भेष।।

ज्ञान बिन नर मुक्ति नाहिं, यह विषय संसार।

रूप रेख, न नाम जल थल, बरन अबरन सार।।[120]

और सुनौ गोपी हरि कौ संदेस।

करि समाधि अंतरगति ध्यावहु, यह उनकौ उपदेस।।

तत्वज्ञान बिनु मुक्ति नहीं है, वेद पुराननि गाइ।

सगुन रूप तजि निरगुन ध्यावहु, इक चित इक मन लाइ।।[121]

The gopīs do not relish all these sermons full of cold reason. They are not prepared to believe that Krishṇa would have sent such a cut and dried message to them. They request Uddhava to tell them the fact, as they are not interested in listening to the dry words pertaining to *Nirguṇa Brahma*. They are keen to have a glimpse of Krishṇa in person.

Madhupa kahāṅ niraguna gāvahi.

Ye priya kathā nagar-nārini sauṅ Kahahi jahāṅ kacchu pāvahi.

Jānati marama naṅdanaṅdana kau aura prasaṅga chalāvahī.

—— —— —— —— —— —— ——

Ati vichitra larikā kī nāīṅ gura dikhāi baurāvahi.

मधुप कहां निरगुन गावहि।
ये प्रिय कथा नगर नारिनि सौं कहहि जहां कछु पावहि।।
जानति मरम नंदनंदन कौ और प्रंसग चलावहि।
अति विचित्र लरिका की नाईं गुर दिखाइ बौरावहि।।[122]

It suddenly strikes to them that it is just possible that Uddhava might not have been sent here by Krishṇa. It is only either through mistake that he (Uddhava) has come here or Krishṇa might have smiled a little and thus befooled him (Uddhava). This reflects the poet's sense of subtle humour as well.

Uddhau jāhu tumahiṅ hama jānai.

Syāma tumhaiṅ hyāṅko nahi paṭhyau tuma hī bīch bhulāne.

—— —— —— —— —— —— ——

Sūra syāma jaba tumahiṅ paṭhāyau taba naiṅkahuṅ musakāne.

ऊधौ जाहु तुमहिं हम जाने।
स्याम तुम्हैं ह्याको नहि पठ्यौ तुमही बीच भुलाने।
......
सूर स्याम जब तुमहिं पठायौ तब नैंकहुं मुसकाने।।[123]

Gopīs feel least inclined towards Uddhava's moralizing homilies and preachings for the attainment of *Nirguṇa Brahma* through jṅāna and tell him frankly to mind his own business and get his insanity cured (जाइ करो उपचार आपनौ–jāi karo upachāra āpanau-10,4229).

Āpu dekhi dekhi re madhukara, taba aurani sikha dehuṅ

Bitaigo tabahīṅ jānaigau, mahākaṭhin hai nehu.

आपु देखि देखि रे मधुकर, तब औरनि सिख देहुं।
बीतैगो तबहीं जानैगौ, महाकठिन है नेहु।।[124]

They even go to the length of brandishing both Krishṇa and Akrūra as seasoned theives, sly and black (10,4380).

They have completely surrendered themselves to Krishṇa in thought, word and deed and have nothing to do with his (Krishṇa) *jñāna* and *yoga*.

Hama ali gokulanātha ārāḍhyau

Mana bacha-krama hari sauṅ dhari pativrata premajoga tapa sādhyau.

हम अलि गोकुलनाथ आराध्यौ।

मन-बच-क्रम हरि सौं धरि पतिव्रत प्रेमजोग तप साध्यौ।।[125]

They have so much contempt for Uddhava's nonsensical and incoherent twaddle that they damn him and even go to the extent of ridiculing the utility of *jñāna*. They even question the very existence of *Nirguṇa* (formless) *Brahma*.

Niraguna kauna desa kau bāsī?

____ ____ ____ ____ ____ ____

Ko hai janaka, kauna hai jananī, kaun nāri, ko dāsī.

Kaise barana, bheṣa hai kaisauṅ, kihiṅ rasa maiṅ abhilāṣī

Pāvaigau puni kiyo āpanau, jo re karaigo gāṅsī

निरगुन कौन देस कौ बासी ?

. . . .

को है जनक, कौन है जननी, कौन नारि, को दासी।।

कैसे बरन, भेष है कैसौं, किहिं रस मैं अभिलाषी।

पावैगौ पुनि कियौ आपनौ, जो रे करैगो गांसी।।[126]

They only believe in 'Saguṇa Brahma' stretching before them like the ring of the radiant 'Sumeru' mountain.

They are keen to follow & tread the easy and straight path of *love* and *bhakti* (devotion) to be in close proximity of Krishṇa since the path of *Nirguṇa* is a royal one full of thorns. They further observe that Akrūra has taken away the principal and that Uddhava wants to charge even the interest.

Kahai kauṅ rokata māraga sūdhau.

Sunahu madhupa niraguna kaṅṭaka taiṅ, rājapaṅtha kyauṅ rūṅdhauṅ

—— —— —— —— —— —— ——

Sūra mūra akrura gayau lai, byāja niberata ūddhau

काहै कौं रोंकत मारग सूधौ ।

सुनहु मधुप निरगुन कंटक तैं, राजपंथ क्यौं रूंधौं ।

सूर मूर अक्रूर गयौ लै, ब्याज निबेरत ऊधौ ।।[127]

When Uddhava continues to tax their minds with his difficult and unpalatable philosophy of *jṅāna,* the gopis refuse to believe that it was actually Krishṇa's message for them. They thought that it was nothing but a brain-child of *Kubjā* (humpback). They further advised him to take his wise sermons back to Kubjā's home.

Krishṇa is their ultimate goal and it is easy for them to attain him through their unflinching bhakti (devotion) for him. It is a matter of one's liking and any compulsion here won't do.

Ūdhau manamāne kī bāta

Dākha chhuhāra chhāṅḍi amritaphala, biṣkīrā biṣa khāta

Sūradāsa jāko mana jāsauṅ, soī tāhi suhāta.

ऊधौ मनमाने की बात।

दाख छुहारा छांडि अमृतफल, बिषकीरा बिष खात।

सूरदास जाकौ मन जासौं, सोई ताहि सुहात।।[128]

Though the hearts of gopīs are extremely tormented and oppressed with the restiveness of separation yet they have in any way to give an adequate and befitting reply to Uddhava. They emphatically state that they are not at all impressed by Uddhava's dry assertions. They are keen (hungry) to have Krishṇa and Krishṇa alone enshrined in their hearts.

Aṅkhiyāṅ hari darasana kī bhūkhīṅ.

Kaise rahati rūpa-rasa rānchīṅ ye batiyāṅ suni rūkhī.

अंखियां हरि दरसन की भूखीं।

कैसै रहति रूप रस रांची ये बतियां सुनि रूखी।।[129]

They have only one heart which is taken away by Krishṇa and is intently fixed on him alone. If they had ten or twenty hearts, they would have worshipped him. They, therefore, do not bother about any one else.

Uddhau mana na bhaye dasa bīsa

Eka hutau so gayau shyāma saṅga ko avarādhai īsa.

ऊधौ मन न भए दस बीस।

एक हुतौ सो गयौ स्याम संग को अवराधै ईस।।[130]

The sole concern of the gopīs is that their loved-one Krishṇa must come back to them somehow. A glimpse of him once will satisfy them all and will fulfil their long cherished desire.

At last Uḍdhava has to yield to the arguments of gopīs and comes round. His attitude thus undergoes a sea change and he becomes an ardent follower of *Saguṇa Brahma*–Krishṇa.

Aba ati chakitavaṅta mana merau.

Āyau hauṅ niraguṇa upadesana bhayau saguna kau cherau.

and

Uḍdhau mauna sādhi rahe

Joga kahi pacchitāta mana-mana, bahuri kacchu na kahe.

अब अति चकितवंत मन मेरौ।

आयौ हौं निरगुन उपदेसन भयौ सगुन कौ चेरौ।[131]

ऊधौ मौन साधि रहे।

जोग कहि पछितात मन-मन, बहुरि कछु न कहे।।[132]

Uddhava finally leaves for Mathurā to narrate the woeful and pathetic condition of Braja in its true colours. He tells Krishṇa that the eyes of all the inhabitants there always remain drenched in tears without him. They are mentally disturbed and are unable to sleep even for a moment at night. Especially the plight of Rādhā's mind is pitiable and woeful.

Tumhre biraha brajanātha rādhikā nain nadi baḍhī

Līne jāta nimeṣa kūla doū ete māna chaḍhī.

Chali na sakata golaka naukā lauṅ sīṅva palaka bara borati.

Āṅsūsalila būḍata saba gokula sūra sukara gahi lījai.

तुम्हरे बिरह ब्रजनाथ राधिका नैन नदी बढ़ी।

लीने जात निमेष कूल दोउ एते मान चढ़ी।।

चलि न सकत गोलक नौका, सींव पलक बर बोरति ।
आंसुसलिल बूड़त सब गोकुल, सूर सुकर गहि लीजै ।।[133]

Uḍdhava is now totally a changed person so much so that he appeals to Krishṇa to return to Braja. But Krishṇa declines his request and goes to Dwārikā, even far beyond Mathurā. This is the climax of the whole episode. The gopīs heave deep sighs of disappointment and despair. They accuse Krishṇa of having made them liefeless once again, though already dead.

Nainā bhaye anātha hamāre.

Madana gupāla uhāṅ taiṅ sajanī suniyata dūri sidhāre

—— —— —— —— —— —— —— ——

Madhubana basata āsa darsana kī, joi naina maga hāre

Sūra syāma prabhu karī priya aisī mritakahuṅ taiṅ puni māre.

नैना भए अनाथ हमारे ।

मदन गुपाल उहां तैं सजनी, सुनियत दूरि सिधारे ।।
मधुबन बसत आस दरसन की, जोइ नैन मग हारे
सूरस्याम प्रभु करी प्रिय ऐसी, मृतकहुं तैं पुनि मारे ।।[134]

'*Bhramaragīta*' is Sūra's magnum opus. No other love-poem can match this attractive poetry of reproach (Upālambha Kāvya). Herein *Viyoga Shriṁgāra* and *Saguṇa Bhakti* (devotion of God with attributes) both have been portrayed in a satirical or humorous and emotional style. It is really a real pleasure to see poetry bursting out of each pada of '*Sūrasāgara*'. Sūra composed these songs through intution. His honeyed, heart-quietening lyrics have charm and vigour. They are vividly and intensely original and retain the power of enchantment. His lyrics especially in *Bhramaragīta* are at once sensuous and transcendental. They depict Krishṇa as the embodiment of *Supreme Deity* in human form.

To conclude, Sūra is a lyricist par excellence. The childhood pranks of Krishṇa, his eagerness to grow to take out the cows for grazing, the child-mother-father and the brother relationship, the beauty of Rādhā, the erotic love of the milk-maids for their loved-one Krishṇa, their love-sports with Krishṇa etc. as exhibited in 'Bhramaragīta' are the main subjects of his lyrics—'Adbhuta eka anūpama bāgha' (10,2729) wherein Rādhā's body has been compared with a grarden; Hamare prabhu auguna chita na dharo (1,220) in which the devotee entreats the Lord to forget and forgive his sins so that he becomes as pure and sublime as the Lord, having completely surrendered to Him; Āye yoga sikhāvana pāṅḍe—10,3606/4224 (Here comes the pontific preacher of yoga—mind-control) which sustains the sweetness of the taunts hurled by the milk-maids deeply steeped in love for his beloved Krishṇa.

Sūra's Style

As has been stated earlier, Sūra has composed all his *padas* (verses) in a lyrical style. In fact his style is most suited to a sentimental and devotional poet like him. He is simple, straight but effective. He is imaginative. Take for instance his descriptions in *'Bhramaragīta'*. *Bhramaragīta* is just an ordinary topic. *Srīmadbhāgavata Purāṇa* also has not dealt this topic so extensively as Sūra has done in *Sūrasāgara*. He has made use of his subtle power of imagination in portraying the various feelings and emotions of Rādhā and gopīs in respect of their complete involvement and dedication to their most dear one, Krishṇa. Without Krishṇa the dark night appears to be as dreadful as a black female serpent to the gopīs. It is no secret that the upper portion of the female serpent is black in colour and the belly-lower portion is white. The moment she bites someone, she also turns over. Thus its black upper portion i.e. back comes down and the white portion-belly goes up. The gopīs mistaking the upper white portion shining as moonlight start feeling plunged in inexpressible frenzy of separation.

Piya binu nāginī rāta.

Kabahuṅka jāmini Uata junhaiyā, dasi ulati hvai jāta.

पिय बिनु नागिनी रात।

कबहुंक जामिनि उअत जुन्हैया, डसि उलटि ह्वै जात।।[135]

The flight of Sūra's imagination is really fantastic. On another occasion Sūra describes Rādhā's attractive body wrapped in blue sārī and the black (looking) body of Krishṇa with a yellow robe as the lightning glittering in the midst of clouds and the dark clouds sparkling in the midst of lightning respectively.

Nīlāmbara syāmala tanu kī chhabi, tanu chhabi pīta subāsa.

Ghana bhītara dāminī prakāsita, dāmini ghana chahuṅ-pāsa.

नीलाम्बर स्यामल तनु की छबि, तनु छबि पीत सुबास।

घन भीतर दामिनी प्रकासित, दामिनि घन चहुं-पास।।[136]

Sūra is a past master in the art of creating specific images. The image of 'Tribhaṅgī (triangular posture) is here noteworthy. The butter-thief is stuck up in the hearts of the gopis and it cannot be pulled out in spite of best efforts.

Ihiṅ ura mākhana chora gaḍe

Aba kaisaiṅ nikasata suni ūdhauṅ, tirachhe hvai ju aḍe.

इहिं उर माखन चोर गड़े।

अब कैसैं निकसत सुनि ऊधौं, तिरछे है जु अड़े।।[137]

The poet in the following pada imagined that the river Yamunā is turned black, as if burnt by the fever of separation from Krishṇa.

Dekhiata kāliṅdī ati kārī.

Kahiyau pathika jāya una hari sauṅ, bhaī biraha jvara jārī.

देखिअत कालिन्दीं अति कारी।

कहियौ पथिक जाय उन हरि सौं, भई विरह ज्वर जारी।।[138]

Thick dark clouds are gathering all around as if elephants of cupid have run amuck and forcibly broken the chains. Neither the *mahāvata* (elephant-driver) nor the wind nor his hook is able to stop them or bend them. Sūra thus describes the dark clouds in the sky as looking awful and painful to the separated lovers.

Dekhiata chahūṅ disi taiṅ ghana ghore.

Mānahuṅ matta madana ke hathiyani, bala kari baṅdhana tore.

____ ____ ____ ____ ____ ____

Rukata na pauna mahāvatahūṅ pai, murata na aṅkusa more.

देखिअत चहूं दिसि तैं घन घोरे।

मानहुं मत्त मदन के हथियनि, बल करि बंधन तोरे

. . . .

रुकत न पौन महावतहूं पै, मुरत न अंकुस मोरे ।।[139]

The tremendous reflex of the dangling ear-rings on the bright cheeks of Krishṇa appear as if the crocodile is playing about in the ocean of nectar and also as if the moon is moving there with a slow pace. The poet has in these lines depicted a dynamic picture of the beauty of Krishṇa through the medium of the flight of his creative imagination.

Chalita kuṅdala, gaṅda maṅdala jhalaka lalita kapola

Sudhā sara janu makara krīḍata indu ḍaha ḍaha ḍola.

चलित कुंडल, गंड मंडल झलक ललित कपोल ।

सुधा सर जनु मकर क्रीड़त इन्दु डह डह डोल ।।[140]

Again, Rādhā's eyes have planted the creeper of separation. Its roots have gone deep into the nether world. While it grew in a natural way, the shades beneath it have become thick. It is difficult to be weeded out since it has spread over all her body. Here the intensity of love on the part of the gopīs is expressed through eye-gestures.

Mere nainā biraha kī beli baī

Sīṅchata naina nīra ke sajanī, mūra patāla gaī.

Vigasita latā subhāi āpanai, chhāyā saghana bhaī.

Aba kaise niravārauṅ sajanī, saba tana pasari gaī

मेरे नैना बिरह की बेलि बई ।

सींचत नैन नीर के सजनी, मूर पताल गई ।।

विगसित सता सुभाइ आपनै, छाया सधन भई ।

अब कैसे निरवारौं सजनी, सब तन पसरि गई ।।[141]

In short, Sūra's imaginative skill is evident from the descriptions of the bewitching beauty of Rādhā especially that of large and twinkling eyes and also that of the winsome figure and graceful personality of Krishṇa. The protrayals too of the bitter outpourings of the cow-girls on hearing the melodious notes of Krishṇa's musical flute, which they look upon as co-wife (10/1889,1976,1921) display the poet's remarkable ingenuity for imagination

A poet of masses (Lokakavi)

Sūra was well-versed in classical Indian music and had a thorough knowledge of this art. In spite of this his poetry does not lack the touch of folk-art, the reason being that he was a poet of the masses and that he always selected the rural environments as the sites of sports of Krishṇa and the milkmaids. He was not writing for the *rājās, rānīs, nawābs* and all that. He was writing for the rustic and the low, who were the real children of his *'Master'*. He has created their world in a masterly manner, depicting the following occasions:

1. Of rituals e.g. child's *janma* (brith), *nāma-karaṇa* (name giving or baptism), *annaprāshana* (administering of food etc.), *Karṇachhedana* (piercing of the ear), *yajṅyopavīta* (thread-wearing), *Vivāha* (marriage) etc.

2. Of festivals and ceremonies e.g. *holi, govardhana* festivals.

3. Of seasonal songs e.g. *malhāras of shrāvaṇa* and *jhoola (hindolas).*

4. Of amusements etc. (*rasiyā*)

5. Of depicting the emotive feelings such as *viraha* (separation)

In the tenth *skandha* of *Sūrasāgara* different types of rituals connected with the life of Krishṇa have been vividly delineated. These rituals depict the real ways of life. All their attraction and jubilation are centred round them. On the occasion of Krishṇa's birth there is merry-making throughout Gokula. Women decked in their best garments flock together one by one in front of Nandā's house which is bristling with the sweet notes of auspicious songs to felicitate him. Melodious *'sohar'* and congratulatory songs are heard all around. A traditional *sohara* song is given below which reflects the exuberance of joy on the birth of a son after the completion of nine months of pregnancy. in respect of Yashodā wherein the poet inserts folk-notes such as 'Ho' in between the lines.

Gauri ganesvara bīnaūṅ (ho) devī sārada tohiṅ

Gāvauṅ hari ko sohilau (ho), mana-ākhara dai mohiṅ

Haraṣa badhāvā mana bhayau (ho), rānī jāyau pūta

Ghara-bāhara māṅge sabai (ho), ṭhaḍhe māgadha-sūta.

Āṭha māsa chaṅdana piyau (ho), navaiṅ piyau kapūra.

Dasaeṅ mohana bhae (ho), āṅgana bājai tūra.

गौरि गनेस्वर बीनऊं (हो) , देवी सारद तोहिं ।

गावौं हरि को सोहिलौ (हो) , मन-आखर दै मोहिं ।

हरष बधावा मन भयौ (हो) , रानी जायौ पूत ।

घर-बाहर मांगै सबै (हो) , ठाढ़े मागध-सूत ।

आठ मास चन्दन पियौ (हो) , नवएं पियौ कपूर ।

दसएं मोहन भए (हो) , आंगन बाजै तूर । ।[142]

Songs congratulating both Nanda and Yashodā on this auspicious occasion are equally heart-catching. See for illustration:

Dhani dhani Nanda-Jasomati, dhani jaga pāvana re.

Dhani hari liyau avatāra, su dhani dina āvana re

Dasaeṅ māsa bhayau pūta, punīta suhāvana re

Saṅkha-chakra-gadā padmā, chaturabhuja pāvan re

Bani braja-sundari chalīṅ su gāi badhāvana re

Kanaka-thāra rochana-daḍhi, tilaka banāvana re

Nand-gharahiṅ chalī gaī mahari jahaṅ pāvana re

—— —— —— —— ——

Jasumati dhani yaha kokhi, jahaṅ rahe bāvana re

Juga-juga jīvahu kāṅha sabani mana bhāvana re

—— —— —— —— ——

Sūradāsa prabhu janame bhakta hulasāvana re.

धनि धनि नन्द-जसोमति, धनि जग पावन रे।

धनि हरि लियौ अवतार, सु धनि दिन आवन रे।

दसएं मास भयै पूत, पुनीत सुहावन रे।

संख-चक्र-गदा पद्मा चतुर भुज पावन रे।

बनि ब्रज-सुन्दरि चलीं, सु गाइ बधावन रे।

कनक-थार रोचन दधि, तिलक बनावन रे।

नन्द-घरहिं चली गई महरि जहं पावन रे।

. . . .

जसुमति धनि यह कोखि, जहां रहे बावन रे।

. . . .

जुग जुग जीवहुं कान्ह, सबनि मन भावन रे।

सूरदास प्रभु जनमे, भक्त हुलसावन रे।[143]

The songs sung on the occasion of *annaprāshana, nāmakaraṇa, Karṇachhedana* etc. are no less alluring and attractive. The wedding ceremony (*gāṅdharva Vivāha)* of Krishṇa and Rādhā has been depicted in its entirety in typical folk tunes by Sūra with great pomp and show. The poet has narrated almost all the traditions such as playing of music on dundubhi and mridaṅga, scattering or giving away of coins to ward off trouble, tying of festoons of flowers (torana haṅdhāi), wedlock ceremony (pāṇī-grahaṇa), circumambulation around the fire (bhāṅvareṅ lenā), putting the chaplet (maura) made of peacock-feathers on the bridegroom's head etc. followed in *Barsānā*, situated to the west of Mathurā, the birth place of Rādhā, at the time of marriage.

Sanakādika nārada muni, siva viraṅchi jāna

Deva-duṅdubhī mridaṅga, bāje bara nisāna.

Bārana torana baṅdhāi, hari kīnha ucchāha

Braja kī saba rīti bhaī, barasāneṅ vyāha.

सनकादिक नारद मुनि, सिव विरंचि जान।

देव-दुन्दुभी मृदंग, बाजे बर निसान।

बारन तोरन बंधाइ, हरि कीन्ह उछाह।

ब्रज की सब रीति भई, बरसानैं व्याह।।[144]

Mora-mukuta rachi maura banāyau.

Māthe para ḍhari hari bara āyau.

मोर मुकुट रचि मौर बनायौ।

माथे पर धरि हरि बर आयौ।।[145]

Manamatha sainika bhaye barātī, druma phūle bana anupama bhāṅtī.

Sura bandījana mili jasa gāye, mādhavā bājana ananda bajāe.

मनमथ सैनिक भये बरातीं, द्रुम फूले बन अनुपम भांती।
सुर बन्दीजन मिलि जस गाए, मधवा बाजन अनन्द बजाए।।[146]

and

Tāpara pānigrahaṇa vidhi kīṅhīṅ.

Taba maṅdapa bhrami bhāṅvari dīnhīṅ.

तापर पानिग्रहण विधि कीन्हीं।
तब मण्डप भ्रमि भांवरि दीन्हीं।।[147]

The Holī festival is indicative of joyful and hilarious mood of the Indian people. It is celebrated in the spring season. Holī songs (*dhamāra*) are sung by men and women alike to the accompaniment of different kinds of musical instruments e.g. *muraja, rabāba, kinnarī, beena, dhapa, jhāṅjha, mridaṅga, Kartāla* and *benu*. During Holī days the atmoshpere all around is replete with erotic sentiments. The following song depicts in detail the abounding joy, rupture, and ecstasy of men and women folk (milk-maids) belonging to Braja. The song is so much heart-captivating and exciting that it makes them all jump, dance and hug one another in merriment in the sweet company of their beloved Krishṇa. Both men and women are playing *phāga* in the markets of Braja and are sprinkling coloured waters mixed with sandal scent by gem-studded syrings on one another without any reservation or fear of elderly persons.

Yā gokula ke chauhaṭaiṅ raṅga bhījī gvālini.

Hari saṅga khelaiṅ phāga, naina salone rī raṅgarāchī gvālini

Darati na gurujana lāja kauṅ raṅgabhījī gvālini.

Mohan kaiṅ anurāga, naina salone rī raṅgarāchī gvālini.

Duṅdubhī bājai gahagahī, raṅgabhījī gvālini.

——— ——— ——— ——— ——— ———

Ratnajaṭita pichakāriyāṅ raṅgabhījī gvālini.

Kara liye gokulanātha naina salone rī gvālini.

या गोकुल के चौहटैं रंगभीजी ग्वालिनि।

हरि-संग खेलैं फाग, नैन सलोने री रंगराची ग्वालिनि।

डरति न गुरुजन लाज कौं, रंगभीजी ग्वालिनि।

मोहन कैं अनुराग, नैन सलोने री रंगराची ग्वालिनि।

दुन्दुभी बाजे गहगही रंगभीजी ग्वालिनि।

. . . .

रत्नजटित पिचकारियां रंगभीजी ग्वालिनि।

कर लिए गोकुलनाथ नैन सलोने री ग्वालिनि।।[148]

The streets of Braja resound with the words like Ho, Ho, Ho, Ho, Ho, Ho, Horī,[149] Hari Horī Hai[150] uttered in chorus by the inhabitants of Braja. The songs sung at the time of worshipping Govaradhan, a hillock celebrated in Krishṇa—lore, which is popularly known as 'Godhanotsava' are no less artistic and fascinating than Holī songs.

Among the songs that are sung during different seasons *malhāra* is very popular. These songs which are sung in groups by the ladies during rainy season, are extremely touching. They arouse emotional feelings when sung in chorus on having a ride on the gem-studded hindolā (swing) in the company of Krishṇa. Such songs tend to relieve the human beings of their tension and worries for some time at least.

Hiṅdore hari saṅga jhuliye (ho) aru piya kauṅ dehuṅ jhulāi

Gaī bīti grīṣma garada-hita ritu, sarasa barasā āi

——— ——— ——— ——— ——— ———

Gopaṅgnā gopāla ju sauṅ kahati gahi gahi pāi.

Aba gaḍhanahāra hinḍoranā ko, tāhiṅ lehu bulāi

Hama ramaki hinḍorai chaḍhaiṅ, aru tumahiṅ dehu jhulāi.

Ghana Ghatā kārī, sveta bagapaṅgati nirakha nabha ora.

Taisiyai damakati dāmini taisoi ambara ghora.

—— —— —— —— —— ——

jhūlata jhulāvata, kaṅṭha lāvata, baḍhī ānaṅda beli

हिंडोरे हरि संग झूलिये (हो) अरु पिय कौं देहुं झुलाइ।

गई बीति ग्रीषम गरद-हित रितु, सरस बरसा आइ।

—— —— —— —— —— ——

गोपांगना गोपाल जू सौं कहति गहि गहि पाइ।

अब गढ़नहार हिडोरना को, ताहिं लेहु बुलाइ।।

हम रमकि हिंडोरे चढ़ै, अरु तुमहिं देहु झुलाइ।

घन घटा कारी स्वेत बग पंगति निरख नभ ओर।

तैसियै दमकति दामिनि तैसोइ अम्बर घोर।

—— —— —— —— —— ——

झुलत झुलावत, कंठ लावत, बढ़ी आनन्द बेलि।।[151]

Rasiyās: These songs are the real representatives of the folk-people of Braja. Such songs are included in *jalakrīḍā, dānalīlā* and *mānalīlā*. They are love-songs depicting the amorous activities of Rādhā and Krishṇa. Gopīs also share such activities with Krishṇa. They feel that they are destined to live in this world and live a purposeful life. The theme, rhythm and vocabulary are all the same as found in the folk songs. They are composed in *viraha* style of the folk songs.

Gwāla gītas: The songs of the cowherds again are very popular folk songs. They are sung in local tunes to the accompaniment of folk dances on the occasions of different festivals like *gochāraṇa* (grazing of the cows), etc. Such songs are part and parcel of the lives of the happy, lucky and carefree cowherds.

Literature is the most powerful medium for getting at the authentic picture of the people living in a particular region. *'Sūrasāgara'* is no exception to this. Herein we find such references in abundance as throw a considerable light on the beliefs, living patterns, occupations, food materials, dresses and the means of entertainments of the people during the life-time of Sūra.

Beliefs

Sūra has strongly raised his voice against evils of the then prevalent *Varṇavyavasthā* (classification of society into four castes). He is of the opinion that racial discrimination is the root cause of backwardness of the society. He attaches no importance to caste, gotra or family. To him it also does not matter whether he is a king or a pauper (1,11). He treats the high and the low alike (7,427). He, however, points out some of the values and prejudices of caste society. People from the upper castes i.e. the brāhmaṇas were not supposed to take meals or inter-marry with the lower castes i.e. the shūdras. A shūdra dining with a Brāhmana was like a crow living with a haṅsa or garlic in the company of camphor or glass with gold (10,3770). Sūra regards love which transcends all as the essence of *dharma*. High officials are regarded as oppressors. The paṭwārīs (Village officer who maintains the land records) are described as great cheats and exploiters of the poor farmers. They habitually make false entries into their account books (bahī). Whatever they say becomes the truth.

Prabhu jū, Yauṅ kīnhīṅ hama khetī.

Baṅjara bhūmi, gāuṅ hara jote, aru jetī kī tetī.

—— —— —— —— —— ——

Ahaṅkāra paṭawārī kapaṭī, jhuṭhī likhata bahī.

Lāgai dharama, batāvai adharama, bākī sabai rahī.

प्रभु जू, यौं कीन्हीं हम खेती।

बंजर भूमि, गाऊं हर जोते, अरु जेती की तेती।

— — — — —

अंहकार पटवारी कपटी, झूठी लिखत बही।

लागै धरम, बतावै अधरम, बाकी सबै रही।।[152]

People believe that the worship of Indra is very beneficial to them as he, being the rain-god, grants them food-grains, is the main source of their sustenance and also provides water to their cattle. The farmers in particular take pride in celebrating the *Godhanotsava* for the safety and long life of their cattle (cow). Both the Gods *Shivu* and *Sūrya* are adored by the ladies particularly to have their blessings for getting a befitting husband or a son. This is a general feeling among these people that the birth of a son is the result of righteous acts done in previous births. All his actions like weeping, laughing, moving of the lips, sudden getting up startingly from sleep, sucking of the thumb and toe are all related to some or the other belief. The parents or some of the elders frighten their children by creating a false terror in their minds so that they may not go out to a far off place all alone. That the Hāū (houshold watchword of fear) cuts off the ears of children is treated as a matter of superstition or blind faith.

Khelana dūri jāta kata kāṅhā?

Āja sunyau maiṅ 'hāū' āyau tuma nahiṅ jānata kānhā.

Ika larikā abahiṅ bhaji āyau rovata dekhyau tāhi

Kāna tori vaha leta sabani kai, larikā jānata jāhi

Chalau na, vega savārai jaiyai bhāji āpanaiṅ dhāma

Sūra syāma yaha bāta sunata hī boli liye balarāma.

खेलन दूरि जात कत कान्हा ?
आज सुन्यौ मैं 'हाऊ'आयौ, तुम नहिं जानत कान्हा।
इक लरिका अबहिं भजि आयौ रोवत देख्यौ ताहि।
कान तोरि वह लेत सबनि कै, लरिका जानत जाहि।
चलौ न, वेगि सवारै जैयै, भाजि आपनैं धाम।
सूर स्याम यह बात सुनत ड़ी बोलि लिए बलराम।।[153]

Daughter is treated on a par with the son. She moves about freely in childhood but she is not allowed to step out of her house as soon as she advances in age. She is more close to the mother than the father. She is not afraid of her mother and does not even bother about her intimidation at times. It is generally seen that parents name their children as *Kurā Mal*, Gohar Mal, Kālū Rāma, Chūhar Rāma etc. to ward off any evil spirit that may harm them. The names like *Raiṅtā* (रैंता), *Paiṅtā* (पैंता), *Manā* (मना), *Mansukha* found in *'Sūrasāgara'* are in conformity with this practice.

Auspicious and inauspicious omens

Different kinds of omens prevalent in the masses are based on some or the other belief. Some of them are auspicious and others inauspicious. Crowing of the crow in the courtyard,[154] humming of the bees beside the ear of a lovely woman,[155] throbbing of the arms, cracking of the bodice of women on account of great thrill of joy and keen desire to hear sweet words[156] etc. are some of the auspicious omens which indicate the arrival of the lover. Throbbing of the left eye of women or that of the right eye of men is also a good omen.[157] Sneezing, cat's cutting across of someone's path while setting out on some business, crowing of the crow and also braying of an ass on the left side and fluttering of dog's ears at one's door[159] etc. are all included in inauspicious omens. *Bhāgya* (Destiny) also plays a major role in the lives of the common people in the days of Sūra[160]

Superstitious devices (Ṭone-Ṭoṭake)

Ṭoṭakas are generally employed without any fuss by women for the welfare and safety of their children. Yashodā all the time fears lest her dear son Krishṇa should fall a prey to an evil eye. So she is seen moving a mixture of mustard and salt concealed in her fist round his (Krishṇa's) head and consigning that to the flames for countering the influence of evil glances.[161] She puts a black sooty mark also on his forehead to guard him off any evil or calamity.[162] The *Kaṭhulā* and the *lion's nail* too are hung around the neck of a baby simply to neutralize the effect of an evil.[163]

Ṭonas are also used for counter-acting the impact of evil. Quite contrary to the *ṭoṭakas,* these are practised by the *Siddhas* and *Ojhās* for *māraṇa* (causing someone to be killed), for *ucchātana* (magical incantation causing someone to get the mind diverted) and for *Vashīkaraṇa* (charming someone into submission). Sometimes an innocent person or a creature is even sacrificed in order to achieve the desired goal of the *ṭonās*. Rādhā is one day beaten by a snake. Krishṇa is called and he then acts like a *Gārudī* (who draws out someone's poison by chanting mantras) who cures her of the snake's venom.[164]

Social Life

It is a loveable setting painted by Sūra. It consists of mother *(Māṅ)*, father *(bābā)*, brother *(dāu)*, lover *(Krishṇa)*, beloved *(Rādhā)* and companions, neighbours, maid-servants, other relatives, friends and foes. The child is the pivot of the whole society. Every character here is also related to him in some form or the other. *'Sūrasāgara'* presents a true and factual picture of the society in those days through the medium of these characters. Four castes as usual have been mentioned. Ahīra is the main caste. Ahīras have been described as living in perfect unity and harmony. Cows are their most precious treasure.[165] Nanda Bābā is not only head of his family but also the chieftain of the village (*Kṣetrapa*) who is held in great esteem by old and young alike. The Ahīras advocate the joint family system without any reservation. All the persons there respect the sentiments of each other and their mutual relationship is very cordial. They celebrate their festive occasions collectively with great enthusiasm and jubilation, without caring for any racial discrimination. Braja was a unit which included both village and towns. The common people lived mostly in village whereas people from higher strata i.e. chieftains, high officials etc. had their places of residence in towns. The common people consisted of village artisans and low-caste persons, cowherds and cultivators (Kisāna). The lives of the common people was full of misery. On the other hand the upper class enjoyed a special privilege. On the whole the people seem to be very simple and innocent[166] of the intricacies and ostentations of the city life.

Women always feel very helpless and uncomfortable in the house of their in-laws, since their mothers-in-law and their brothers and sisters are a constant source of unending pin-pricks, troubles and miseries to them. They all the time go on interfering in day to day life of their daughters-in-law and would not even spare to taunt or pass sarcastical remarks against them if or not there is an occasion for such things.[167] They are kept under strict control.

The economic condition of the people is depicted as just average. They are somehow able to pull on and meet their daily expenses. Cattle (Cow)-breeding, agriculture and business on small scale are their principal occupations. Though milk, ghee, butter etc. are available in plenty but thier sale outside Gokula is the main source of income.

They attach due importance to ethical values. They are God-fearing and would never try to resort to vicious ways of life. They hate and avoid the company of those who are sinful and immoral.[168]

Both men and women put on simple dress. Men mostly put on *shirt, kurtā, dhotī* (upto knees), jacket, cap or ear-cap (*kaṅtopā*) and women's chief dress is a long loose skirt (lahaṅgā-red, yellow or blue in colour), a red-coloured bodice and a coloured over-cloth (*chunarī*). pītāmbara (yellow cloth) across the back is used by men and women alike. On ceremonious occasions they wear gaudy and variegated dresses. No doubt there is a marked difference between the life-style of rural people and the chief such as Nanda and other officials. Men and women both are fond of putting on various types of ornaments. Normally they are in the habit of taking simple food but on the occasion of festivals and other ceremonies a variety of dishes e.g. luchai (a special type of pūrī), bāṭis in curd, cakes made of gram flour, lentils and sweets viz. hesamī, khurme, phenī, ghevara, jalebī, mālpūā, sakkharpāre, dry fruits[169] etc. are liked by them.

People are optimistic and interested in leading a life full of joys and merriments. Āṅkha mudavvala (hide and seek)[170], chaugāna (modern hockey or polo),[171] racing, chaka-dorī[172] (playing with top and string), chaupaḍa (playing with dice),[173] playing on lute (venu) and viṣāna (a wind instrument made of horns) are their main means of entertainment.

The above study shows that Sūra is undoubtedly a poet of the masses in letter and spirit. He, as keen observer of various instincts and states of human mind has faithfully echoed the sentiments of the common man. There is no other source as authentic as Sūra who can give such a graphic and picturesque account of the cultural, social, religio-philosophical and psychological mood of the people of Braja.

Sūra's greatness lies in his art of portraying life as it is and human feelings and emotions. As far as the subject-matter of 'Sūrasāgara' is concerned Sūra has got an inspiration to some extent from the Bhāgavata Purāṇa but he has developed it in his own way and given an original touch with his creative imagination. His padas mirror his keen insight into different sorts of human moods and attitudes. In their delineation in the right perspective lies his poetic craft and excellence. His padas, in fact, will neither wither or perish. They will remain ever fresh and ever green, since they reflect and epitomize all the sufferings and love-pangs of humanity. Besides, they suggest that the only easier path of the attainment of salvation (mukti) is the worship of 'Saguṇa Brahma'. As for language used it is simple, communicative, sweet and devoid of any superficiality and verbosity. The style too is uncumbersome, lucid and effective. Thus the great blind poet excels in all respects. Above all Sūra's message of love–paternal, friendly as well as divine, humility, self-surrender and equality has still the same significance or relevance as it had during his life-time. Sūra is no longer with us to day but he will ever remain enshrined in the hearts of all the world over as one who had completely identified himself with the general masses.

References

1. For details see chapters 2.
2. Ibid,
3. Ibid,
4. Ibid,
5. Ibid,
6. Ibid,
7. Ibid,
8. Bhāgavata, Skandha 2, Chapter 10, Shloka 4.
9. Sūrasāgara (Nāgarī Prachāriṇi Sabhā) edition, V. S. 2021 (Vol I) and 2018 (Vol. II), Skandha I, Pada 35.
10. Ibid, Sk. 1, pada, 36.
11. Ibid, Sk. 10, pada, 3727
12. Ibid
13. Sūrsāgara, Skandha 10, padas 2305 and 4911.
14. Ibids Sk., 1, pada, 134
15. Ibid, pada, 133
16. Ibid, pada, 132
17. Ibid, pada, 4911
18. Quoted in 'The Mainstream' December, 1923, 1978, pp. 22-23
19. Ibid
20. Ibid
21. Ibid
22. Ibid
23. Ibid
24. Ibid

25. Sūrasāgara, Skandha 1, pada, 225
26. Ibid, SK 1, pada1
27. A. Ibid, SK. 10, pada 717, and 27 B Sk. 10, pada 1190
28. Ibid, SK, 10 pada 838
29. Ibid, SK, 10, pada 1214
30. Ibid, pada, 1233
31. Ibid, pada, 1471
32. Ibid, pada, 1488
33. Ibid, pada, 4159
34. Ibid, pada, 4111
35. Ibid, pada, 3788
36. Ibid, pada, 4292
37. Ibid, pada, 3624
38. Ibid, pada, 4165
39. Ibid, pada, 4259
40. Ibid, pada, 4259
41. Ibid, pada, 835
42. Ibid, pada, 3021
43. Ibid, pada, 4578
44. Ibid, pada, 4585
45. Ibid, pada, 4259
46. Ibid, pada, 4609
47. Ibid, pada, 3804
48. Ibid, pada, 4175
49. Ibid, pada, 4587
50. Ibid, pada, 4163
51. Ibid, pada, 4173
52. Ibid, pada, 4176
53. Ibid, pada, 4587
54. Ibid, pada, 4224

55. Ibid, pada, 2341
56. Ibid, pada, 2404
57. Ibid, pada, 3213
58. Ibid, pada, 2462
59. Ibid, pada, 1922
60. Ibid, pada, 1473
61. Ibid, pada, 1475
62. Ibid, Skandha 1,pada, 270
63. Ibid, SK, 10, pada, 2590
64. Ibid, pada, 4585
65. Ibid, pada, 4141
66. Ibid, SK 10 pada, 733
67. Ibid, pada, 1479
68. Ibid, pada, 2716
69. Ibid, pada, 4757
70. Ibid, pada, 1245
71. Ibid SK, 1, pada 1.
72. Ibid, SK 10 pada,811
73. Ibid, pada, 8113
74. Ibid, pada, 2729
75. Ibid, pada, 2723
76. Ibid, pada, 897.
77. Ibid, pada, 2432
78. Ibid, pada, 2493
79. Ibid, pada, 752
80. Ibid, pada, 723
81. Ibid, pada, 717
82. Ibid, pada, 769
83. Ibid, pada, 795
84. Ibid, pada, 728

85. Ibid, pada, 661
86. Ibid, pada, 855
87. Ibid, pada, 798
88. Ibid, pada, 1320
89. Ibid, pada, 897
90. Ibid, pada, 952
91. Ibid, pada, 833
92. Ibid, pada, 793
93. Ibid, pada, 811
94. Ibid, pada, 3795
95. Ibid, pada, 3793
96. Ibid, pada, 3592
97. Ibid, pada, 3754
98. Ibid, pada, 1290
99. Ibid, pada, 1299
100. Ibid, pada, 1300
101. Ibid, pada, 1300
102. Ibid, pada, 4912
103. Ibid, pada, 4913
104. Ibid, pada, 3614
105. Ibid, pada, 3619
106. Ibid, pada, 3628
107. Ibid, pada, 3624
108. Ibid, pada, 3777
109. Ibid, pada, 3821
110. Ibid, pada, 3830
111. Ibid, pada, 4110
112. Ibid, pada, 3920
113. Ibid, pada, 3928
114. Ibid, pada, 3892

115. Ibid, pada, 4688
116. Ibid, pada, 3784
117. Ibid, pada, 3619
118. Ibid, pada, 3840
119. Ibid, pada, 3858
120. Ibid, pada, 4305
121. Ibid, pada, 4122
122. Ibid, pada, 4118
123. Ibid, pada, 4141
124. Ibid, pada, 4233
125. Ibid, pada, 4150
126. Ibid, pada, 4251
127. Ibid, pada, 4510
128. Ibid, pada, 4641
129. Ibid, pada, 4177
130. Ibid, pada, 4346
131. Ibid, pada, 4699
132. Ibid, pada, 4502
133. Ibid, pada, 4733
134. Ibid, pada, 4872
135. Ibid, pada, 3892
136. Ibid, pada, 2686
137. Ibid, pada, 4351
138. Ibid, pada, 3811
139. Ibid, pada, 3923
140. Ibid, pada, 1245
141. Ibid, pada, 3866
142. Ibid, pada, 658
143. Ibid, pada, 646
144. Ibid, pada, 1692

145. Ibid, pada, 1690
146. Ibid, pada, 1690
147. Ibid, pada, 1690
148. Ibid, pada, 3487
149. Ibid, pada, 3488
150. Ibid, pada, 3534
151. Ibid, pada, 3450
152. Ibid, Skandha, pada,185
153. Ibid Skandha 10, pada 838
154. Tere āvaige āju sakhi hari khelana ko phāgu rī.
    Saguna saṅdeso hauṅ sunyau, tairaiṅ āṅgana bole kāga rī. 10, 3479

    तेरे आवैगे आजु सखि हरि खेलन को फागु री।

    सगुन संदेसो हौं सुन्यौ, तैरैं आंगन बोले काग री।।10, 3479
155. Āja koū nīkī bāta sunāvaiṅ
    Kai madhubana taiṅ naṅda lāḍilau kai aba deta koū āvai
    Bhauṅra eka chahuṅ disi taiṅ uḍi uḍi kānani lagi lagi āvai 10,4075

    आज कोऊ नीकी बात सुनावैं।

    कै मधुबन तैं नंद लाडिलौ कै अब देत कोउ आवै।

    भौंर एक चहुं दिसि तैं उड़ि उड़ि काननि लगि लगि आवै।।10,4075
156. Bhuja pharakata aṅgiyā tarakati koṅu mīṭhī bāta sunāvai
    Syāma sundara ko āgama jāniya, vai nischaya ghara āvai 10, 4074

    भुज फरकत अंगिया तरकति कोंउ मीठी बात सुनोवे।

    श्याम सुन्दर को आगम जानिय, वै निश्चय घर आवै।। 10,4074
157. Bāta na dharati kāna tānati hain bhauṅha bāna
    Tau na chalati bāma aṅkhiyāṅ pharaki rahīṅ. 10, 3406

    बात न धरति कान, तानति हैं भौंह बान।

    तउ न चलति बाम अंखियां फरकि रहीं।।10,3406
158. Jasumati chali rasoī bhītara, tabahīṅ gvāli eka chhīṅkī

Ṭhaṭhaka rahī dvāre para thāḍī, bāta nahiṅ kacchu nīkī

Āi ajira nikasī naṅdarānī bahurī dosa mitāī

Maṅjārī āge hvai āī, puni phiri āṅgana āī

Vyākula bhaī, nikasa gaī bāhira, kaha dhauṅ gaye kanhāyī

Bāeṅ kāga, dāhinai khara-swara, vyākula ghara phiri āī

Khana bhītara khana bāhira āvata khana āṅgana ihiṅ bhāṅti

Sūra syāma koṅ ṭerati jananī naiṅkuṅ nahiṅ mana sāṅti 10, 1158

जसुमति चली रसोई भीतर, तबहीं ग्वालि एक छींकी ।

ठठक रही द्वारे पर ठाढ़ी, बात नहीं कछु नीकी ।

आइ अजिर निकसी नन्दरानी, बहुरी दोष मिटाइ ।

मंजारी आगे ह्वै आई, पुनि फिर आंगन आइ ।

व्याकुल भई, निकस गई बाहिर, कह धौं गये कन्हाई

बाएं काग, दाहिनै खर-स्वर, व्याकुल धर फिरि आइ ।

खन भीतर खन बाहिर आवत, खन आंगन इहिं भांति ।

सूर श्याम कों टेरति जननी नैंकुं नहीं मन सान्ति 10,1158

159. Phaṭakata sravanana svāna dwāre para 10, 1159

फटकत स्रवनन स्वान द्वारे पर । 10,1159

160. (i) Apanau apanau bhāgya sakhī rī 10, 2404

(ii) Pāvai kauna likhai binu bhāla 10, 2405

(क) अपनौ अपनौ भाग्य सखी री । 10,2404

(ख) पावै कौन लिखै बिनु भाल । 10,2405

161. (i) Kabahuṅ aṅga bhuṣana banāvati, rāī-ona utārati 10,736

(ii) khelata maiṅ koi dīṭhi lagāī lai-lai rāī-lona utārati 10, 818

कबहुं अंग भूषन बनावति, राइ-लोन उतारति । 10,736

खेलत मैं कोइ दीठि लगाई, लै-लै राइ-लोन उतारति 10,818

162. Lālana, vārī yā mukha ūpara
Māī morihi dīṭhi na lāgai, tātaiṅ maṅsi-biṅdā diyau bhupara 10,710

लालन वारी या मुख ऊपर।

माई मोरिहि दीठि न लागै, तातैं मंसि-बिंदा दियौ भूपर 10,710

163. Kaṭhulā kaṅṭha bajra-kehari-nakha,

Masi-biṅdukā sumrīgamada bhāla 10, 702

कठुला कंठ ब्रज-केहरि-नख, मसि-बिन्दुका सुमृगमद भाल 10,702

164. (i) Mahari gāruḍī kuṅvara kaṅhāī 10,1372

(ii) Kahūṅ rādhikā kāraiṅ khāyau jahu na āvau jhāri

Jaṅtra-maṅtra kachhu jānata hau tuma, sūra syāma banavāri 10, 1373

(iii) Sūra syāma mere baḍau gāruḍi, rādhā lyāvahu jāī 10, 1374

(क) महरि, गारुड़ी कुंवर कन्हाई ।10,1372

(ख) कहूं राधिका कारैं खायौ जाहु न आवौ झारि

जंत्र-मंत्र कछु जानत हौ तुम, सूर श्याम बनवारि 10,1373

(ग) सूर श्याम मेरे बड़ौ गारुड़ी राधा ल्यावहु जाई । 10,1374

165. Ahīra jāti godhana kauṅ mānaiṅ 10, 2544

अहीर जाति गोधन कौं मानैं ।10,2544

166. Chhaṅda kapaṭa kachhu jānati nāhiṅ na

Sūdhī hai, braja kī saba bāla 10,2397

छंद कपट कछु जानति नहिं न, सूधी है, ब्रज की सब बाल 10,2397

167. (i) Vai kachhu kahaiṅ, karaiṅ kachhu aurai,

Sāsu nanada tina para jhaharai 10,2539

(ii) Sāsu nanada ghara trāsa dikhāvai 10,2540

(क) वै कछु कहैं, करैं कछु औरै, सासु ननद तिन पर झहरै 10,2539

(ख) सासु ननद घर त्रास दिखावैं । 10,2540

168. Vimukha janani kau saṅga na kījai,

Inke vimukha bachana suni sravanani

dina-dina dehī chhījai 10, 2546

विमुख जननि कौ संग न कीजै।

इनके विमुख बचन सुनि स्रवननि

दिन-दिन देही छीजै। 10,2546

169. Sūrasāgara, Skandha 10, pada 801, 829, 830, 859

170. Ibid, Ibid, 858

171. Ibid, Ibid, 861, 4786

172. Ibid, Ibid, 1287

173. Ibid, Skandha 1, 60

174. Ibid, Skandha 10, 1066

5

THE MUSICIAN

Besides being a poet of great eminence Sūra was also a skilled musician very well acquainted with the classical and folk-music of his times. Both the internal and external evidences bear testimony to this. The basic internal evidence is provided by the structural form of the compositions, the names of the rāga-rāginīs mentioned on the top of most of the padas and by musical terms used in these padas. The external evidence is found in the personal accounts regarding the group of eight poet-musicians known as Aṣṭachhāpa as well as in the oral musical tradition of the temples of the Vallabha Sampradāya.

The flexibility, soft flow and melodiousness of Sūra's language has played a very significant role in making his compositions musical. All his padas especially available in Bhramaragītā are cast in musical pattern classical or popular (folk) to suit the general tone of the themes dealt therein. In 'Sūrasāgara' the poet has made use of almost all the rāga-rāginīs mentioned in the ancient works of Indian musicology. He has always been inspired more by his emotive instincts and impulses than any thing else in composing his padas. That is why he has used tadbhava words (derived from saṁskrit) such as नोन (लवण)[1], माहिं[2] (मध्य), भौंरा,[3] भंवर[4] (भ्रमर), भक्तवछल[5] (भक्तवत्सल), सुभाइ[6]

(स्वभाव), माधौ[7] (माधव), सोभित[8] (शोभित) and रेनु (रेणु), आसा[9] (आशा), औगुन (अवगुण), समदरसी[10] (समदर्शी) in large numbers to suit the necessary requirements of rhythm which is considered as the chief characteristic of 'Braja Bhāṣhā'. It is thus natural for the poet to avoid the use of conjunct words and also such words as are jarring to the ear as far as possible so that his padas could be sung with greater ease and flueney. In some of his padas he has employed words like री[11], अरी अरी[12], ए[13], एरी[14], रे[15], हो[16], है[17] हैं [18] etc. to give them a musical touch. Sūra has more often repeated the same sound once or more than once or the syllables uttered from the same place of articulation to lend melody and rhythm to his language. As for instance:

1. चारु कपोल लोल लोचन
लट लटकनि मनु मत्त मधुप गन मादक मधुहिं पिये ।[19]
2. चोरत चितहिं चारु चित्त चितवनियां ।[20]
3. कारो हि कजरा कारो हि बदरा, कारे हि स्याम हमारे ।[21]
4. घटा घनघोर घहरात अररात ।
दररात थररात ब्रज लोग डरपाए ।[22]

As Sūra is a gifted musician he has been able to conveniently repeat similar words in his padas, conveying different meanings each time to give them a musical flow e.g.

सारंग पर सारंग खेलत हैं,
सारंग ही सौं हंसि-हंसि जात ।
अरि सारंग राखि सारंग कौं
सारंग गहि सारंग कौ जात[23]

He has also used the same words or syllables in the beginning or at the end of each pada to create musical effect e.g.

जब जब मुरली कान्ह बजावत
तब तब राधा नाम उचारत,
बार बार रिझावत। [24]

and

निकसि कुंवर खेलन चले रंगहोरी,
मोहन नंदकिसोर लाल रंगहोरी। [25]

Sūra is very much fond of using pure saṁskrit words (tatsama) relying more on compound words while depicting beauty of Krishṇa and Rādhā. So Sūrasāgara abounds in tatsama words which render the padas musical. As for example:

नवल निकुंज नवल नवला मिलि,
नवल निकेतन रुचिर बनाए। [26]

The following lines portray a lively pen picture of Krishṇa's dancing postures and gesticulations on the occasion of performing the Dance Divine (Rāsalīlā) for the pleasure of Rādhā with the help of appropriate words in Rāga Rāmkalī e.g.

नृत्यत स्याग स्यांगा-हेत
मुकुट-लटकनि भृकुटि मटकन
नारीमन सुख देत
कबहुं चलत सुगंध गति सौं कबहुं उधटत नैन। [27]

Whenever the poet happens to delineate the furious and devastating wild-fire as well as the stormy and thundering clouds[29] he succesfully employs harsher sounds.

As a poet Sūra has made use of almost all the Varṇika and Mātrika metres handed down by tradition in his compositions viz. Dohā, Chaupāi, Rolā, Hari-Priyā, Ghanāksharī, Savaiyā, Daṅḍaka, lāvaṇī, Hari-gītikā, Viṣṇupada, Chancharī etc. He is more interested in using Dohā, Rolā and Chaupāi for his compositions. At places he has not lagged behind in making certain modfications in the words to fit in the scheme of rhythm. He has introduced Dohā after the first two lines of the pada in between his songs by inserting 're' and 'Pai' to give a musical tone to the metre, as for example:

मन रे, माधव सौं करि प्रीति।

काम-क्रोध-मद-लोभ तू, छांड़ि सबै बिपरीति।।

भौंरा भोगी बन भ्रमे, (रे) मोद न भानै ताप।

सब कुसुमनि मिलि रस करै, कमल बंधावै आप।।[30]

On the whole Sūra has faithfully followed the established scheme of a particular metre adopted by him but in very rare padas he has also coined words for the purpose of terminal alliteration (तुक) alone. This in fact, has totally marred their beauty and excellence e.g.

आए जोग सिखावन पाँड़े।

परमारथी पुराननि लादे, ज्यौं बनजारे टांड़े।

हमरे गति पति कमल नयन की, जोग सिखैते रांड़े।

— — — — —

कहुं षट्पद कैसे खैयत है, हाथिनि कै संग गांड़े।

— — — — —

सूरदास तीनौ नहिं उपजत, धनिया, धाव कुम्हांड़े।[31]

There is no denying the fact that there is a close relationship between Rasa and Rāga. Each rāga originates from the combination of particular notes (swaras). The nature of a rāga whether *gambhīra* or *chapala* depends on such a combination of a cluster of notes. Rāgas such as Hindolā, Shrī, Mālakauṅs, Bhairava etc are considered male in character where as Gaurī, Ghanāshrī, Jai-Jaivantī, Āsāvarī, Rāmakalī,

Bhairavaī, Jaitashrī are treated as female in character. It is the rāga expressing various mental states through the medium of notes that attains to the state of rasa.

The pitch, intensity, frequency, lapeṭa (लपेट) Khaṭakā (खटका)and Kampana (कम्पन)of the notes create a particular atmosphere which ultimately leads to the manifestation of that particular rasa. The ancient Indian musicologists have recognised seven swaras. They mention 'सारे' as signifying the Heoric (वीर), the Furious (रौद्र) and the marvellous (अद्‌भुत), 'ध' as representing Disgutful (वीभत्स)and the Terible (भयानक),'गनि' as the Pathetic (करुणा) and lastly 'मप' as denoting comic (हास्य).

Sūra has composed his songs both sweet and sad in various rāga-rāginīs, mostly keeping in view the theme either prayer or Krishṇa's childhood pranks and his winsone beauty or his amorous love-sports (līlā). But in some of his songs he has not strictly adhered to any such hard and fast principle. He has adopted a variety of rāgas to depict the same subject. At times he has chosen the same one rāga for depicting different sentiments. Under the first category he has composed padas having the same subject-matter–humility (Vinaya) in different rāgas stated below:

राग नट

हरि सौं ठाकुर और न जन कौं।

जिहिं जिहिं विधि सेवक सुख पावै, तिहिं विधि राखत मन कौं।[32]

राग केदारौ

जाकौं हरि अंगीकार कियौ।

ताके कोटि विधन हरि हरि कै अभै प्रताप दियौ।[33]

राग सोरठ

अब कैं राखि लेहु भगवान।

हौं अनाथ बैठ्यो द्रुम-डरिया, पारधि साधे बान।[34]

राग कान्हरौ

अबिगत-गति कछु कहत न आवै

ज्यों गूंगें मीठे फल को रस अन्तरगत हीं भावै।[35]

राग कल्याण

जैसें राखहु तैसें रहौं।

जानत हो सब दुख-सुख सब जन के,

मुख करि कहा कहौं।[36]

राग मलार

तुम तजि और कौन पै जाऊं

काकै द्वार जाइ सिर नाऊं, पर हथ कहां बिकाऊँ।[37]

As for the second category he has used rāga mārū (which is traditionally used to describe heroic sentiments alone) for portraying the Erotic[38] and Pathetic[39] sentiments. He has used this rāga for describing the Heroic[40] sentiment as well.

Sūra's Vinayapadas display his deep sense of devotion grounded in love and finally his total surrender to his adorable Lord for getting salvation. He emphasized the virtue of the repetition of Rama's name and declares that he owns his devotees and provides them shelter and converts even an ordinary man into a perfectly purified man. Sūra plainly tells him that he is the greatest sinner alive and it is upto Him to salvage him. Such utterances of humility form the subject of those professional singers (कीर्तनकार) who sing songs in His praise as well as in the praise of the devotees and saints of the later generation after Sūra till today. At the instance of his preceptor Vallabhāchārya he gave up the stance of humility and servility and absorbed himself in remembering and glorifying his Lord, thus attaining the level of love based on comeradeship.

With the exception of the narrative part of the story of Lord Rāma (Ninth Skandha) the remaining narrative part along with a few Vinayapadas is composed in Vilāvala rāga. The rest of the Vinayapadas relating to the topics–love for the devotee (भक्तवत्सलता),greatness of His name (नाममहिमा),supplications (विनती), renunciation (वैराग्य) etc are composed in other rāgas with soft notes like Kedārau, RāmaKalī, Ghanāshrī, Kānharau, Vihāgarau etc.

The second segment of Sūra's padas after the Vinayapadas pertains to Krishṇa's birth, and his christening (नामकरण)and piercing of the ears (कर्णछेदन)and other childhood scenes like crawling upon the knees, throwing about the feet and turning over, grapping the big toe and sucking it, stealing curd and butter, rivalry and competion, the extra-ordinary beauty of his face and figure have been the themes of singers of later period who sang them in rāgas like Kānharau, Ghanāshrī, Rāmkalī, lalita, Āsāwarī, Bhairawa etc. Krishṇa's exploits and adventurous deeds as a child e.g. killing of the fierce and terrible monsters, subdueing the serpent (Kālī-damana), drinking of the forest-fire (Dāvānala-pāna) etc. are expressive of Sūra's skill in depicting the heroic sentiment in Gaurī,[41] Māru[42] and Kānharau[43] rāgas respectively.

The joy of Yashodā and Nanda knows no bounds on seeing the child-like pranks of their son and also his extraordinary deeds in such a tender age and embrace him again and again out of affection. Sūra thus stands unrivalled in the portrayals of parental love (वात्सल्य) in suitable rāgas. The child Krishṇa gradually grows into a handsome cowherd. He has been playing and frolicking with Rādhā and other gopīs in the alleys of Braja since his childhood. Rādhā gets attracted towards Krishṇa and Krishṇa towards her. They fall in love with each other and start exchanging visits. Thus the bond of love between both of them born in childhood becomes so strong that it is not possible to be forsaken. This love of the couple goes on deepening day by day. The venu is the scenic bank of Yamunā in Vrindābana where they indulge in all sorts of conceivable love-sports. Thus the entire life of Krishṇa, Rādhā and cow-maids is full of fun and merry-making. This aspect of their union (संयोग) is described in appropriate rāgas like Kānharau, Kalyāna, malāra, Vasanta, Āsāvarī, Bhairava, Kedārau, Vihāgarau etc.

Sūra is equally superb in portraying the aspect of separation (वियोग).All the possible psychic states during separation have also been extensively delineated in apt rāgas like Ghanāshrī Sārañga, Jaitshrī, Bhupālī, Kalyāna. Aḍānā etc. The deep feeling of frustration, anguish and despair caused in the minds of irritated Yashodā, Nanda, the cow-boys and the milk-maids bears testimony to Sūra's deft handling of the sentiments of pathos (करुण). In spite of the repeated messages despatched when Krishṇa does not return from Mathurā to Braja both the menfolk and womenfolk feel restless and impatient. Even the moralizing theme of Non-dualism (अद्वैतवाद)preached by Uddhava, a constant companion of Krishṇa, does not produce the desired effect in the minds of the emotionally charged milk-maids. "Shyāma did not send you to Gokula. You have only blundered on the way.[44] Our eyes rain day and night in the frenzy of separation from Krishṇa".[45] Saying so and such other words full of sarcasm the milk-maids play a practical joke on him and ask him to go back and listen again to what the son of Nanda had told him. They even go to the extent of asking him to get himself treated for his insanity (जाइ करौ आपनौ उपचार).[46] They outright reject the idea of accepting as formless (निरगुन कौन देस को बासी मधुकर कहि समुझाय सौंह दे.)[47] The whole dialouge between a great vedāntist Uddhava and the naive cow-girls occurring in 'Bhramaragīta' is depicted in rāgās with soft notes e.g. Kalyāni, Kedārau, Gaurī, Gujara, Adānau, malāra, Kānhahrā suited to the occasion. The life-like description of the advent of rains in the context of upholding the Govardhana hillocks is composed in rāga malār[48] which is in tune with the musical tradition. Rāgas soft in nature like Kedārau, Gaurī, Āsāvarī, Ghanashrī etc. are gainfully adopted in depicting the pathetic moments whereas Shuddha Kānharā and Darabārī are used in describing sober and serious situations. Now it comes to this that Sūra has expresed his emotions through the medium of various rāga-rāginīs which have added exceptional sweetness and charm to his lyrical poetry.

On going through the padas of Sūra one notices that he has advocated the 'Time-theory' enunciated in the ancient works of musicology while composing them. According to the mode of service (सेवाविधि) propounded in the Bhakti cult into which the poet was initiated by Vallabhāchārya, there were eight occasions from morning till evening when such service (अष्टयाम सेवा) were performed with suitable rites and rituals. This began in the early hours of morning with the ceremony of waking up of the deity (Shrīnāthji) and ended at night on going of the deity to bed.

Sūra has adopted a variety of rāga-rāginīs as per requirements or situations of a particular rāga-rāginī.

Padas pertaining to the occasion of Krishṇa's waking up, taking of bath and his dressing up and decoration and also that of his breakfast are composed in rāgas- lalita, Vibhāsa, Rāmakalī, Bhairava, Bhairavī to suit the early hours of morning. Next comes the occasion for milking the cows for which generally rāgas such as Kānharau[49], Ghanāshrī[50] and Sāraṅga[51]are adopted by Sūra. At noon even the deity is offered delicious meals befitting the status of a deity. After the close of the first part of the day rāgas soft in nature viz. Āsāvarī, Jaunpurī, Toḍī are employed. At twilight the evening prayers are composed in Gauri[52]. The first part of the night when the deity goes to sleep Sūra likens rāga Kedārau[53]. Songs sung on the occasion of seasonal festivals are composed in the rāgas in accordance with those prescribed in the treatises on Indian musicology.

Sūra has by and large employed those very rāgas which suit the timings recognized for their singing in the ancient shastras of Indian music. Besides the occasions stated earlier the padas relating to the churning of curd and butter, playing the flute, the Holi festival and the Dance Divine (Rāsa Līlā) are composed in rāgas like Āsāvarī[54] Ghanāshri, Sāraṅga,[55] Toḍi[56] and Adānā[57] respectively according to the set timings of their singing.

Sūra has composed his padas in those rhythms (लय) which suit the theme. In depicting the parental love and other joyful festivities connected with Krishṇa's childhood the poet has adopted *madhya* laya. The ***druta*** laya is used in those padas which convey the feelings of ecstasy, adventure, courage and the'vilamita laya' is employed for describing depression, pathetic and pensive moments. Take for instance the pada—

मैया मोहि दाऊ बहुत खिजायौ।

मों सों कहत मोल कौ लीन्हौ

तू जसुमति कब जायौ।।[58] (राग गौरी)

is composed in 'Madhya laya'. The words रंग होरी utilized in portraying the Holī carnival in the following pada:

निकसि कुंवर खेलन चले, रंग होरी।

मोहन नंद किसोर, लाल रंग होरी।

कंचन माट भराइ कै, रंग होरी।। इत्यादि[59] (राग सारंग)

rightly fits in the scheme of 'Druta laya.' The tempo of the lines given below :

ऊधौ इतनी जाइ कहौ।

सबै विरहणी पा लागति हैं, मथुरा कान्ह रहौ।।

भूलिहिं जनि आवहु इहिं गोकुल, तपति तरनि ज्यों चंद।

सुन्दर बदन स्याम कोमलतन, क्यौं सहिहैं नंदनंद।।[60]

इत्यादि (राग नट)

is slow (Vilambita)

In 'Sūrasāgara' the number of rāgas mentioned is six and that of rāginīs is thirty six (छहौ राग छत्तीसौ रागिनि। इक इक नीकै गावैं री)[61]. But 'Sūrasārāvalī' has stated that the number of rāga-rāginīs is thirty six only[62]. This reference to rāga-rāginīs suggests that Sūra recognized the rāga-rāginī classification but names given on the top of the padas always mention rāga even in the cases of 'Gaurī', Ghanāshrī which are feminine in gender. However a close scrutiny of the padas (songs) reveals that the actual number of rāga-rāginīs employed by the poet stands as eighty six, It appears that the poet treats 'Horī' and 'Dhamāra' as two different rāgas. They are in fact two styles of singing adopted on the occasion of spring season. Sūra has employed some obsolete rāgas as well e.g. Sūhā, Sūhī, Sānuta, Desākha, Jaṅgalā, Sugharai, Nāyakī, Kuraṅga, Devagiri, Karṅāti, Vairāti, Saṅkābharana. Some other rāgas, unknown to both the Northern and Southern styles of music are also found in his work viz. Rājṅī (राज्ञी),Haṭhīlī, Rājṅī Shrī Haṭhī, Rājṅī malāra, Rājṅi Rāmagiri, Vasanti. Mixed (मिश्र) rāgas are also used in some of the padas viz. mixture of Sūhā and Vilāvala[63], of Mulatānī and Ghanāshrī[64], of Vilāvala and Rāmakalī[65], of Vilāvala and Alahiyā[66], of Malāra and Kamoda[67] and that of Rājṅī and Rāmagirī[68]. Of the recognized six rāgas Sūra has mentioned only four rāgas– Bhairava, Malkauṅs, Shrī and Megha. It is really surprising to note that most popular rāgas such as Bhīmapalāsī, Dīpaka and Vāgashrī are untraceable in his padas. He has made certain changes in the names of some of the rāgas e.g. Kānharau (कान्हरा), Kedārau (केदार), Vihāgarau (विहागरौ), Sūhī, Sūhāu (सूहा), Bhairon (भैरव), Gunda Malāra (गौड़मल्हार), Malāra (मल्हार) to adapt to the phonological structure of Braja language. Vilāvala covers the largest number of padas is Sūra's poetry, irrespective of the content and context but this name does not occur in the extant works of musicology in that period. Next in number comes rāgas like Sāraṅga, Ghanāshri, Malāra, Gaurī, Kāṅharau, RāmaKalī, Vihāgarau, Kedārau, Soraṭha, Āsāvarī, Kalayāna, Jaitashrī, Sūhi or Sūhau, Gunda or Gauḍa malāra etc. in descending order. Some other rāgas viz. Multānī, Khamabhāvatī, Īmana, Bhairava, Adānā, Kāphī, Karnāti, Mālkauṅs, Kamoda, Saṁkīrṇa, Kuraṅga, Gunakalī, Gunasāraṅga, Rāma Giri, Rājṅī Shrī Haṭhi, Shrī-Haṭha, Alahiya, etc are used only once. Rāgas like Ahīrī, Vihāga, JaiJaivantī[69] are adopted twice each. Padas having burden (टेक) such as तो पर वारि हौं नन्दलाल [69] are also found here and there, as the padas are primarily meant for musical rendering.

The references to the names of rāga-rāginīs[70] and their visual contemplation (dhyāna)[71] and other general terms like seven swaras[72], forty nine tānas, three grāmas and twenty one mūrchhanas[73] are noticeable in Sūra's padas. Besides the two tālas viz tital (त्रिताल)[74] and jhapatāra (झपताल),[75] other terms pertaining to tāla like Atītā-anāgata[76] and anāghātā[77] are also found in Sūra's padas.

In Pushti-cult music is regarded as part and parcel of devotion of eight routine occasions of services offered for Shrīnātha ji and also on other annual seasonal festivals songs are sung in praise of the deity to the accompaniment of different musical instruments. Thus it is natural that Sūra has made use of stringed, wind or percussion type of instruments in his compositions e.g. Mridaṅga, Jhānjhara, Veenā Venu, Bānsurī (Muralī), Muraja, Rabāba, Tala, Pakhāwaja, Ghūnghuru, Dundubhī, Dimadima, Kinnarī, Jhālarī, Saṅkha Dapha, Manjīra, Chaṅga, Upaṅga, Vishāṇa[78], Nishāna[79], Pataha, Shahanāi, Bherī, Jantra, Dhola, Ghaṅtā etc.

That Sūra was well-versed in the dance form of music too is amply evident from the gestures of the hands, eyes, eye-brows and footwork of Krishṇa, Rādhā and the gopīs during the performance of Rāsa Līlā as portrayed in the pada given below:

राग गुंड़मलार

धरनि पग पटकि, कर झटकि भौंहनि मटकि,

अटकि मन तहां रीझे कन्हाई ।

तब चलत हरि मटकि, रहीं जुवति अटकि, लटकि

लटकनि छटकि छवि विचारे ।[80]

The bolas of the mridaṅga like त तता दिक दिमन द्रिम द्रिम मृदंग[81] and those of the dance such as होड़ा-होड़ी नृत्य करैं—ता ता थई थई[82] indicate that Sūra had a good knowledge of instrumental music and dance.

Like the ancient musicologists Sūra also holds the view that the word music includes song (गीत), instrument (वाद्य) and dance (नृत्य) as is borne out by the following pada:

राग पूरबी

नंद नंदन सुधराई बांसुरी बजाई ।

सर गमा पधनी सा में, सप्त सुरनिगाई ।।

अतीत अनागत संगीत, बिच तान मिलाई ।

सुर तालऽरूनृत्य ध्याइ, पुनि मृदंग बजाई ।।[83]

In sum, Sūra was an accomplished poet-musician and was fully conversant with both classical and popular (folk) styles of singing of his times.

References

Sūrasāgara Skandha Number of Pada

1. Ibid. 1 148

2. Ibid 10 753

3. Ibid 10 4371

4. Ibid 10 4369,4370

5. Ibid 1 6

6. Ibid 1 8

7. Ibid 10 4751,4897

8. Ibid 10 717

9. Ibid 1 53

10. Ibid 1 220

11. Ibid 10 2432

12. Ibid 9 488

13. Ibid 10 4317

14. Ibid 10 2726

15. Ibid 1 311

16. Ibid 10 3869

17. Ibid 10 2571

18. Ibid 10 2564

19. Ibid 10 771

20. Ibid 10 724

21. Ibid 10 3856

22. Ibid 10 1473

23. Ibid 10 1813

24. Ibid 10 1976
25. Ibid 10 3486
26. Ibid 10 2606
27. Ibid 10 1766
28. Ibid 10 1214
29. Ibid 10 1471,1473
30. Ibid 1 325
31. Ibid 10 4224
32. Ibid 1 9
33. Ibid 1 38
34. Ibid 1 97
35. Ibid 1 2
36. Ibid 1 161
37. Ibid 1 164
38. Ibid 10 2370
39. Ibid 10 3963
40 Ibid 10 1170
41. Ibid 10 1175
42. Ibid 10 1208
43. Ibid 10 1210,1213
44. Ibid 10 4141
45. Ibid 10 3856
46. Ibid 10 4231
47. Ibid 10 4251
48. Ibid 10 1471-1477
49. Ibid 10 1019
50. Ibid 10 1018,1284
51. Ibid 10 1285

52. Ibid 10 1125
53. Ibid 10 815
54. Ibid 10 96, 1714
55. Ibid 10 1835
56. Ibid 10 1836
57. Ibid 10 1768
58. Ibid 10 833
59. Ibid 10 3486
60. Ibid 10 4661
61. Ibid 10 1856
62. Sūrasārāvalī, 1012-1018
63. Sūrasāgara, 1 69
64. Ibid 1 219
65. Ibid 10 1832
66. Ibid 10 2239
67. Ibid 10 1767
68. Ibid 10 3455
69. Ibid 10 1799
70. Ibid 10 2761-62
71. Ibid 10 1798
72. Ibid 10 1762,2759
73. Ibid 10 1971
74. Ibid 10 32,87,219-221
75. Ibid 10 1798
76. Ibid 10 1769
77. Ibid 10 1834
78. Ibid 10 2113
79. Ibid 10 1663

80. Ibid 10 1659

81. Sūra Sahitya Sādhanā (Bhagavat Swaroop Mishra) page 124

82. Sūrasāgara 10 1767

83. Ibid 10 1769

6

CONCLUSIONS

We have endeavoured in our own humble way to answer the following questions in the preceding pages:

-What are the sources to study the life and work of Sūradāsa?

-Where was he born and on what date?

-What was his actual name and what family did he belong to?

-What was his caste?

-How did he spend his childhood?

-Why did he leave his home and renounce the world?

-Why did he join the order of Vallabhāchārya and elected to be a Kīrtanakāra?

-Did he really meet with Akbar as is generally believed?

-How many works did he compose?

-How great was he as a poet?

-How proficient was he as a musician?

-And finally, what place does he enjoy in history?

Our purpose in seeking to answer these questions was to portray a real Sūradāsa—a Sūradāsa in colours true to history. How far we have succeeded in this endeavour, it is for the readers to judge.

Sūra was bron in a poor family. He was blind. He did not get parental affection or care. Even the family root was snatched from him in early childhood. He was an 'orphan' by all standards.

A man confronted with such problems reacts normally in three ways: (I) he completely breaks under their pressure, (II) he breaks, recovers, again breaks and again recovers—and these processes go in all through his life; and (III) he overcomes his problems. Sūra belonged to the third category. With his infinite power of creativity he did away with his 'deprivation' and created what he did not get in life. He became a full man by dint of his ability to create.

II

Sūra selected to be a singer (*Kīrtanakāra*) in the court of Lord Krishṇa. He fully utilized his knowledge of classical as well as folk-music of his times in singing songs in praise of his Lord in as many as six *rāgas* and thirty-six *rāginīs* as mentioned in the ancient works of Indian Musicology. The mention of musical terms within the padas of Sūrasāgara and employment of bolas pertaining to dance on the occasion of Krishṇa's Rāsa Līlā with the gopīs are sufficient enough to prove that Sūra had a profound knowledge of all the three aspects of music viz. Gīta, Vādya and Nritya. It is his really a substantial contribution to the enrichiment of Indian Music. He composed fine poetry and sang it with deep and ardent devotion. There was nothing else he was interested in or worked for. Day and night he sang his beautiful and scintillating *padas* to his Master, to please Him and to please himself. Sūra's poetry is, however, not a dialogue between him and his God but it concerns us also a great deal.

To sum up, Sūra is a perfect symbol of medieval cultural Renaissance. He brought about a unique synthesis of the two cultures viz the classical culture of the Bhāgavata and the folk culture of Braja region. From the very beginning of his life till his last moment Sūra had been an ardent devotee but when his devotion reached its climax and bore fruit he became a poet of excellence, philosopher who did not prefer to strictly adhere to any sectarian principles and dogmas and above all an elevated and noble soul–all rolled into one.

Appendix

SOME IMPORTANT *PADAS* OF SŪRADĀSA WITH ENGLISH VERSION

1

Charaṇa-kamala bandauṅ Harirāi.

Jāki kripā paṅgu giri laṅghai aṅdhe kauṅ saba kachhu darasāi.

Bahirau sunai, gūṅga puni bolai, raṅka chalai sira chhatra dharāi.

Sūradāsa swāmī karunāmaya, bārabāra tihiṅ pāi.

चरन-कमल बन्दौं हरि राइ।

जाकी कृपा गिरि लंघै, अंधे कौं सब कछु दरसाइ।।

भहिरौ सुनै, गूंग पुनि बोलै, रंक चलै सिर छत्र धराइ।

सूरदास स्वामी करुनामय, बारबार बन्दौ तिहिं पाइ।।

(स्कंध 1, पद संख्या 8)

I bow to the lotus-feet of Hari, the Lord,
By His grace the lame can climb up a mountain.
The blind can have a full view of things.

The dumb can speak, the deaf can hear,

The pauper marches under a royal canopy,

O merciful Lord, I offer my salutations to your feet time and again, says Sūradāsa.

2

Hari, hauṅ saba patitani ko nāyaka

Ko kari sakai barābari merī aura nahīṅ kau lāyaka

Jo prabhu ajāmīla kauṅ dīnhau so pātau likhi pāūṅ.

Tau bisvāsa hoi mana meraiṅ aurau patita bulāūṅ.

Yaha suna jahāṅ jahān taiṅ simiṭaiṅ, āi hoi ika ṭhaura.

Aba kai tau itane lai āyau, bera bahura kī aura.

Hoḍā-Hoḍī manahiṅ bhāvate kiye kiye pāpa bhari peṭa.

Te saba patita pāya-tara ḍārau, yahai hamārī bheṅṭa.

Bahuta bharosau jāni tumhārau, agha kīnhe bhari bhāṅdau

Lījai begi niberi turatahiṅ Sūra patita kauṅ ṭāṅḍau.

हरि, हौं सब पतितनि को नायक ।

को करि राकै बराबरि गेरी, और नहीं कोउ लायक ।

जो प्रभु अजामील कौं दीन्हौ सो पाटौ लिखि पाऊं ।

तौ बिस्वास होइ मन मेरैं, औरौ पतित बुलाऊं ।

यह सुन जहां जहां तैं सिमिटैं, आइ होइ इक ठौर ।

अब कै तौ इतने लै आयौ, बेर बहुर की और ।

होड़ा-होड़ी मनहिं भावते किए, किए पाप भरि पेट ।

ते सब पतित पाय-तर डारौ, यहै हमारी भेंट ।

बहुत भरोसौ जानि तुम्हारौ, अध कीन्हे भरि भांड़ौ ।

लीजै बेगि निबेरि तुरतहिं सूर पतित कौ टाडौ ।।

(स्कंध 1,पद संख्या 146)

O Lord, I am the chief of sinners;

There is none to match me in this.

Who else is there so deserving?

If You can give me a gaurantee.

That You can save me as You saved Ajāmila,

My trust in You will increase,

And I shall call other sinners like myself

(To be sanctified by you.)

Having heard of your glory people from all over would have gathered together.

And this time I have brought these only to you and next time I would bring others too

Who have committed excessive sins in competition ahead of others.

O Lord, I shall make them

fall at your feet.

And this is my offering to You.

I have committed innumerable acts having full faith in You

Save me immediately this time, O master

For I am the chief of sinners.

Says Sūradāsa.

3

Aba maiṅ nāchyo bahuta gupāla.

Kāma-krodha kau pahiri cholanā, kaṅṭha viṣaya kī māla.

Mahāmoha ke nupura bājata, niṅdā-sabda-rasāla.

Bhrama bhayau mana bhayau pakhāvaja, chalata asaṅgata chāla.

Tṛṣnā nāda karati ghaṭa bhītara, nānā vidhi dai tāla.

Māyā ko kati phaiṅṭā bāṅdhyau, lobha-tilaka diyau bhāla.

Kotika kalā kācchi dikharāī jala-thala sudhi nahiṅ kāla.

Sūradāsa kī sabai avidyā dūri karau naṅdalāla.

अब नैं नाच्यो बहुत गुपाल।

काम-क्रोध कौ पहिरि चोलना, कंठ विषय की माल।

महामोह के नुपुर बाजत, निन्दा-सब्द-रसाल।

भ्रम भयौ मन भयौ पखावज, चलत असंगत चाल।

तृष्ना नाद करति घट भीतर, नाना विधि दै ताल।

माया को कटि फैंटा बांध्यौ, लोभ-तिलक दियौ भाल।

कोटिक कला काछि दिखराई जल-थल सुधि नहिं काल।

सुरदास की सबै अविद्या दूरि करौ नंदलाल।

(स्कंध 1, प. सं.153)

O Gopāla, I have danced a great deal.

I have put on the cloak of desire and wrath

And the garland of sense objects is waving at my neck.

My anklets of infatuation are jingling,

And are ringing with the harsh tones of censure and abuse,

My erring mind is the sounding pakhāvaja (timbrel-musical instrument)

And treading the evil path.

The drums of desire reverberate through my whole body

To many and various a beat.

I have bound the cloth of Māyā (illusion) round my waist

And applied to my forehead the tilaka of avarice,

Absorbed in my own artistic performance,

I have lost all sense of reality

And of the swift march of time

O son of Nanda,

Dissipate the nescience (ignorance) of Sūradāsa.

4

Kauna sunai yaha bāta hamārī?

Samaratha aura na dekhauṅ tuma bīna kāsauṅ vithā kahauṅ banavārī?

Tuma avigata, anātha ke swāmi, dīna-dayāla, nikuṅja-bihārī.

Sadā sahāi kari dāsani kī, jo ura dharī soi pratipārī.

Aba kihiṅ sarana jāūṅ jādaupati, rākhi leū bali, trāsa, nivārī

Sūradāsa charanani kī bali-bali kauna khatā taiṅ kripā bisārī.

कौन सुनै यह बात हमारी ?
समरथ और न देखौं तुम बिन कासौं बिथा कहौं बनवारी ?
तुम अविगत, अनाथ के स्वामी, दीन-दयाल, निकुंज-बिहारी।
सदा सहाइ करी दासनि की, जो उर धरी सोइ प्रतिपारी।।
अब किहिं सरण जाऊं जादौपति, राखि लेऊ बलि, त्रास, निवारी।
'सूरदास' चरननि की बलिबलि कौन खता तैं कृपा बिसारी।।
(स्कंध 1, प.सं. 160)

Who is there to hear the sad note of my plaint?

I can see none other than You as omnipotent and kind, O Banawārī!

You are indescribable or invisible (beyond comprehension), the Lord of the helpless, kindly to the depressed, dweller in the bowers of Braja!.

Enough witnesses testify that ever You have helped

The suppliants and fulfilled their cherished desires.

If You are going to reject a suppliant like me, who has surrendered totally at Your feet, tell me to whom should I turn to, O yadupati (Krishṇa).

Says Sūradāsa "I am fully devoted to You. For what fault of mine have you forsaken me?"

5

Jo hama bhale bure tau tere

Tumhaiṅ hamārī lāja-baḍāī, binatī suno prabhu mere.

Saba taji tuma sarṅāgati āyau, driḍha kara charana gahe re

Tuma pratāpa-bala-badata na kāhūṅ niḍara bhaye ghara-chere

Aura deva saba raṅka-bhikhārī tyāge bahuta anere

Sūradāsa prabhu tumharī kripā taiṅ, pāye sukha ju ghanere

जो हम भले बुरे तौ तेरे !

तुम्हैं हमारी लाज-बड़ाई, बिनती सुनो प्रभु मेरे ।।

सब तजि तुम शरणागति आयौ, दृढ़ कर चरन गहे रे ।

तुम प्रताप-बल बदत न काहूं, निडर भये घर-चेरे ।।

और देव सब रंक-भिखारी त्यागे बहुत अनेरे ।

'सूरदास' प्रभु तुम्हरी कृपा तैं, पाये सुख जु धनेरे ।।

(स्कंध 1, प.सं. 170)

Good or Bad, whatever I am I belong to You.

I beg of You, Lord! it is in Your hands to save me from dishonour and calumny.

Renouncing all I have approached You and clasped your Lotus-Feet close to my heart.

Fearless have I become enboldened, girded as I am in the thought of your strength.

This truth is also revealed to me that all other devās (gods) are beggars at Your door and I have abandoned them.

Says Sūradāsa, O Lord, I have much comfort with your Grace.

6

Jaisaiṅ rākhavahu taisaiṅ rahauṅ

Jānata ho dukha-sukha saba jana ke, mukha kari kahā kahauṅ?

Kabahuṅka bhojana lahauṁ kripānidhi, kabhuṅka bhūkha sahauṅ.

Kabahuṅka chaḍhauṅ turaṅga, mahā gaja, kabahuṅka bhāra bahauṅ.

Kamalanayana ghana-syāma-manohara, anuchara bhayau rahauṅ.

Sūradāsa prabhu bhakta kripānidhi, tumhare charana gahauṅ

जैसै राखवहु तैसै रहौं ।

जानत हो दुख-सुख सब जन के, मुख करि कहा कहौं ?

कबहुंक भोजन लहौं कृपानिधि, कबहुकं भूख सहौं ।
कबहुंक चढ़ौं तुरंग, महा गज, कबहुंक भार बहौं ।।
कमलनयन घन-स्याम-मनोहर, अनुचर भयौ रहौं ।
'सूरदास' प्रभु भक्त कृपानिधि, तुम्हरे चरन गहौं ।।

(स्कंध 1, प.सं.161)

I shall pass my days with You, living as You wish me to live. You know every pain and pleasure of all, so why should I repeat them?

What does it matter, O compassionate One! whether I get plenty of food to eat or none at all?

What if, one day I ride on an elephant or on a horse, on another day carry another's load?

I ever live as a slave to You, O Dark complexioned Lotus-Eyed Darling! You are a boon, a blessing to the devotees. I offer myself at Your Feet, Says Sūradāsa.

7

Binatī karata marata hauṅ lāja
Nakha-sikha lauṅ merī yaha dehī hai pāpa kī jahāja
Aura patita āvata na āṅkhi-tara dekhata apanau sāja
Tīnauṅ pana bhari ora nibāhyau taū na āyau bāja
Pācche bhayau na āgai hvai hai, saba patitani siratāja
Narakau bhajayau nāma suni mero pīṭhi daī jamarāja
Aba lauṅ nānheṅ-nanheṅ tāre, saba brithā akāja
Sāṅche birada sūra ke tārata, lokan-loka avāja

बिनती करत मरत हौं लाज।
नख-सिख लौं मेरी यह देही है पाप की जहाज।।
और पतित आवत न आंखि-तर देखत अपनौ साज।
तीनौं पन भरि ओर निबाह्यौ तऊ न आयौ बाज।।
पाछे भयौ न आगै ह्वै है, सब पति तनि सिरताज।
नरकौ भज्यौ नाम सुनि मेरो, पीठि दई जमराज।।
अब लौं नन्हें-नन्हें तारे, सब बृथा अकाज।
सांचे बिरद 'सूर' के तारत, लोकन-लोक अवाज।।

(स्कंध 1, प.सं.96)

I die of shame and dare not appear and pray for your forgiveness.

From head to foot I am steeped in sins

So mean and repellent am I that You will seek in vain to find my compeer.

The three stages of life, childhood, manhood and old age

I passed in sin. Even then I never desisted from indulging in.

My acts are so degraded that none before me has

committed them, nor shall any one do so in the future.

Even hell has fled and Yamarāja (God of Death) has also turned his face (is averse) to give shelter to me, on hearing my name so fallen.

Lord ! really you have no cause to feel pride in your name. For you have so far reclaimed only the small sinners. People will see justification in Your name only if

One fallen like him is redeemed by you.

8

Tuma prabhu mosauṅ bahuta karī

Nara-dehī dīnī sumirana kauṅ, mo pāpī taiṅ kacchu na sarī

Garbha-bāsa ati trāsa, adhomukha, tahāṅ na merī sudhi bisarī

Pāvaka-jaṭhara jarana nahiṅ dīnhauṅ, kaṅchana sī mama deha karī

Jaga maiṅ janami pāpa bahu kīnhe, ādi aṅta lauṅ saba bigarī

Sūra patita, tuma patita udhārana, apane birada kī lāja dharī

तुम प्रभु मोसौं बहुत करी।
नर-देही दीनी सुमिरन कौं, मो पापी तैं कछु न सरी।।
गर्भ-बास अति त्रास, अधोमुख, तहां न मेरी सुधि बिसरी।
पावक-जठर जरन नहिं दीन्हौं, कंचन सी मम देह करी।।
जग मैं जनमि पाप बहु कीन्हे, आदि अन्त लौं सब बिगरी।
'सूर' पतित, तुम पतित उधारन, अपने बिरद की लाजधरी।।

(स्कंध 1, प.सं. 116)

Lord! very great service have you rendered me

A human birth you conferred to pass in contemplation

But alas! as a sinner I wasted it.

You did not overlook me when upturned I hung

in the mother's womb, terrified (As veritably in a Hell).

You protected me from the burning fire in the stomach

And helped my body to keep its gloss like gold.

Many a sin have I committed since my brith and am indeed ruined.

You are the redeemer of the fallen, save me, prays Sūradāsa

9

Hari bina kauna sauṅ kahiye

Mansija bithā arani lauṅ jārati ura antara dahiyai

Kānana bhavana raini aru bāsara, kahūṅ na sachu lahiyai

Mūka ju bhaye jagya ke pasu lauṅ, kahaṅ lauṅ dukha sahiyai

Kabahuṅka upajai jiya maiṅ aisī, jāi jamuna bahiyai

Sūradāsa prabhu kamalanaina binu, kaise braja rahiyai

हरि बिन कौन सौं कहिए।

मनसिज बिथा अरनि लौं, जारति उर अंतर दहियै।।

कानन भवन रैनि अरु बासर, कहूं न सचु लहियै।

मूक जु भये जज्ञ के पसु लौं, कहं लौं दुख सहियै।।

कबहुंक उपजै जिय मैं ऐसी, जाइ जमुन बहियै।

'सूरदास' प्रभु कलमनैन बिनु, कैसे ब्रज रहियै।।

(स्कंध 10, प.सं. 3392/4010)

To whom except-Hari are we to repeat our tale of woe?

My mental agony consumes me, the heart within burns like the oven.

I know no rest at home or in the woods (wilderness) for all night and all day I am afire.

For how long would have I to bear my despondency like a dumb animal meant for sacrifice in the yajña?

Some times, it strikes to my mind to seek peace by drowning in the river Yamunā.

How can one pass the time in Baraja without the Lotus-Eyed

Syāma by one's side? asks Sūradāsa.

10

Karī gopāla kī saba hoi

Jo apano puruṣārtha mānata, ati jhūṭhau hai soi

Sādhana, mantra, jantrā, udyama, bala, ye saba ḍārau dhoi

Jo kacchu likhi rākhī nandanandana, meti sake nahin koi

Dukha-sukha lābha-alābha, samujha tuma, katahin marata hau roi

Sūradāsa swāmī karunāmaya, syāma charana mana poi

करी गोपाल की सब होइ।

जो अपनो पुरुषारथ मानत, अति झूठौ है सोइ।।

साधन, मंत्र, जंत्र उद्यम, बल, ये सब डारौ धोइ।

जो कछु लिखि राखी नन्दनंदन, मेटि सके नहिं कोइ।।

दुख-सुख लाभ-अलाभ, समुझ तुम, कतहिं मरत हौ रोइ।

'सूरदास' स्वामी करुनामय, स्याम चरन मन पोइ।।

(स्कंध 1, प.सं.262)

Whatever is destined by the Lord Gopāla will come to pass, whatever may happen.

If one seeks by personal effort to change the course of

destiny he is sadly mistaken (a great liar).

Therefore wash away all faith in effort, mantras talismans and the like.

Whatever Lord Nandanandana has inscribed in your lot,

There is none who can erase it.

Then why waste time pondering over gain or loss good and evil consequences of the deeds that may fall to your lot?

Believe me, says Sūradāsa, God is kindness incarnate.

Therefore let your mind dwell on His Lotus-Feet.

11

Dekhi sakhī mohana mana chorata

Nain-kaṭāccha-vilokani madhurī, subhaga bhrakuṭi bibi morata

Chandana khauri laḷāṭa syāma kaiṅ, nirakhata ati sukhadāī

Mānahu ardha-chaṅdra taṭa ahinī sudhā churāvana āī

Malayaja bhāla bhrakuṭi rekhā kī kabi upamā ika pāī

Mānau eka saṅga gaṅga jamuna nabha, tiracchī dhāra bahāi

Bhrakuti chāru nirakhi braja sundari yaha mana karati bichāra

Sūradāsa prabhu sobhā-sāgara kou na pāvata pāra

देखि सखी मोहन मन चोरत।

नैन-कटाच्छ-विलोकनि मधुरी, सुभग भ्रकुटि बिबि मोरत।।

चन्दन खौरि ललाट स्याम कैं, निरखत अति सुखदाई।

मानहु अर्धचन्द्र तट अहिनी सुधा चुरावन आई।।

मलयज भाल भ्रकुटि-रेखा की कबि उपमा इक पाई।

मानौ एक संग गंग जमुन नभ, तिरछी धार बहाई।।

भ्रुकुटि चारु निरखि ब्रज सुन्दरि, यह मन करति बिचार।

'सूरदास' प्रभु सोभा-सागर कोउ न पावत पार।।

(स्कंध 10, प.सं.1815/2433)

Watch my friend! Mohana makes my heart a prisoner by spreading His beauty's net!

Watch His captivating glances and observe how He twists His curved eye-brows.

The sandal paste on His forehead shoots cooling rays. (is pleasant to look at)

If simile can be offered it is as if His locks are like serpents

come to drink the nectar on His crescent-like forehead.

His twin eye-brows may be compared to the two rivers—Ganges and Jamunā flowing slantwise on the face.

When such charm is witnessed by the gopīs, they feel themselves drowned deep in the blue ocean of---Shyama's beauty and are unable to cross over it.

12

Syāma! sakhī nīkaiṅ dekhe nāhīṅ

Chitavata hī lochana bhari āye, bāra-bāra pacchitāhīṅ

Kaisaihuṅ kari ika ṭaka maiṅ rākhati, naikahuṅ akulāhiṅ

Nimisa manau chhabi para rakhavāre tāte atihi darāhiṅ

Kahā karaiṅ ina kau kaha dūṣana, ina apanī sī kīnhīn

Sūra syāma chhabi para mana aṭakyo, ina saba sobhā līnhīṅ

स्याम ! सखी नीकें देखे नाहिं ।
चितवत ही लोचन भरि आये, बार-बार पछिताहिं । ।
कैसैहुं करि इक टक मैं राखति, नैकहुं मैं अकुलाहिं ।
निमिष मनौ छबि पर रखवारे, ताते अतिहि डराहिं । ।
कहा करैं इन कौ कह दूषन, इन अपनी सी कीन्हीं ।
'सूरस्याम' छबि पर मन अटक्यो, उन सब सोभा लीन्हीं । ।

(स्कंध 10, प.सं.1841/2459)

Laments Rādhā, 'Sakhīs! I could not enjoy to the full the beauty of Shyāma.

I am now repenting again and again

At the mere sight of Him my eyes were filled with tears of happiness

I was very disturbed at their obstructing my vision but however much I tried to hold them back, they continued to flow.

Perhaps they feared the reprimand of the eye-lids that served as sentinels.

Say the Gopīs to Rādhā "Why murmur at (blame) their behaviour? They have done whatever they could do.

The fault is of
Shyāma who exhibits such charming loveliness
that our hearts are stuck up there.

13

Dekhau māī suṅdaratā kau sāgara

Buddhi-viveka-bala pāra na pāvata magana hota mana-nāgara.

Tanu ati syāma agāḍha ambunidhi, kaṭi paṭa pīṭa taraṅga

Chitavata chalta adhika ruchi upajati, bhaṅvara parati saba aṅga.

Naina-mīni, makarākrita, kuṅḍala, bhujabala subhaga bhujaṅga

Mukutamāla milīṅ mānau surasari dvai lie saṅga

Moramukuṭa maṇi naga ābhuṣana, kaṭi kiṅkina nakha chaṅda

Manau adola bāridha maiṅ bimbita rākā udaganabriṅda

Badana chandra maṅdala kī shobhā avalokana sukhadeta

Janu jalanidhi madhi prakaṭa kiyau sasi, shrī aru sudhā sameta

Dekhi sarūpa sakala gopījana, rahīṅ bichāri bichāri

Tadapi sūra tari sakīṅ na sobhā, rahīṅ prema pachi hāri

देखो माई सुन्दरता कौ सागर।

बुद्धि-विवेक-बल पार न पावत, मगन होत मन-नागर।।

तनु अति स्याम अगाध अम्बुनिधि, कटि पट पीत तरंग।

चितवत चलत अधिक रुचि उपजति, भंवर परति सब अंग।।
नैन-मीन, मक्राकृत कुंडल, भुजबल सुभंग भुजंग।
मुकुतमाल मिलीं मानौ सुरसरि द्वै लिए संग।।
मोरमुकुट मणि नग आभूषण, कटि किंकिन नखचंद।
मनौ अडोल बारिध मैं बिंबित राका उडगन बृंद।।
बदन चंद्र मण्डल की शोभा अवलोकन सुख देत।
जनु जलनिधि मधि प्रकट कियौ ससि, श्री अरु सुधा समेत।।
देखि सरूप सकल गोपीजन, रहीं बिचारि-बिचारि।
तदपि 'सूर' तरि सकीं न सोभा, रहीं प्रेम पचि हारि।।
(स्कंध 10, प.सं.628/1246)

Sakhi! observe Syāma—a veritable sea of beauty which

With all His intelligence and knowledge even the intelligent person cannot cross it and is drowned in the sea of beauty.

Like the blue deep sea is His dark complexion in which His pitāmbara on the waist flits like the waves.

Like the whirlpool is His gait as he walks majestically

His eyes are like two fish, the ear-rings like the

crocodiles and like the snakes are His supple graceful arms

On his chest the pearly-necklaces like twin Ganges appear.

His shining nails, His glorious crown and ornaments like

the moon and stars cast reflections in the deep waters.

Is this beautiful Form, then, made by the creator by kneading the Divine Sea of Nectar?

The Gopīs seeing such Form, seek to ponder over it and enjoy it.

But they are lost to themselves as they gaze at it and cannot cross that sea of beauty.

14

Prīti kara kāhū sukha na lahyau

Prīti pataṅga karī dīpaka sauṅ āpe prāṇa dahyau

Alisuta prīti karī jalasuta sauṅ sampatti hātha gahyau

Sāraṅga prīti karī ju nāda sauṅ sanmukha bāna sahyau

Hama jau prīti karī mādhau sauṅ chalata na kacchu kahyau

Sūradāsa prabhu binu dukha dūnau, nainani nīra bahyau

प्रीति कर काहू सुख न लह्यौ।

प्रीति पतंग करी दीपक सौं, आपे प्राण दह्यौ।।

अलिसुत प्रीति करी जलसुत सौ, सम्पत्ति हाथ गह्यौ।

सारंग प्रीति करी जु नाद सौं, सन्मुख बान सह्यौ।

हम जौ प्रीति करि माधौ सौ, चलत न कछू कह्यौ।

'सूरदास' प्रभु बिनु दुख दूनौ, नैननि नीर बह्यौ।।

(स्कंध 10, प.सं. 2390/3908)

None, who fell into the snare of love has enjoyed life.

The moth made love to the lamp, death came as the reward.

The bhramara made love to the lotus, it lost the wealth of life.

The deer made love to the sweetness of the hunter's musical note, it fell into the snare that cost it its life.

As for us gopīs who made love to Mādhava, we now find ourselves forsaken and helpless

So as for me, says Sūradāsa, I surrendered to Him and in the end tears fell to my lot and my grief doubled all the more.

15

Hari darasana kau tarasatin aṅkhiyāṅ

Jhānkati jhānpati jharokhā baiṭhī, kara mīṅḍita jyauṅ makhiyāṅ

Bicchuri badana sudhānidhi risate lāgata nahiṅ palakhiyāṅ

Ika ṭaka chitavati uḍa na sakata janu, thakita bhaī lakha sakhiyāṅ

Bāra bāra sira dhunati bisūrati, grāha janu bhakhiyāṅ

Sūra surūpa mile taiṅ jīvahiṅ, kāḍhi kināre nakhiyāṅ

हरि दरसन कौ तरसतिं अंखियां ।
झांकति झांपति झरोखा बैठी, कर मींडित ज्यौं मखियां ।।
बिछुरी बदन सुधानिधि रिसते लागत नहिं पलखियां ।
इक टक चितवति उड़ न सकत जनु, थकित भई लख सखियां ।।
बार बार सिर धुनति बिसूरति, बिरह ग्राह जनु भखियां ।
'सूर' सुरूप मिले तैं जीवहिं काढ़ि किनारे नखियां ।।

(स्कंध 10, प.सं.3242/3860)

Our eyes yearn to enjoy the glimpse of (the beautiful form of) Hari, say the gopīs.

Our eye-lids flutter as the wings of a fly that is held snared by the hand.

Having been cut off from the Moon-faced Hari we are unable to have a wink of sleep due to anger.

Tired after long searching we sakhis, are unable to flee.

Victims of the pangs of separation like a trapped crocodile we strike our heads repeatedly.

"Only if the Lord returns", says Sūradāsa "shall we be relieved and regain life. Then shall we feel as the fish thrown back into the sea."

16

Aba yā tanahiṅ rākhi kaha kījai

Suni rī sakhi syāmasundara binu, bānṭi biṣama biṣa pījai

Kai giriyai giri chaḍhi suni sajanī sīsa saṅkarahi dījai

Kai dahiyai dāruna dāvānal jāi jamuna dhasi lījai

Dusaha viyaga, viraha mādhau ke, ko dina hī dina chhījai

Sūrasyāma prītama binu rādhe, sochi sochi jiya jījai

अब या तनहिं राखि कह कीजै।
सुनि री सखी स्यामसुन्दर बिनु, बांटि बिषम बिष पीजै।।
कै गिरियै गिरि चढ़ि सुनि सजनी, सीस संकरहि दीजै।
कै दहियै दारुन दावानल, जाइ जमुन धसि लीजै।।
दुसह वियोग, विरह माधौ के को दिन ही दिन छीजै।

'सूरस्याम' प्रीतम बिनु राधे, सोचि सोचि जिय जीजै ।।

(स्कंध 10, प.सं.3364/3982)

"To what purpose do you retain, listen O sakhi, this body without Shyāma?"

It behoves us rather to drink poison and end our life.

Either let us climb to the mountain top and falling therefrom bid adieu to this existence.

Or let us burn ourselves to ashes or die drowning ourselves in the waters of Yamunā.

Very difficult it is to pass these moments of agony without Mādhava!

Thus saying, Rādhā pines away for Shyāma! says Sūradāsa

17

Aṅkhiyāṅ hari darasana kī pyāsī

Daikhyau chāhatiṅ kamala naina kauṅ, nisi dina rahatiṅ udāsī

Āye ūdhau phiri gae aṅganā, dāri gae gara phāṅsī

Kesari ko tilaka motini kī mālā, briṅdābana ke bāsī

Kāhū ke mana kī kau na jānata, logani ke mana hāṅsī

Sūradāsa prabhu tumhare darasa kauṅ, jāi karavata laiṅhauṅ kāsī

अंखियां हरि दरसन की प्यासी ।

दैख्यौ चाहतिं कमलनैन कौं, निसि दिन रहतिं उदासी ।।

आए ऊधौ फिरि गए अंगना, डारि गए गर फांसी ।

केसरि को तिलक मोतिनि की माला, बृन्दावन के बासी ।।

काहू के मन की कोऊ न जानत, लोगिन के मन हांसी ।
सूरदास प्रभु तुम्हरे दरस कौं जाइ करवत लैंहौं कासी ।।
(स्कंध 10, प.सं.3560/4178)

These eyes yearn for a vision of Shyāma!

They suffer and are sad, waiting the whole day for the Lotus-Eyed Syāma,

When Uddhava came with a message from Him, old memories were aroused and only served to awaken our pain.

It reminded us of those happy days when our beloved dwelt amongst us in Vrindābana, having a saffron tilaka on his forehead and a pearl-studded neeklace around his neck.

Says Sūradāsa, it is difficult to understand the feelings of the separated one. People simply mock at it.

The lover longs to go to Kāsi and end his life by having his head cut off on the scaffold.

18

Ūḍhau nā hama birahini nā tuma dāsa

kahata sunata ghaṭa prāṇa rahata haiṅ, hari taji bhajahu akāsa

Birahī mīna marai jala bicchuraiṅ, cchāṅḍi jiyana kī āsa

Dāsa bhāva nahiṅ tajata papīhā, barasahi rahata piyāsa

Paṅkaja parama kamala maiṅ biharata, vidhi kiyau nīra nīrāsa

Rājiva rabi ko doṣa na mānata sāsi sauṅ sahaja udāsa

Pragata prīti dasaratha pratipālī, prītama ko banavāsa

Sūrasyāma so driḍha vrata rākhyo, cchāṅdi jagata upahāsa

ऊधौ ना हम बिरहिनि ना तुम दास।
कहत सुनत घट प्राण रहत है, हरि तजि भजहु अकास।।
बिरही मीन भरै जल बिछुरैं, छांडि जियन की आस।
दास भाव नहिं तजत पपीहा, बरसहि रहत पियास।।
पंकज परम कमल मैं विहरत, विधि कियौ नीर निरास।
राजिव रबि को दोष न मानत, ससि सौं सहज उदास।।
प्रगट प्रीति दसरथ प्रतिपाली, प्रीतम को बनवास।
'सूरस्याम' सो दृढ़ व्रत राख्यो, छांडि जगत उपहास।।

(स्कंध 10, प.सं.3815/4433)

Uddhava! Neither we gopīs are really languishing in separation for our beloved nor you are His faithful servant.

Do you not consider the meaninglessness of the yoga message,

to give up Hari the Lord in manifest form for the worship of the Formless?

Neither the fish survives separated from the beloved water nor papihā lives without rain.

Yours is the helpless position like that of a lotus which in its ignorance

loves not the water from which it is born.

Does the lotus for fear of the fire and heat turn its face from the Sun?

Daśaratha really understood love and gave up life when the beloved Rāma parted,

Love's demand is fulfilled if life is sacrificed at the altar of love, without heeding the world's opinion (ridicule), says Sūradāsa.

19

Uddhau kahī su bahuri na kahiye

Jau tuma hamaiṅ jivāyau chāhata, anabole hvai rahiyai

Prāna hamāre ghāta ḥota haiṅ, tumhare bhāvaiṅ hāṅsī

Yā jīvana soṅ marana bhalau hai, karavata laīhaiṅ kāsī

Puraba prīti saṅbhāri hamārī, tuma kauṅ kahana paṭhāyau

Hama to jari-bari bhasma bhaī tuma. ānī masāna jagāyau

Kai Hari hama kauṅ ānı milāvahuṅ kai lai chaliye sāthai

Sūrasyāma binu prāna tajata haiṅ doṣa tumhāre māthai.

ऊधौ कही सु बहुरि न कहिये।

जौ तुम हमैं जिवायौ चाहत, अनबोले ह्वै रहिये।।

प्रान हमारे घात होत हैं, तुम्हरे भावैं हांसी।

या जीवन सों मरन भलौ है, करवत लैहैं कासी।।

पूरब प्रीति संभारि हमारी, तुम कौं कहन पठायौ।

हम तो जरि-बरि भस्म भई तुम, आनि मसान जगायौ।।

कै हरि हम कौं आनि मिलावहुं, कै लै चलिये साथै।

'सूरस्याम' बिनु प्रान तजत हैं दोष तुम्हारे माथै ।।

(स्कंध 10, प.सं. 3609/4227)

Uddhava! repeat not the painful yoga message again.

Remain silent if you desire us to live a little.

You revel, enjoy, while we suffer tortures when you ask us to devote ourselves to the Formless Lord.

Better we give up our life than our faith in worship of Shyāma of the beautiful Form by having our heads cut off on the scaffold at Kāsī

Remembering our past love He sent you as a messenger.

And you come to fan in us the smouldering fire of separation.

Either take us to Hari or bring Hari here or else we shall sacrifice our lives and the blame will lie on Your head.

20

Ati malīna Briṣabhānu kumārī

Hari srama jala bhījyau ura aṅchala, tihiṅ lālacha na dhuāvati sārī

Adhamukha rahati uradha nahiṅ chitavata jyauṅ gathahāre thakita juvārī

Chhūṭe chikura badana kumhilāne, jyauṅ nalinī himakara kī mārī

Hari saṅdeśa suni sahaja mritaka bhai, ika birahini dūje alijāri

Sūrasyāma binu yoṅ jīvata haiṅ, braja banitā saba syāmadulārī

अति मलीन वृषभानु कुमारी।
हरि स्त्रम जल भीज्यौं उर अंचल, तिहिं लालच न धुआवति सारी।।
अधमुख रहति उरध नहिं चितवत, ज्यौं गथहारे थकित जुवारी।
छुटे चिकुर बदन कुम्हिलाने, ज्यौ नलिनी हिमकर की मारी।।
हरि संदेश सुनि सहज मृतक भइ, इक बिरहिनि दूजे अलिजारी।
"सूरस्याम" बिनु यों जीवत है, ब्रज बनिता सब स्याम दुलारी।।
(स्कंध 10, प.सं.4075/4693)

Says Uddhava to Shri Krishṇa:

Very fatigued is the daughter of Brisabhāna—Rādhā, today.

Donning on her breast garments drenched with Krishṇa's sweats and reluctant to have them washed for fear

of losing from them the marks left by touches of Shyāma, when he danced the Rāsa-dance with her.

Her eyes are always downcast and she never raises them.

As a gambler feels dejected, having lost his capital amount,

Her hairs are dishevelled and body has lost all its glow as a lotus plant crushed with hailstones.

On hearing the message of Hari-Krishṇa even the last breath of life seemed to leave her.

Thus in agony she passes her time along with her dearly beloved women of Braja, O! Shyāma

21

Hari ju āye so bhalī kīnhī

Mohiṅ dekhata kahi uṭhi rādhikā, aṅka timira kauṅ dīnhī

Tana ati kampita biraha ati vyākula, ura dhuka-dhuki kheda kīnhī

Chalata charana gahi rahi gaī giri, sweda salila bhaī bhīnī

Chūti vaha bhuja tūtī balayāvali phatī kaṅchukī jhīnī

Manau prema kī parani parevā, yā hī taiṅ paḍhi līnī

Avalokati ihiṅ bhāṅti ramāpati, mānau chūtī ahi mani chīnī

Sūradāsa prabhu kahauṅ kahāṅ lagi, bhaī ayāna mati hīnī

हरि जु आये सो भली कीन्ही।

मोहिं देखत कहि उठि राधिका, अंक तिमिर कौं दीन्ही।।

तन अति कंपित बिरह अति व्याकुल, उर धुक-धुकि खेद कीन्ही।

चलत चरन गहि रहि गई गिरि, स्वेद सलिल भई भीनी।।

छूटी वह भुज टूटी बलयावलि, फटी कंचुकी झीनी।

मनौ प्रेम की परनि परेवा, या ही तैं पढ़ि लीनी।।

अवलोकित इहिं भांति रमापति, मानौ छूटी अहि मनि छीनी

सूरदास प्रभु कहौं कहां लगि, भई अयान मति हीनी।।

(स्कंध 10, प.सं. 4105/4723)

Says Uddhava:

Upon my appearance Rādhā thinking you have come,

with closed eyes, stretched out her arms to greet you,

O' Krishṇa.

Her body all shivering, her legs unsteady, her heart throbbing,

She stepped forth deeply distressed due to separation and drenched with sweats

But unable to keep her balance, she fell injuring her arms and breaking her bangles, her hair

dishevelled and her brassieres torn out.

It was as if she read love's message from a distance.

She was as miserable as a snake deprived of his crest jewel.

Uddhava was unable to express in words the gravity of the scene he saw, says Sūradāsa.

22

Sunahu syāma yaha bāta aura kou kyauṅ samujhāi kahai

Duhuṅ disi kau ati biraha birahanī, kaisaiṅ kai ju sahai

Jaba Rādhā taba hīṅ mukha mādhau, mādhau raṭata rahai

Jaba mādhau hoī jata sakala tana, Rādhā biraha dahai

Ubhai agra dava dāru kīṭa jyauṅ, sītalatāhi chahai

Sūradāsa ati vikala birahani, kaisaihūṅ sukha na lahai

सुनहु स्याम यह बात और कोउ क्यों समुझाइ कहै।

दुहुं दिसि कौ अति बिरह बिरहनी, कैसैं कै जु सहै।।

जब राधा तब हीं मुख माधौ, माधौ रटत रहै।।

जब माधौ होई जात सकल तन, राधा बिरह दहै।।

उभै अग्र दव दारु कीट ज्यौं, सीतलताहि चहै ।
सूरदास अति विकल बिरहनी, कैसैहुं सुख न लहै ।।

(स्कंध 10. प.सं. 4108/4726)

Says Uddhava:

Shyāma! who is there besides you who

can understand the state of Rādhā's pining?

How, do what she may, she burns and languishes in separation

When she is in her senses she repeats your

name incessantly—Shyāma! Shyāma.

And as a result of such recollection she loses herself and she believes she is turned to a veritable Shyāma.

Thus changed into You (Mādhava), Rādhā laments.

Like an insect held in a hollow bamboo between a fire at either end.

She suffers, finding no escape from the fire of separation. She knows no rest.

23

Jo pai kau madhubana lauṅ jāya

Patiyāṅ likhī syāmasuṅdara ko, kara kaṅkana daihauṅ tāī

Aba vaha prīti kahāṅ gaī, mādhava milate benu bajāi

Nayana nīra saba sejyā bhījai, dukha sauṅ raina bihāi

Sūna bhavana mohe kharo ḍarāvai yaha ritu bana na suhāi

Sūradāsa yaha samau gaye taiṅ puni kāhi laihaiṅ āi

जो पै कोउ मधुबन लौं जाय।
पतियां लिखी स्याम सुन्दर को, कर कंकन देहौं ताइ।।
अब वह प्रीति कहां गई, माधव मिलते बेनु बजाइ।
नयन नीर सब सेज्या भीजै, दुख सौं रैन बिहाइ।।
सून भवन मोहे खरो डरावै, यह ऋतु बन न सुहाइ।
सूरदास यह समौ गये तैं पुनि कहि लैहैं आइ।।

(स्कंध 10, प.सं.3946/4563)

Says Rādhā:

If any one goes (as pilgrim) to Mathurā

Let him take to my Shyāmasundara the letter I have written for him.

In token I shall give him my bangles.

In my letter I have written, Mādhava! where is that love gone which urged you to meet me playing the flute?

You know that night is now passed in shedding tears, the bed drenched by them.

The spring has no charm for me, the palace looks dreary and forbidding.

Mādhava! if You do not return now, what will You find coming later? (Rādhā will have passed away by then)?" says Sūradāsa.

24

Binu mādhau Rādhā tana sajanī, saba viparīti bhaī

Gaī cchapāi cchapākara kī cchavi, rahī kalaṅka maī

Aṅkhiyāṅ hutīṅ kamala paṅkhurī sī succhabi nichori laī

Āṅcha lagai chūigo sonā jyoṅ tyauṅ tanu dhātu hai

Kadalī dala sī pīṭhi manohara, so janu ulaṭa gaī

Sampati saba hari harī sūra prabhu, bipadā deha daī

बिनु माधौ राधा तन सजनी, सब विपरीति भई ।
गई छपाइ छपाकर की छबि, रही कलंक मई ।।
अंखियां हुतीं कमल पँखरी सी, सुछबि निचोरि लई ।
आंच लगै चूइगो सोना ज्यों त्यौं तनु धातु हई ।।
कदली दल सी पीठि मनोहर, सो जनु उलट गई ।
सम्पति सब हरि हरी 'सूर' प्रभु, बिपदा देह दई ।।

(स्कंध 10, प.सं.3406/4024)

Sakhi! without Mādhava! Radha's body has suffered a great change (everything has turned against Rādhā).

The moon-like beauty of her rosy face turned sallow and pale pining for shyāma

The eyes that were like lotuses in bloom, appear as pale as dry leaves

The one golden-hued body now appears as if the gold's lustre had been robbed by fire.

The beautiful back that vied with the glorious plantain trunk appears as if turned inside out

Thus by parting from Sri Rādhā the Lord took away all her beauty from her, says Sūradāsa

25

Uddhava jo kou yā tana pheri banāvai

Toū naṅdanaṅdana taji madhukara, aura na kacchu mana āvai

Jau yā tan kī tvachā kāḍhi kai, suṅdara duṅḍubhi sājai

Vividha utaṅga tāna raṅga se syāma syāma kahi bājai

Yā tanu kī koī karai kīṅgarī aura nasana ke tāra

Āṭhoṅ jāma madhura dhvani nikasai sundara syāma murāra

Nikasaiṅ prāna hoya tana māṭi, druma lāgai tihiṅ ṭhāma

Sūradāsa sākhā phala, patra, leta uṭhaiṅ hari nāma

ऊधौ जो कोउ या तन फेरि बनावै।
तोऊ नन्दनन्दन तजि मधुकर, और न कछु मन आवै।।
जौ या तन की त्वचा काढ़ि कै, सुंदर दुन्दुभि साजै।
विविध उतंग तान रंग से स्याम स्याम कहि बाजै।।
या तनु की कोई करै कींगरी और नसन के तार।
आठों जाम मधुर ध्वनि निकसै, सुन्दर श्याम मुरार।।
निकसैं प्रान होय तन माटी, द्रुम लागै तिंहि ठाम।
सूरदास साखा, फल, पत्र, लेत उठैं हरि नाम।।

(स्कंध 10, प.सं. 3809/4427)

Says Rādhā:

Uddhava! if this body should again be incarnate

This I pray, that my mind should love none besides Naṅdanaṅdana

That of the skin of this body a drum should be made so that when struck

It would melodiously utter Shyāma, Shyāma!

That of its veins, a stringed instrument be made

so that at all hours it would reverberate with the music of Shyāma Murārī's name.

And that when this body is turned into dust, a creeper with lovely flowers may appear out of it.

The branches, fruits, leaves and flowers when plucked by him would produce the sound 'Shyāma! Shyāma', says Sūradāsa

26

Uddhau dekhata ho jaise brajabāsī

Leta usāṅsa nain jala pūrita, sumari sumari abināsī

Bhuli na uṭhata Jasodā jananī, manau bhuaṅgama ḍāsī

Chhuṭati nahiṅ prāna kyauṅ aṭakai, kaṭhina prema kī phāṅsī

Āvata nahiṅ naṅda maṅdira maiṅ bhayau phirata banavāsī

Parama malīna dhenu durbala bhaīṅ, syāma biraha kī trāsī

Gopī gvāla sakhā bālaka saba, kahūṅ na suniyata hāsī

Kāhaiṅ diyau Sūra sukha maiṅ dukha, kapaṭi kāṅha bisāsī

ऊधौ देखत हो जैसे ब्रजवासी ।

लेत उसांस नैन जल पूरित, सुमिरि सुमिरि अबिनासी ।।

भूलि न उठत जसोदा जननी, मनौ भुअंगम डासी ।

छूटति नहीं प्रान क्यौं अटकै, कठिन प्रेम की फांसी ।।

आवत नहिं नंद मन्दिर मैं, भयौ फिरत बनवासी ।

परम मलीन धेनु दुर्बल भईं, स्याम विरह की त्रासी।।
गोपी ग्वाल सखा बालक सब, कहूं न सुनियत हांसी।
काहैं दियौ 'सूर' सुख मैं दुख, कपटी कान्ह बिसासी।।
(स्कंध 10, प.सं. 4093/4711)

Says Mother Yasodā:

Uddhava! Do you observe the condition of the dwellers of Braja?

How heavily they draw their breath, as tears fill their eyes, remembering the Eternal Beloved?

The condition of mother Yasodā is lamentable. She looks as if a snake had bitten her. It is difficult to understand as to why they do not die. It is so because the bonds of love are very strong.

As for Naṅda, he roams about lonely aimlessly and does not return home.

The cows seized by the agony of separation feel depressed and have become lean and thin without Shyāma

Today not so much as a smile is ever seen on the faces of even the gopis, cow-boys, friends and the children.

Why O Lord! after having once conferred the joy of Your company, have You thus brought amongst them the agony of separation? asks Sūradāsa. Krishṇa is a fraud.

27

Gopālahiṅ pāvauṅ dhauṅ kehiṅ desa

Sriṅgī mudrā kara khappara lai, karihauṅ jogini bhesa

Kaṅthā pahari bibhūti lagāūṅ, jaṭā bandhāuṅ kesa

Hari kārana gorakhahiṅ jagāūṅ, jaisaiṅ swāṅga mahesa

Tana mana jārūṅ bhasma chaḍhāūṅ birahani guru upadesa

Sūra syāma binu hama haiṅ aisī, jaishaiṅ mani binu sesa

गोपालहिं पावौं धौं केहिं देस।

स्रिंगी मुद्रा कर खप्पर लै, करि हौं जोगिनि भेस।।

कंथा पहरि बिभूति लगाऊं, जटा बन्धाऊं केस।

हरि कारन गोरखहिं जगाऊं, जैसें स्वांग महेस।।

तन मन जारूं भस्म चढ़ाऊं, विरहनि गुरु उपदेस।

'सूर' स्याम बिनु हम हैं ऐसै, जैसें मनि बिनु सेस

(स्कंध 10, प.सं.3228/3846)

Says Rādhā:

Tell me where shall I meet my Gopāla?

I will don the yogi's dress, wear long matted hair, take the bowl and the horn in hand, wear the glass ring in the ear, dress up in patched-cloth garment and besmear ashes on my body.

For my Beloved Hari's sake I will wander in the world, invoking Gorakha by name, attired as Shiva.

Separation–which is my guru-has imparted this lesson to me—burn yourself thus for His sake.

'The lamentable plight of the gopīs is like the snake (Sheṣanga) that has lost its crest jewel', says Sūradāsa.

28

Uddhava itanī kahiyahu jāi

Ati krisa gāta bhaīṅ ye tuma binu, parama dukhārī gāi

Jala samūha barasati doū aṅkhiyāṅ, hūnkati līṅhaiṅ nāūṅ

Jahaṅ jahaṅ go dūhana kīnhau, sūṅghati soī ṭhāuṅ

Paratiṅ pacchāra khāi cchinahīṅ cchina, ati ātura hvai dīna

Mānahuṅ Sūra kāḍhi ḍārī haiṅ, vāri madhya taiṅ mīna

ऊधौ इतनी कहियहु जाइ।
अति कृस गात भईं ये तुम बिनु, परम दुखारी गाइ।।
जल समूह बरसति दोऊ अंखियां, हूंकति लीन्हैं नाऊं।
जहँ जहँ गो दूहन कीन्हौ, सूंघति सोई ठाऊँ।।
परतिं पछार खाइ छिनहीं छिन, अति आतुर ह्वै दीन।
मानहुं सूर काढ़ि डारी हैं, वारि मध्य तैं मीन।।
(स्कंध 10, प.सं. 4072/4690)

Say the gopīs:

Uddhava! please carry to Mādhava this simple message of ours! "Without Your sight, the cows have become very lean and grown very melancholy

On the mere mention of His name, they cry in pain of separation.

The tears flow from their eyes.

They smell the spots where You sat milching them.

They fall senseless to the ground unable to endure the agony.

Their condition is as that of a fish taken out of water (and cast on to the burning sands), says Sūradāsa

29

Kahā hauṅ aise hī mari jai hauṅ

Yahi āṅgana gopāl lāla ko, kabahuṅka kaniyā laihauṅ

Kaba vaha mukha bahurau dekhauṅgī, kaba vaiso sachu paihauṅ

Kaba mo pai mākhana māṅgaigo, kaba roṭī dhari dai hauṅ

Milana āsa tana prāna rahata haiṅ, dina dasa māraga chaihauṅ

Jau na sūra kaṅha āihaiṅ tau, jāī jamuna dhaṅsi laihaiṅ

कहा हौं ऐसे ही मरि जैहौं ।
यहि आंगन गोपाल लाल को, कबहुंक कनियां लैहौं ।।
कब वह मुख बहुरौ देखौंगी, कब वैसो सचु पैहौं ।
कब मो पै माखन मांगैगो, कब रोटी धरि देहौं ।।
मिलन आस तन प्रान रहत हैं, दिन दस मारग चैहौं ।
जौ न सूर कान्ह आइहैं तौ, जाई जमुन धंसि लैहौं ।।

(स्कंध 10, प.सं. 3013/3631)

Mother Yasodā laments:

Shall I thus die yearning in vain for my Krishṇa?

Will he never come back to my courtyard and shall I never hold Him with affection in my lap?

When shall I comfort my eyes gazing affectionately into His sweet face?

When again will He ask of me bread and butter and offer them to Him with affection?

In the hope of meeting Him I will survive for a few days more.

But if he returns not, I shall surely plunge into the waters of Jamunā and drown myself. Says Sūradāsa.

30

Kehiṅ māraga maiṅ jāūṅ sakhī rī, māraga mohiṅ bisaryau

Nā jānau kita hvai gae mohan, jāta na jāni paryau

Apanau piya ḍhūṅḍhati phirauṅ, rī mohiṅ milane kau chāva

Kānṭo lāgyauṅ prema kau, piya, yaha pāyau dāva

Bana dauṅgara ḍhuṅḍhati phirī, ghara māraga, taji gāṅva

Būjhauṅ druma prati beli kou, kahai na piya ko nāṅva

Chakita bhaī, chitavata phirī vyākula atihiṅ anātha

Ab kai jau kaisehuṅ milauṅ, palaka na tajihauṅ sātha

Hridaya māṅjha piya-ghara karauṅ rī nainana baiṭhaka deūṅ

Sūradāsa prabhu saṅga milauṅ, bahuri rāsa-rasa leūṅ

केहिं मारग मैं जाऊं सखी री, मारग मोहिं बिसरयौ।
ना जानौं कित ह्वै गए मोहन, जात न जानि पर्‌यौ।।
अपनौ पिय ढूंढ़ति फिरौं, री मोहिं मिलने कौ चाव।
कांटो लाग्यौं प्रेम कौ, पिय, यह पायौ दाव।।

बन डोंगर ढूंढ़ति फिरी, घर मारग तजि गांव।
बूझौं द्रुम प्रति बेलि कोउ, कहै न पिय को नांव।।
चकित भई, चितवत फिरी, व्याकुल अतिहिं अनाथ।
अब कै जौ कैसेहुं मिलौं, पलक न तजिहौं साथ।।
हृदय मांझ पिय-घर करौं री नैनन बैठक देऊं।
'सूरदास' प्रभु संग मिलौं, बहुरि रास-रस लेऊं
(स्कंध 10, प.सं. 1111/1729)

Which way am I to proceed, sakhi? for I have lost the trail?

I did not observe which way He escaped, as I was so lost in contemplation of Him.

I am seeking my beloved in the wilderness for I am pining for Him.

As I was absorbed tending the wound of love, he found excuse to slip away.

I seek Him in the jungle, forsaking my home and the town.

I ask the very trees and creepers which way my beloved went but, Alas! none shows me the way.

A helpless maniac, I wander seeking Him, as if stunned.

If this time I find Him, not for one moment I will leave Him again.

I shall seat Him in my heart and close the doors of my eyes.

Thus having met, says Rādhā, I shall enjoy again the Rāsa-Dance Divine with Him, sings Sūradāsa.

31

Braja ke birahī loga dukhāre

Bina gopāla ṭhage se ṭhāḍhe, ati durbala tana kāre

Naṅda, jasodā māraga jovatiṅ, nita uṭhi sāñjha sakāre

Chahuṅ disi kānha kānha kari ṭerata, aṅsuana bahata panāre

Gopī gāi, gvāla, gosuta saba, atihiṅ dīna bichāre

Sūradāsa prabhu binu yauṅ sobhita, chaṅdra binā jyauṅ tāre

ब्रज के बिरही लोग दुखारे ।

बिन गोपास ठगे से ठाढ़े, अति दुर्बल तन कारे ।।

नंद, जसोदा मारग जोवतिं नित उठि सांझ सकारे ।

चहुं दिसि कान्ह कान्ह करि टेरत, अंसुअन बहत पनारे ।।

गोपी, गाइ, ग्वाल, गोसुत सब, अतिहिं दीन बिचारे ।

'सूरदास' प्रभु बनु यौं सोभित, चंद्र बिना ज्यौं तारे ।।

(स्कंध 10, प.सं.4101.4719)

The separated ones of Braja pining for their beloved Gopāla are turned dark and thin and look as if cheated in the absence of Gopāla (in anticipation of His return to Braja).

Every morning and evening Naṅda and Yasodā awaiting for His return stand and watch the path.

The tears stream from eyes as "Kaṅhā", "kaṅhā" they call Him plaintively by name.

The Gopīs, the cowherds and the cows are all grown lean and helpless waiting for Gopāla!

They look as forlorn as the stars in the sky at the night without the moon in their midst, says Sūradāsa.

32

Nātha anāthani kī sudhi lījai

Gopī, gāi, gvāla, gosuta saba dīna malīna dinahiṅ din cchījai

Nainani jal dhārā bāḍhī ati, buḍata braja kina kara gahi lījai

Itanī binatī sunahu hamārī, bārakahūṅ patiyāṅ likhi dījai

Charana kamala darasana nava nauṅkā, karunā-siṅdhu jagata asa lījai

Sūradāsa prabhu āsa milana kī, eka bāra āvana braja kījai

नाथ अनाथनि की सुधि लीजे।

गोपी, गाइ, ग्वाल, गोसुत सब, दीन मलीन दिनहिं दिन छीजै।।

नैननि जल धारा बाढ़ी अति, बूडत ब्रज किन कर गहि लीजे।

इतनी बिनती सुनहु हमारी, बारकहूं पतियां लिखि दीजै।।

चरन कमल दरसन नव नौंका, करुनासिन्धु जगत अस लीजे।

'सूरदास' प्रभु आस मिलन की, एक बार आवन ब्रज कीजै।।

(स्कंध 10, प.सं. 3192/3810)

Take heed of the helpless ones, O Lord!

The gopīs of Braja, the cowherds and the calves are all grown so lean, poorly and depressed pining for You day in and day out.

From their eyes, tears in floods are gushing out. It seems that they will inundate Braja unless you succour them by extending Your benign (gracious) hands.

Pray accede to their prayers and write a letter only once to the gopīs.

Pray lend to them the canoe of Your Lotus-Feet so that catching it they may cross the dreary ocean of Your separation.

Fulfil their hope and bless them with Your vision by going over only once to Braja, Sūradāsa prays.

33

Nisi dina barasata naina hamāre

Sadā rahata baraṣā ritu hama para, jaba taiṅ Syāma sidhāre

Naina aṅjana na rahata nisi bāsara, kara kapola bhaye kāre

Kaṅchukī paṭa sūkhata nahiṅ kabahūṅ, ura bicha bahata panāre

Āṅsū salila sabai bhaī kāyā, pala na jāta risa ṭāre

Sūradāsa prabhu gokula būḍata kāhe na leta ubāre

निसि दिन बरसत नैन हमारे ।

सदा रहत वरषा रितु हम पर, जब तैं स्याम सिधारे ।।

नैन अंजन न रहत निसि बासर, कर कपोल भए कारे ।

कंचुकि पट सूखत नहिं कबहूं, उर बिच बहत पनारे ।।

आंसू सलिल सबै भई काया, पल न जात रिस टारे ।

सूरदास प्रभु गोकुल बूड़त काहे न लेत उबारे ।।

(स्कंध 10, प.सं. 3238/3856)

Day and night, tears rain from our eyes incessantly.

Since Shyāma left us, our eyes rain like the clouds in the rainy season.

The collyrim of the eyes is washed away and the cheeks are coloured black.

Our under-garment supporting the breasts are drenched and can never be dried.

Our body is wet with tears day and night.

Our anguish diminishes not even for a moment

Sūradāsa pleads to you, O Lord! save Braja from drowning in the sea of the agony of Your separation.

34

Nayana salone syāma, Hari kaba āvahiṅge

Vai jo dekhata rāte rāte, phulana phule dāri

Hari bina phula jharī sī lāgata, jhari jhari parata aṅgāra

Phūla binana nā jāūṅ sakhī rī, Hari bina kaise phūla

Suni rī sakhī mohiṅ Rāma dohāī, lāgata phūla triśūla

Jaba te panaghaṭa jāūṅ sakhī rī, vā jamunā ke tīra

Bhari bhari jamunā umaḍi chalata hai, ina nainana ke nīra

Ina nainana ke nīra sakhī rī, seja bhaī ghara nāva

Chāhata hauṅ tāhī para chaḍhi kai hari jī ke dhiṅga jāva

Lāla pyāre prāṇa hamāre, rahe adhara para āī

Sūradāsa prabhu kuṅja bihārī, milata nahiṅ kyauṅ dhāī

नयन सलोने श्याम, हरि कब आवहिंगे।।
वै जो देखत राते राते, फूलन फूले डारि।
हरि बिन फूल झरी सी लागत, झरि झरि परत अंगार।।
फूल बिनन ना जाऊं सखी री, हरि बिन कैसे फूल।
सुनि री सखी मोहिं राम दोहाई, लागत फूल त्रिशूल।।
जब ते पनघट जाऊं सखी री, वा जमुना के तीर।
भरि भरि जमुना उमड़ि चलत है, इन नैनन के नीर।।

इन नैनन के नीर सखी री, सेज भई धर नाव।
चाहत हौं ताही पर चढ़ि कै, हरि जी के ढिंग जाव।।
लाल प्यारे प्राण हमारे, रहे अधर पर आई।
सूरदास प्रभु कुञ्ज विहारी, मिलत नहीं क्यों धाई।।
(स्कंध 10, प.सं.3277/3895)

When will He of the beautiful Lotus Eyes—my Shyāma visit me?

The blooming red flowers that with Him by our side gave us joy. Without Him they now burn us like scintillating fire.

What avails it, our going now to gather flowers in the garden?

When Hari is not there with us, flowers prick us like thorns. When I go to the periphery of a well from where water is drawn on the banks of the Jamunā, my eyes flow in torrents and the very waters make the river Yamunā rise with these accumulated tears.

At times my bed is so covered with tears that I could well make a canoe of it and on it reach my Beloved

Since we are on the verge of death, O our darling Krishṇa, dweller in the groves, why don't you hastily come to us.

35

Kāhe kauṅ piya piyahiṅ raṭata hau, piya kau prema tero prāṇa haraigau

Kāhe kauṅ leta nayana jala bhari bhari, naina bhare kaisaiṅ sūla ṭaraigau

Kāhe kauṅ svāsa usāṅsa leti hau, bairī biraha ko davā baraigau

Kshāra sugaṅdha seja puhupāvali, hāra cchuvai, hiya hāra jaraigau

Badana durāi baiṭhi maṅdir maiṅ, bahura nisāpati udaya karaigau

Sūra sakhī apane ina nainani, chandra chitai jina chanda jaraigau

काहे कौं पिय पियहिं रटत हौ, पिय कौ प्रेम तेरो प्रान हरैगौ ।
काहे कौं लेति नयन जल भरि भरि, नैन भरे कैसैं सूल टरैगौ । ।
काहे कौं स्वास उसांस लेति हौ, बैरी बिरह को दवा बरैगौ ।
क्षार सुगंध सेज पुहुपावलि, हार छुवै, हिय हार जरैगौ । ।
बदन दुराइ बैठि मन्दिर मैं, बहुर निसापति उदय करैगौ ।
'सूर'सखी अपने इन नैननि, चंद्र चितै जिन चंद जरैगौ । ।
(स्कंध 10, प.सं. 3370/3988)

Why do you cry "Beloved! O my Beloved".

This cry of beloved's love, I tell you, shall take away your life.

Why do you fill your eyes with tears? You wrongly think that thus you will gain peace?(How can the tears relieve you of your pain?)

Why do you draw sighs? This shall only highten the flames of the fire of separation

The bedstead, fragrance & the flowers are liable to be reduced to ashes with the fire of separtion in the breast.

As far the garland (on the breast) it would also be burnt with the fire of separation.

Sakhi! go and sit in some corner of the house as the moon is just to rise again.

And do not see the moon then with these eyes of yours otherwise it would also be reduced to ashes by the fire of separation in the breast (Such is your separation).

36

Uddhaua kahaṅ kī prīti hamāraiṅ
Ajahuṅ rahata tana hari ke sidhāraiṅ
Chhidi chhidi jāta biraha sara māraiṅ
Puri puri āvata avadhi bichāraiṅ
Phaṭati na hridaya saṅdesa tumhāraiṅ
Kulisha taiṅ kaṭhina dhukata dou tāre
Barașata naiṅa mahājala dhāraiṅ
Ura paṣāna bidarata na bidāraiṅ
Jīvana marana bhaye doū bhāre
Kahiyata Sūra lāja pati hāre

ऊधौ कहं की प्रीति हमारैं।
अजहुं रहत तन हरि के सिधारैं।।
छिदि छिदि जात बिरह सर मारैं,
पुरि पुरि आवत अवधि बिचारैं।
फटति न हृदय सन्देस तुम्हारैं,
कुलिश तैं कठिन धुकत दोउ तारे।।
वरषत नैन महाजल धारैं,
उर पषान बिदरत न बिदारैं।
जीवन मरन भए दोऊ भारे,
कहियत 'सूर' लाज पति हारे।।
(स्कंध 10, 3624/4242)

Uddhava! No lovers are we!

For even now can a lover's life endure the pangs of separation from the beloved?

But there is reason for life persisting in us in the hope of Krishṇa's return to Vrindābana which would again heal those wounds.

We are surprised that your yoga message to give up the love of Krishṇa's Form for that of the Formless Lord—does not tear our heart asunder.

Perhaps our heart is grown as hard as thunderbolt

These eyes rain torrents and yet the heart melts and pines not away.

Life and death are both heavy loads on our shoulders.

We die of shame that we cannot be called Your lovers, sings Sūradāsa, of the plight of the gopīs.

37

Ihiṅ ura mākhana chora gaḍe

Aba kaisaiṅ nikasata suni uddhava, tiracchai hvai ju gaḍe

Jadapi ahīra Jasodā naṅdanaṅdana kaisaiṅ jāta cchaṅḍe

Hāṅ jādaupati prabhu kahiyati haiṅ, hamaiṅ na lagata baḍe

Ko basudeva devakī naṅdana ko jānai ko būjhe

Sūra naṅdanaṅdana ke dekhata, aura na koū sūjhe

इहिं उर माखन चोर गड़े ।

अब कैसैं निकसत सुनि ऊधौ, तिरछे है जु गड़े ।।

जदपि अहीर जसोदा नंदनन्दन, कैसैं जात छंड़े।
हां जादौपति प्रभु कहियत हैं, हमैं न लगत बड़े।।
को बसुदेव देवकी नंदन, को जानै को बूझे।
सूर नंदनंदन के देखत, और न कोऊ सूझे।।
(स्कंध 10, प.सं. 3733/4351)

The butter-thief is stuck up in our hearts

O Uddhava! hear, how can he now be taken out, as he lies stuck up there obliquely?

Though the son of Yasodā is a cowherd, even then how can he be forsaken?

There he is known as the lord of the yādavas but here does not look to be so great to us.

Who knows and who understands as to who is the son of Vāsudeva and Devakī.

Sūradāsa says, on seeing the son of Naṅda we cannot think of any one else.

38

Uddhau itanī kahyao jāi

Sabai birahinī pāṅ lāgati haiṅ, mathurā kānha rahau

Bhūlahiṅ jani āvahu ihiṅ gokula, tapati tarani jyoṅ chaṅda

Suṅdara badana syāma komala tana kyauṅ sahihaiṅ naṅdanaṅda

Madhukara, mora, prabala pika, chātaka, bana upabana chaḍhi bolata

Manahuṅ siṅha kī garaja sunata go baccha dukhita tana ḍolata

Tuma hauṅ saṅta, sadā upakārī jānata hau saba rīti

Sūra syāma kauṅ kyauṅ bolai braja, binu ṭāre yaha īti

ऊधौ इतनी कह्यौ जाइ

सबै बिरहिनी पां लागति हैं, मथुरा कान्ह रहौ।

भूलहिं जनि आवहु इहिं गोकुल, तपति तरनि ज्यों चंद।

सुन्दर बदन स्याम कोमल तन, क्यौं सहिहैं नन्दनंद।

मधुकर, मोर प्रबल पिक, चातक, बन उपबन चढ़ि बोलत।

मनहु सिंह की गरज सुनत गो बच्छ दुखित तन डोलत।

तुम हौ संत सदा उपकारी, जानत हौ सब रीति।

सूर स्याम कौं क्यौं बोलै ब्रज, बिनु टारे यह ईति।।

(स्कंध 10, प.सं.4096/4684)

Go and tell this, Uddhava

All your beloved ones entreat you to stay at Mathurā

Do not think of coming to Gokula even by mistake

You know how the moon burns like the sun.

How can the dark-coloured, delicate-bodied, Nandanandana bear it?

The bee, peacock, chātak and the cuckoo have turned furious, shriek violently in forests and gardens.

On hearing the roars of the lion, the cows and the calves move as if distressed in the woods of Braja.

Simple and soft-hearted, you know all these things.

Why Shyāma, says Sūra, should come to Braja without ending the days of disasters.

39

Āyau ghoṣa baḍau vyāupārī

Khepa lādi guru jṅāna joga kī, braja maiṅ āni utārī

Phāṭaka dai kai haṭaka māṅgata bhorau nipaṭa sudhārī

Dhurahiṅ taiṅ khoṭo khāyau hai, lie phirata sira bhārī

Inakaiṅ kaha kauna ḍahakāvai aisī kauna anārī.

Apanau dudhi cchāṅḍi ko pīvai, khāre kūpa ko bārī

Uddhau jāhu sabāraiṅ hyāṅ taiṅ, begi gaharu jani lāvahu

Mukhamāṅgau paihau sūraja prabhu, sāhuhiṅ āni dikhāvahu

आयौ घोष बड़ौ व्यौपारी।

खेप लादि गुरु ज्ञान जोग की, ब्रज मैं आनि उतारी।।

फाटक दै कै हाटक मांगत, भोरौ निपट सुधारी।

धुरहीं तैं खोटो खायौ है, लिए फिरत सिर भारी।

इनकैं कह कौन डहकावे, ऐसी कौन अनारी।

अपनौ दूधि छांड़ि को पीवै, खारे कूप कौ बारी।।

ऊधौ जाहु सबारैं ह्यां तैं, बेगि गहरु जनि लावहु।

मुखमांगौ पैहौ सूरज प्रभु, साहुहिं आनि दिखावहु

(स्कंध 10, प.सं. 3967/4582)

A big merchant has come to the village.

In Braja he has unloaded the commodity of yoga

In return for his chaff this simple innocent creature demands gold.

From the very beginning he has made profit out of the sale of adulterated goods carrying on his head.

Who is that much of a simpleton who would be deceived by him?

Who would like to drink the saltish water from the well in preference to milk available.

Uddhava, get away from here immediately.

Do not make any further delay.

Says Sūra, you would get the price, asked for, if you show us the master (Money-lender) here.

40

Adbhuta eka anupama bāga

Jugala kamala para gajabara krīḍata, tāpara siṅha karata anurāga.

Hari para sarabara, sara para giribara, giri para phūle kañja parāga.

Ruchira kapota basata tā ūpara, amrita phala lāga

Phala para puhupa, puhupa para pallava, tā para suka, pika, mrigamada kāga.

Khañjana, dhanuṣa, chandramā ūpara, tā ūpara ika manidhara nāga

Aṅga Aṅga prati aura aura cchabi, upamā tākauṅ karata na tyāga

Sūradāsa prabhu piyau sudhārasa, mānau, adharani kai bada bhāga.

अद्‌भुत एक अनुपम बाग।

जुगल कमल पर गजबर क्रीड़त, तापर सिंह करत अनुराग।।

हरि पर सरबर, सर पर गिरिबर, गिरि पर फूले कंज पराग।

रुचिर कपोत बसत ता ऊपर, ता ऊपर अमृत फल लाग।।

फल पर पुहुप, पुहुप पर पल्लव, ता पर सुक, पिक, मृगमद काग।

खंजन, धनुष, चन्द्रमा ऊपर, ता ऊपर इक मनिधर नाग।

अंग अंग प्रति और और छबि, उपमा ताकौं करत न त्याग।

सूरदास प्रभु पियौ सुधारस, मानौ, अधरनि कै बड़ भाग।।

(स्कंध 10, प.सं.2111/2729)

Lalitā (Gopī) says, "O Mādhava, I will show you a wonderful garden.

In this garden elephants i.e. the thighs are seen playing on the two lotus flowers i.e. the feet. A lion i.e. the waist above them fondles the elephants.

There is a pond i.e. the deep naval over the lion. On the pond there are hillocks i.e. the breasts and on the hillocks the filaments (pollen) of the lotus flowers i.e. the golden-hued ṇipples of the breasts bloom.

There iṣ a beautiful pigeon i.e. the neck on the breasts and a neçtar fruit i.e. the face on the pigeon.

There are flowers i.e. the chin on the fruits and leaves i.e. the lips on the flowers, parrots i.e. the nose, cockoo i.e. the voice, crow i.e. the black round mark on the forehead are there on the leaves.

Khañjan bird i.e. the eyes and bow i.e. the eye-brows are there on the moon i.e. the forehead. Over the head there is a crest-jewelled black snake i.e. the locks of hair.

Thus each and every limb of Rādhā's body possesses extra-ordinary beauty and needs no other *upamās* for comparison i.e. all the similes are quite apt.

Her lips are really very lucky, as Krishṇa himself tasted (drank) the nectar from her lips, says Sūradāsa.

41

Baḍi hai Rāma nāma kī oṭa

Sarana gaeṅ prabhu kāḍhi-deta nahiṅ karata kripā kaiṅ koṭa

Baiṭhata sabai sabhā Hari jū kī, kauna baḍau ko chhoṭa?

Sūradāsa pa̋rasa ke parasaiṅ miṭati loha kī khoṭa

बड़ी है राम नाम की ओट।

सरन गएं प्रभु काढ़ि देत नहिं करत कृपा कैं कोट।

बैठत सबै सभा हरि जू की, कौन बड़ौ को छोट?

सूरदास पारस के परसैं मिटति लोह की खोट। (1/232)

Rāma's name is a mighty force.
He who takes refuge in Hari is never abaondoned
The castle of His grace becomes his shelter.
All, great and small, resort to it.
As with the touch of the mythical stone
Iron becomes gold, says Sūradāsa.

BIBLIOGRAPHY

Abul Fazl: *Āin-i-Akbarī,* Ed. Blochman, Calcutta, 1939.

—*Akbar Nāmā,* Ed. Baveridge, Calcutta, 1912.

Agrawal, Sarayu Prasada: *Akabarī Darabāra Ke Hindi Kavi,* Lucknow, 1951.

Ahivasi, Jagan Nath: *Kīrtana Sangraha,* Bombay, V.S. 1998.

Anand Kumar: *Hindi Kavitā Kā Vikāsa,* Prayāga, 1940.

Bajpai, Nand Dulare: *Mahākavī Sūradāsa,* Delhi, V.S. 1952.

Banerjee, Jitendranath: *The development of Hindu Iconography,* Calcutta, 1956.

Bhatt, G.H.: *A Further Note on Vishṇusvāmī and Vallabhāchārya,* Mysore, 1953.

Bhatt, Ratan Gopal : *Tatvārtha Deep Āvarna Bhaṅga Tīkā Shāstrārtha Prakaraṇa Tathā Sarva Nirṇaya Prakaraṇa,* Bombay, N.D.

Bhatt, Shri Nath: *Sanskrit Vartāmanimālā,* Kākrolī N.D.

Bhatt, Viṭṭhal: *Sampradāya Kalpadruma,* Kākrolī, N.D.

Bharat, Mahamuni: *Nāṭyashāstra,* Barodā, 1926.

Bhandarkar, R.G.: *Vaiṣṇavism, Shaivism and Minor Religious Systems,* Vārānasī, 1965.

Bhatnagar, Ram Ratna: *Sūradāsa Eka Adhyayana,* Prayāga, V.S.1946.

—*Sūra Sāhitya Kī Bhūmikā,* Prayāga, V.S.1941

—, *Hindi Bhakti kāvya*, Prayāga V.S. 1941.

Brahma Bhatt, Nar Singh Das,: *Sūra Nu Jīwana Chritra, Ahmedābād*, V.S. 1980.

Brahamchārī, Prabu Dutt (Ed.): *Bhagat Charitrāvalī, Prayāga*, V.S. 1913.

Brown, Percy: *Indian Architecture*, Bombay, 1964.

Chaturbuj Dass: *Govardhanavāsī*, Mathurā, N.D.

Chaturvedi Dat Ram (Ed.): *Amrita Kī Būnda*, Bombay, V.S. 1915.

Chaturvedi, Jawahar Lal (Ed.): *Basanta Ke Kirtana*, Bombay, V.S.1992.

—*Basanta Ke Pada*, Bombay, 1992.

Chaturvedi, Sharma: *Mahāprabhu Srimadvallabhāchārya aur Puṣṭi Mārga*, Vārānasī, 1961.

Denielou, Alain: *Hindu Polytheism*, New York, 1964.

Dass, Braj Ratna: *Hindi Sāhitya Kā Vikāsa*, Kāshī, V.S. 1989.

Dass, Veni Madhav: *Mūla Gusāaiṅ Charitra*, Gorakhpur, V.S. 1993.

Das Gupta, Surender Nath: *A History of Indian Philosophy*, Cambridge, 1961.

Dass, Shayam Sundar (Ed.): *Saṁkshipta Padmāvata*, Prayāga, 1921.

—*Sāhityālochana*, Prayāga, V.S. 1994.

— (Ed.): *Hastalikhita Hindī Pustakon Kā Saṁkshipta Vivaraṇa*, Kāshī, V.S. 1980.

—*Hindi Bhāsā aur Sāhitya*, Prayāga, V.1994.

Dey, Nand Lal: *The Geographical History of Ancient and Medieval India* 1899.

De, Sushil Kumar: *Early History of the Vaiṣṇava Faith and Movement in Bengal*, Calcutta, 1961.

Desai, Lalu Bhai, Chhagan Lal (Ed.): *Nija Vārtā, Chāru Vārtā Tathā Chaubīsa Badken Ke Charitra*, Ahmedabad, V.S. 1979.

Dhawrikesh: *Bhāva Saṅgrah*, Mewar, N.D.

Dhruva Dass: *Bhakta Nāmāvalī*, Kāshī, V.S. 1919.

Devi Parshad: *Sūradāsa Kā Jīwan Charitra*, Muradabad, V.S. 1903.

– *Hālāte Hayāt-Bābā Sūradāsa*, Ajmer, N.D. (Urdu)

Dikshit, Rajesh (Ed.): *Kumbhanadāsa Ke Pada, Mathūra*, 1926.

Demock, Edward: *The Place of Hidden Moon*, Chicago, 1966.

Din Kinkar: *Shri Gokul Nātha Jī Nā Hasya Prasaṅga* Vol. I, Ahmedabad, N.D.

Dixit, Appaya (Pub.): *Sidhāntalesha, Kāshī*, N.D.

Dodwell, H.H. (Ed.): *The Cambridge Shorter History of India*, Delhi, 1969.

Dowson, John: *A Classical Dictionary of Hindu Mythology*, London, 1968.

Dube, Lalit Prasad: *Hindi Bhakta Vārtā Sāhitya*, Dehradun, 1967.

Dwivedi, Ganesh Prasad: *Hindi Ke Kavi aur Kāvya*, Prayāga, V.S. 1937.

Dwivedi, Hazari Prasad: *Hindi Sāhitya Kī Bhūmika*, Bombay, 1954.

—*Sūra Sāhitya*, Indore, V.S. 1993.

Dwivedi, R.A. : *A Critical Survey of Hindi Literature*, Vārānasī, 1966.

Eliade, Mircea: *Patterns in comparative Religion*, Cleveland, 1968.

Farquhar, J.N.: *An Outline of the Religious Literature of India*, Delhi, 1966.

Gadadhar Prasad: *Sampradāya Pradeep*, Kākrolī, N.D.

Gaur, Rajinder Singh: *Prāchīna Kaviyon Kī Sāhitya Sādhanā*, Prayāg, V.S. 1950.

Gaur, Chhagan lal: *Nitya Kīrtana*, Bombay, V.S. 1958.

Gautam, Man Mohan: *Sūra Kī Kāvya Kalā*, Delhi, V.S. 1958.

Girdhar Ji: *Śudhādvaita Mārtaṅḍa*, Banaras, N.D.

Gokul Nath: *Aṣṭhachhāpa*, Prayaga, V.S. 1929.

—*Chaurāsī Vaiṣṇavan Kī Vārtā*, Ahmedabad, V.S. 1881.

—*Bhāva Sindhu*, Ahmedabad, V.S. 1979.

Gopilankar: *Vaiṣṇava Vāhini ke Pada*, Kaṅkroli, N.D.

Goswami, Roop: *Laghubhāgavatāmrita*, Bombay, V. S. 1959.

Goswami, Roop: *Bhakti-Rasāmrita-Sindhu*, *Kāshī*, N.D.

Goswami, Sharana Bihari: *Krishṇabhakti Kāvya Meṅ Sakhībhāva*, Vārānasi, 1966.

Goswami, Viṭṭhal Nath: *Bhakti Haṅs*, Bombay, V.S. 1971.

—*Sawāmini Shrota*, Bombay, N.D.

—*Sawāmī nayashataka*, Bombay, N.D.

Goswami, Yadhunāthji : *Vallabha Digvijaya*, *Nātha Dwārā*, V.S. 1975.

Govardhan Nath: *Shri Govardhan Nātha jī Kī Prākatya Ki Vārtā*, Bombay, N.D.

Gulab Rai: *Navarasa*, Āarrā, 1934.

—*Hindi Sāhitya Kā Subodh Itihāsa*, Agra, V.S. 1938.

Grvowse, F.S.: *Mathurā: A District Memoir*, Allahabad, 1883.

Gupta, Dina Dayal: *Aṣṭachāpa aur Vallabha Sampradāya*, Allahabad, 1948.

Gupta, Jagdish: *Rīti kāvya Saṅgraha*, Allahabad, 1961.

Gurti, Subermaniam: *Hindi Sāhitya Samīkshā*, Prayāga, V.S. 1941.

Haig, Wolseley and Burn Richard (Pub.): *The Cambridge History of India*, Delhi, 1963.

Hari Bakshi: *Bhakta Mālā*, Bombay, V.S. 1884.

Harish Chander Bharatendu: *Bhakta Rahasya*, Patnā, V.S. 1983.

—(Ed.): *Sāhitya Lahrī*, Banikipur, V.S. 1892.

—*Shrī Yugala Sarvasva*, Bankipur, N.D.

Hari Dass: *Bhakta Virudāvalī*, Rohtak, V.S. 1929.

Hari Dass (Pub.) Brahmavāda Saṅgraha, Banaras, V.S. 1985.

Hari Ray Ji: Shikhsāpatra, Bombay, 1962.

—Chaurasī Vaiṣṇvana Kī Vārtā, Mathura, 1961

Harishankaraji, Chimmana Lala: *Puṣṭimārgopadeshikā*, Vāranāsi, 1941.

Hari Viyogi: *Braja Mādhurī Sāra*, Paryaga, V.S. 1980.

Himat Dass: *Bhakti Charitāmrita*, Koria, (Gujrat) V.S. 1955.

Ikram, S.M.: *Muslim Civilization in India*, New York, 1964.

Ilango Adigal: *Shilpādikarma*, New York, 1965.

Ingalls Daniel: *Sanskrit Poetry from Vidyākara's Treasury*, Cambridge, 1968.

Jailal Kavisvar Ed.): *Nāgara Samuchchaya*, Bombay, V.S. 1958.

Jain, Shikhar Chand: *Sūra Eka Adhyayana*, Indore, V.1938.

Jhaver, K.M.: *Imperial Farmans*, Bombay, 1928.

Kamat, A.R.: *The Educational Situation*, Economical & Political Weekly, 1972.

Kashi, Gopal Dass (Ed.): *Braja Kī Holī*, Kāshī, V.S. 1948

Kavi, Miya Singh: *Bhakta Vinod*, Lucknow, N.D.

Kavi, Sardar: *Sūradāsa Ke Driṣṭakūṭa*, Lucknow, 1929.

Keith, Arthur B : *The Religion and Philosophy of Veda and Upanishad*, Cambridge, 1925.

Kumbhan Dass: *Dāna Līla*, Mathurā, N.D.

Mahamahopadhyaya Gopinath: *Shāndilya Bhakti Sūtra Vayākhyā, Bhakti Charitra*, Banaras, N.D.

Maharaja, Shrikriṣnapriya Betiji (Ed.): *Pāṭhya-Pustaka*, Two Vols. Vārānasī, 1957.

Marfatia, Mrudula: *The Philosophy of Vallabhāchārya*, Delhi, 1967.

Mate, M.D.: *Temples and Legends of Mahāraṣṭra*, Bombay, 1962.

Member, Bhagat Ram (Ed.): *Rāga Ratanākara*, Bombay, V.S.1983.

Mc Gregor, R.S.: *The Language of Indrajīta of Orcchā*, Cambridge, 1968.

—*Hindi Navratna*, Lucknow V.S. 1967.

Mishra, Bandhu: *Mishra Bhandhu Vinoda*, Lucknow, V.S. 1998.

Mishra, Bandhu: *Hindi Sāhitya Kā Vikāsa*, Lucknow, V.S. 1939.

–: *Hindi Sāhitya Kā Sanskshipta Itihāsa* Prayaga, V.S. 1938.

Mishra, Bhagirath: *Hindi Kāvya Shāstra Kā Itihāsa* Lucknow, V.S. 2005.

Mishra, Ganesh Bihari: *Mishra Bandhu Vinod. Vol. 1,2., Lucknow, V.S. 1983.*

Mishra, Janardan: *Sūradāsa*, Patnā, 1935.

Mittal, Parbhu Dayal: *Aṣṭacchāpa Parichaya*, Mathura, V.S. 2004.

—*Braj Kā Sāṅskritika Itihāsa*, Delhi, 1966.

—*Braj Ke Dharma-Sampradāyoṅ Kā Itihāsa* Delhi, 1968.

—*Chaitanya Maṭha aur Braja Sāhitya*, Mathura, 1962.

Mohammad, Malik: *Ālwāra Bhaktoṅ Kā Tāmil-Prabandham aur Hindi Kṛṣṇa-Kāvya* Agra, 1964.

Monier, Williams Monier: *A Saṅskrit-English Dictionary*, Oxford, 1960.

Mulji, Karsandas: *History of the Sect of Mahārājas or Vallabhāchāryas in Western India*, London, 1865.

Mumat, Somnath: *Aṣṭacchāpa Padāvalī*, Lahore, V.S. 1940.

Murli Dass: *Shrimad Vallabhāchāryas Charitam*, Bombay, N.D.

Nelson, A.E. (Ed.): *Central Provinces District Gazetteer*, Bombay, 1909.

Nijhavana, Rajendra Kumar: *Dwārikā*, 1966, Ed. Shiv Lal, Bombay,V.S. 1955.

Nagri Dasa: *Nāgara Samuchchaya*, Ed. Bombay, V.S. 1955.

Nand Dasa: *Daśam Skandha Bhāṣā*, Amritsar, N.D.

—*Dānalīlā*, Mathurā, 1873.

—*Nāmamālā*, Banāras, N.D.

—*Bhramara Gīta*, Allahābād, 1942.

—*Bhramara Gīta*, Mathurā, N.D.

—*Rāsapañchādhāyī* Ed. V.N. Tiwari, Prayāga, V.S.1993.

— *Rukminī Maṅgala Evam Shyāma Sagāī*, Ed. V.N. Mehrotra, Allahabad N.D.

—*Shyāma Sagāī*, Mathura, N.D.

Nabha Dass: *Bhakta Māla*, Calcutta, V. 1873.

Nar Singh Dass Ji Bhean Bhai: *Shrī Brajamaṅdala*, Kaṭhayawāḍa, N.D.

Pandey, Rajabali: *Hindu Saṅskāra* Vāranāsī, 1966.

Pandeya, S.M. and Zide, N.H.: *The Poems of Sūradasa*, Chicago, 1963.

Paramānandadāsa (G.N. Shukla Ed.): *Parmānaṅda Sāgara*, Aligarh, 1958.

Parikh, Bhai Mani Lal C.: *Śri Vallabhāchārya: Life, Teachings and Movement*, Rajkot, 1943.

Parikha, Dvārakādāsa and Mittala, Prabhu Dayal: *Sūra Nirṇaya*, Mathura, 1962.

Parikha Dvārakā Dāsa Purushottama (Ed.): *Prāchīna Vārtā Sāhitya*, Kāṅkroli, 1940.

Parikha Dvārakā Dāsa: *Aṣṭa Sakhan Kī Vārtā*, Mathura, V.S. 2007.

— (Ed.): *Chaurāsī Vaṣṇavn Kī Vārtā*, Mathura, V.S. 2003.

—(Ed.): *Prāchīn Vārtā Rahasya*, Ahmedabad, V.S. 1996.

— *Vārtā Sāhitya Mīmāṅsā*, Ahmedabad, V.S. 2005.

—(Ed.): Ṣaṭha Ritu Kī Vārtā Ahmedabad, V.S. 2005.

Parikha, Jayanti Lal Magan Lal: *Pushṭimārgiya Sewā Prakāra* (Gujrat) Ahmedabad, V.S. 1994.

Prtap Singh: *Bhakta Mālā,* Lucknow, V.S. 1884.

– *Bhakta Mālā, Bhakta kalpadruma Tikā* Lucknow, 1922.

Priya Dass: *Bhakta Mālā,* Mathura, V.S. 1912.

— *Bhakta Mālā Tika, Bhaktirasa Bodhinī,* Bombay, V.S. 1967.

Poddar, Hanuman Prasad: *Philosophy of Love,* Gorakhpur, N.D.

Poddar, Kanihya Lal: *Kāvya Kalpadruma,* Lucknow, V.S. 1991.

Potter, Karl H: *Presuppositions of India's Philosophies* Englewood, 1963.

Radha Krishna, S. (Ed.): *The Principal Upaniṣads,* London, 1953.

Rāmānuj Dass: *Bhakta Māla,* Bombay, V.S. 1900.

Ranchor Dass Laxmidass (Ed.): *Puṣṭimāragīya Udbodhana,* Mathura, V.S. 1988.

Ray Bahadur Lala Sita Ram: *Hindi Survey Committee Kī Report,* Prayāga, V.S. 1930.

Rupa Goswami: *Bhakti-Rasāmrita Sindhu,* Brindāban, 1900

Sahai, Jagan Nath: *Bhakta-rasāmarita,* Lucknow, V.S. 1888.

Sanayal, Nalini Mohan: *Sūradāsa III Edition,* Prayāga, V.S. 2005.

Sant Dass: *Chaurasī Bhakta Nāmamālā,* Mewar, N.D.

Satyendra: *Sūra Kī Jhāṅkī,* Agra, V.S. 1926.

Sengar, Shiv Singh: *Shiva Siṅgh Saroj,* Lucknow, 1926.

Shah, Gokul Dass Natwar Lal: *A world eye view of Puṣṭimārga,* Ahmedabad, N.D—*A Short Biographical Sketch of Shri Vallabhāchārya Ji's Life,* Ahmedabad, N.D.

Shah, J.G. :*Rāsas Shrikrishṇa*, Ahmedabad, N.D.

— *A Primer of Aṇubhāṣya* Naidyad, N.D.

Sharma, Bhatt Shrirāmanātha (Trans.): *Sevākaumudī*, Bombay, 1919.

Sharma, Bhatt Rama Nath: *Shuddhādvaita Darshana* Bombay, N.D.

— *Shrīmad Vallabhāchārya*, Bombay, N.D.

— *Bhakti aur Prapatti Kā Swarūpagata Bheda*, Nātha Dwārā, N.D.

Sharma, Brij Ratan: *Sūrdasa kā Jīwan Charitra*, Muradabad, V.S. 1903.

Sharma, Brij Vallabha Dass: *Kīrtana Saṅgraha*, Ahmedabad, V.S. 1976.

Sharma, Harbansh Lala: (Ed.): *Sūradāsa*, Delhi, 1966.

Sharma Krishan Dev: *Sūra Vaṅsh Nirṇaya*, Mathura, V.S. 1998.

Sharma, Munshi Ram: *Sūra Saurabha*, Vol. I Kanpur, V.S.2000.

— *Sūra Saurabha*, Vol. II, Kanpur, V.S. 2002.

— *Sūradāsa Aur Bhagvadbhakti*, Prayāga, V.S. 1958.

— *Bhāratīya Sādhanā aur Sūra Sāhitya* Kanpur, 1961.

Sharma, Niranjanadeva (ed.): *Do sau Bāvana Vaiṣṇvana Kī Vārtā*, Mathura, 1966.

Sharma, Parbu Dayal (Ed.): *Dohā Ratnāvali*, Itawa, N.D.

Sharma, Purshotam: *Hindi Rasa Gaṅgādhara*, Prayāga, N.D.

Sharma, Vrajabhushaṇa (Ed.): *Krishṇadāsa (Pada Saṅgraha)* Kāṅkroli, 1963.

—& Kaushik, (Eds.): *Kumbhanadāsa*, Kāṅkroli, 1954.

Shastri, Anandi Lala: *Vaishṇavachinhanirūpaṇa*, Nāthadwārā, 1952.

Shastri, Kanthamani: *Kāṅkarolī Kā Itihāsa*, Kāṅkroli, V.S. 1996.

Shastri, Keshav Ram Kashi Ram: *Puṣṭimārgiya-Kirtana-Prakāra*, Bombay, V.S. 1980.

Shastri, Rāmanāth: *Brahmvāda*, Nāthadwārā, V.S. 1992.

Shastri, Surya Kant: *Hindi Sāhitya Kā Vivechanātmaka Itihāsa* Lahore, V.1931.

Shastri, Vasant Ram: *Kīrtana Kusumākara*, Ahmedabad, V.1990.

Shukla Govardhana Nath: *Kavivara Paramānaṅdadāsa aur Vallabha Sampradāya*, Aligarh, 1964.

Shukla Krishan Chandra: *Hamare Sāhitya Kī Roop Rekhā*, Kashi, N.D.

Shukla, Ram Chandra: *Sūradāsa* Kāshī, V, 2000.

—:*Bhrmaragīta Sāra*, kāshī, V.S. 1983.

—:*Hindi Sāhitya Kā Itihasa*, Kāshī, V.S. 1986.

Shukal, Ram Shankar: *Hindi Sāhitya Kā Itihāsa*, Prayāga, V.S. 1961.

Shukal, Uma Shankar: *Naṅdadāsa* Prayāga, 1942.

Shukal Vishvanātha (Ed.): *Hindi Krishṇa Bhakti Kāvya Para Shrimadbhāgavata kā Prabhāva*, Aligarh, 1966.

Singh, Raghunandan Prasad: *Bhakti Yoga*, Gorakhpur, V.S. 1993.

Singh, Raghu Raj: *Rasa Rasikāvali*, Bombay, V.S. 1971.

Singer, Milton (Ed.): *Krishṇa: Myths, Rites and Attitudes* Honolulu, 1966.

Tod, James (K.K.Thakura) Trans.: *Rājasthāna Kā Itihāsa*, Allahabad, 1965.

Tribuvan Dass Ranchor Dass (Ed.): *Kīrtana Ratnākara*, Ahmedabad, V.S. 1891.

Tripathi, Ramapratapa: *Hinduoṅ Ke Vrata, Parva aur Tyauhāra*. Allahabad, 1966.

Tripathi, Ram Naresh: *Kavitā Kaumudī* Vol. I, Prayāga, V.S 1940.

Tulsi Dass (Shayam Sundar Ed.): *Rāma Charita Mānasa*, Prayāga, N.D.

Ram Naresh Tripathi) Ed.– : *Rāma Charita Mānasa*, Prayāga, N.D.

Tulsi Ram: *Bhaktamāla*, Sohna, V.S. 1867.

Tyāgishananda Swāmi (Trans.) *Aphorisms on the Gospel of Divine Love or Nārada Bhakti Sūtras*, Madras, 1955.

Upādhyāya, Ayodhayā Singh: *Hindi Bhāṣā aur Sāhitya kā Vikāsa*, Kashi, V.S. 1997.

— *Vibhutimati Brajbhāṣā* Vrindābana V.S. 1997.

Vaidya, Chiman Lal, M: *Shrī Vallabhāchārya and His Teachings*, Kapadwanj, 1959.

Vajapeyi Kriṣnadatta (Ed.): *Braja Kā Itihāsa*, Two vols., Mathura, 1959.

Vallabhāchārya: *Shrīmadbrahmasūtrāṇubhāṣyam*, Bombay, 1941.

Vallabhacharya: *Shrisubodhinī*, Ed. N.K. Sharma Nāthadwārā 1928.

— *The Tattvārthadīpa-Nibandha with* Prakāsha, Ed. M.G.Shastri, Bombay, 1943.

Vallabhāchārya: *A Sketch of His Life and Teachings*, Madras, 1918.

— *Tattvadīpanibandha Shaṣtrārthaprakaraṇa*, Ahmedabad. 1926.

— *Chatushloki*, Ed. B.R.N.Sharma, Bombay, V.S. 1979.

— *Nava Ratna*, Ed. B.R.N. Sharma, Bombay V.S. 1979

— *Nirodhalakshaṇa*, Ed. B.R.N. Sharma, Bombay, V.S. 1979.

— *Pañchapāda*, Ed. B.R.N. Sharma, V.S. 1979.

— *Puṣṭipravāha Maryādā*, Ed. B.R.N. Sharma, Bombay, V.S. 1979.

— *Bālabodha*, Ed. B.R.N. Sharma, Bombay, V.S. 1979.

— *Bhakti Vardhinī*, Ed. B.R.N. Sharma, Bombay, V.S. 1979.

— *Yamunāshataka*, Ed. B.R.N. Sharma, Bombay, V.S. 1979.

— *Vallabhashataka*, Ed. B.R.N. Sharma, Bombay V.S. 1979.

— *Sañyāsa Nirṇaya*, Ed. B.R.N. Sharma, Bombay, 1979.

— *Sidhāntamuktāvali*, Ed. B.R.N. Sharma, Bombay, V.S. 1979.

— *Sewāphala*, Ed. B.R.N. Sharma, Bombay, V.S. 1979.

Vaishnav Thakur Dass Sūradāsa (Ed.): *Rāga-Kalpadrum*, Calcutta, N.D.

Verma Brajeshwar: *Sūradāsa*, Prayāga, V.S. 1946.

— *Hindi Ke Vaiṣṇava* Kavi, Prayāga, V.S. 1941.

Verma, Dhirendra (Ed.): *Grāmīṇa Hindi*, Allahabad, 1957.

—(Ed.) *Hindi Sahitya Koṣa*, Vārānasī, 1964. (Two Vols.)

—(Ed.) *Aṣṭacchāapa*, Allahabad, N.D.

—(Ed.): *Pariṣada Nibandhāvali*, Prayāga, N.D.

Verma, Ramchandra: *Mānaka Hindi Koṣa*, (Five Vols.), Allahabad, 1963.

Verma, Ram Kumar: *Hindi Sāhitya Kā Alochanātmaka Itihāsa*, Allahabad, V.S. 1938.

Verma, Ram Kumar: *Hindi Sāhitya Kī Rūparekhā*, Prayāga, V.S. 1938.

Vidyalankar, Jai Chandra: *Itihāsa Praveṣa*, Allahabad, 1939.

Vidhaleshawar (Ed.): *Shriṁagāra Maṅdana*, Bombay, N.D.

Viraj: *Hindi Kaviyaoṅ Kā Ālochanātmaka Itihāsa*, Delhi, N.D.

Vishav Nath: *Sāhitya Darpaṇa*, Lucknow, V.s. 1978.

Vyāsa: *Shrīmadbhāgavata Mahāpurāṇa, Gītā Press*, Gorakhapur, 1965.

— *The Mahābhārata*, 12 Vols., Calcutta N.D.

— *The Srīmadbhāgavatam* (5 Vols.), Calcutta, 1952.

Wach, Joachim: *Sociology of Religion*, Chicago, 1948.

Warren, Henery Clarke: *Buddhism in Translations*, New York, 1969.

Yudhunath: *Vallabha Digvijaya* Kāṅkroli, V.S. 1958.

— *Vallabha Digvijaya*, Kāṅkroli, 1963.